NARRATIVE THEORIES AND POETICS

Other interview books from Automatic Press ♦ $\frac{V}{I}$P

Formal Philosophy
edited by Vincent F. Hendricks & John Symons
November 2005

Masses of Formal Philosophy
edited by Vincent F. Hendricks & John Symons
October 2006

Political Questions: 5 Questions for Political Philosophers
edited by Morten Ebbe Juul Nielsen
December 2006

Philosophy of Technology: 5 Questions
edited by Jan-Kyrre Berg Olsen & Evan Selinger
February 2007

Game Theory: 5 Questions
edited by Vincent F. Hendricks & Pelle Guldborg Hansen
April 2007

Philosophy of Mathematics: 5 Questions
edited by Vincent F. Hendricks & Hannes Leitgeb
January 2008

Philosophy of Computing and Information: 5 Questions
edited by Luciano Floridi
Sepetmber 2008

Philosophy of the Social Sciences: 5 Questions
edited by Diego Ríos & Christoph Schmidt-Petri
September 2008

Epistemology: 5 Questions
edited by Vincent F. Hendricks & Duncan Pritchard
September 2008

Mind and Consciousness: 5 Questions
edited by Patrick Grim
January 2009

Philosophy of Science: 5 Questions
edited by Robert Rosenberger
November 2010

See all published and forthcoming books in the 5 Questions series at
www.vince-inc.com/automatic.html

NARRATIVE THEORIES AND POETICS
5 QUESTIONS

edited by

Peer F. Bundgård
Henrik Skov Nielsen
Frederik Stjernfelt

Automatic Press ♦ $\frac{V}{I}$P

Automatic Press ♦ $\frac{V}{I}$P

Information on this title: www.vince-inc.com/automatic.html

© Automatic Press / VIP 2012

This publication is in copyright. Subject to statuary exception
and to the provisions of relevant collective licensing agreements,
no reproduction of any part may take place without
the written permission of the publisher.

First published 2012

Printed in the United States of America
and the United Kingdom

ISBN-10 87-92130-42-9 paperback
ISBN-13 978-87-92130-42-6 paperback

The publisher has no responsibilities for
the persistence or accuracy of URLs for external or
third party Internet Web sites referred to in this publication
and does not guarantee that any content on such
Web sites is, or will remain, accurate or appropriate.

Typeset in $\LaTeX 2_\varepsilon$
Cover design by Vincent F. Hendricks

Contents

Preface	iii
Acknowledgements	vii
1 H. Porter Abbott	1
2 Jan Alber	11
3 Mieke Bal	21
4 Ann Banfield	29
5 Marisa Bortolussi & Peter Dixon	33
6 Claude Bremond	43
7 Wallace Chafe	53
8 Seymour Chatman	59
9 Jonathan Culler	61
10 Monika Fludernik	65
11 Dorothy J. Hale	69
12 David Herman	73
13 Manfred Jahn	85
14 Susan S. Lanser	95
15 Uri Margolin	103
16 Brian McHale	115
17 David S. Miall	121

18 Jeff Mitscherling	133
19 Ansgar Nünning	141
20 Alan Palmer	151
21 Sylvie Patron	159
22 Thomas Pavel	171
23 James Phelan	175
24 John Pier	187
25 Gerald Prince	195
26 Peter J. Rabinowitz	201
27 Brian Richardson	211
28 Shlomith Rimmon-Kenan	215
29 Franz K. Stanzel	227
30 Peter Stockwell	237
31 Reuven Tsur	245
32 Richard Walsh	257
33 Robyn Warhol	265
General bibliography	273
About the Editors	307

Preface

Narrative Theories and Poetics: 5 Questions
Edited by Peer Bundgaard, Henrik Skov Nielsen and
Frederik Stjernfelt

———————————— ♦ ————————————

In the present interview book, *Narrative Theory and Poetics: 5 Questions*, eminent narratologists, literary scholars, poeticians, stylisticians and philosophers answer five simple and broad questions. As is generally the case in the *5 Questions Series*, the questions are intended to give the authors an occasion to outline their intellectual biography – in whatever detail they find necessary, with or without the anecdotes of life – as well as to lay down their idea of the state of the art of the domain of research to which they have devoted their work including the future challenges and unsolved issues it is still ripe with.

The title of this book does not designate any research program as such. Neither does it suggest that all contributors are brothers in arms, gathered under the same two-colored banner. In a case like the present one, titles are meant to be compromises, vague predicates – as Charles Peirce had it – which roughly indicate the matter of the contributors' intellectual concern, the kind of thing they interrogate and explore, in different directions, with different purposes and in different theoretical frameworks. In other words, not all contributors are specifically involved in narrative theory or poetics *stricto sensu* (although most are), but all of them have developed an original theory by examining the nature of an object we could call the literary artwork: stories, poetry, verbal art in general.

Nonetheless, if "narrative theory" takes on a prominent position in the title, it is of course because the bulk of this book consists of contributions from scholars engaged in the study of stories. Some of them are outstanding pioneers in this research field – we could call them 1st generation narratologists – others have succeeded them by opening new paths, formulating new questions, addressing new issues in the investigation of the stories of humans, what they are, what they do, how they hook up with the human condition, human thinking, acting, cognition and consciousness. As the reader will soon realize, the unity or even identity of the object of investigation – the story – does not entail identity or unidimensionality of theoretical approach: scholars are concerned with rather different (but not for that matter mutually exclusive) things while considering the same kind of object. Probably for the simple reason that stories, like other intentional phenomena, are essentially multifarious objects, susceptible of being examined along different theoretical lines, according to the aspect highlighted in a given type of investigation. Just to mention a few of these aspects: stories are transcultural, universally instantiated phenomena (all cultures seem to construct a type of verbal art where non-trivial events, involving sentient beings, are linked in recurrent types of structure); it seems thus natural to ask, as some of the contributors have done (in the wake of the ancients), what exactly stories are, what is their mechanics, their physics, as it were, what do they consist of, even what must they consist of, to what constraints is the unfolding of the plot submitted, and so on? We could call this the ontology of stories. Now, if humans universally display a propensity for story-telling, stories (and verbal art in general) most likely play an essential anthropological function, so another general line of research consists then in answering the question what do stories do, or what do humans do with stories (fictional as well as non-fictional)? What is the cosmological (mythological) use of stories, what is their social function, what is their intersubjective function, and what is their subjective or psychological function (for example in the construction of what is often called the Self)? We could call this vast field of research the pragmatics of stories. Finally, as someone once put it, the words of stories and poems come out of a head, not out of a hat. This simple fact opens a cognitive line of research aiming at examining verbal art with a view to capturing what stories and poems tell us about the human mind, what it is sensitive to, what is significant for it; what are the means by way of which they give access to the consciousness of a character, what are the tools thanks to which they shape whole worlds or small packets of meaning, and what are the crossovers between plain meaning making, or plain cognition, and aesthetic meaning making and cognition (questions which are also highly relevant outside the realm of narrative theory, in poetics and stylistics)?

This book, of course, does not tell the whole story, but we do think that – through its intellectual flash biographies, its theoretical concerns and crash courses in cognitive poetics, the ontology of art, stylistics and narrative theory – it conveys to the reader a valuable gist of what stories and verbal art in general are, what they do, how they do it and probably also why.

February 2012
Peer Bundgaard, Henrik Skov Nielsen and Frederik Stjernfelt
Editors

WWW.VINCE-INC.COM

Acknowledgements

We are particularly grateful to the contributors for devoting time to writing such erudite, enlightening and often thought-provoking interviews and grateful to the philosophical community in general for showing interest in this project. In addition, we would like to thank editor-in-chief Vincent F. Hendricks and associate editor Henrik A. Boensvang of **Automatic Press** ♦ $\frac{V}{I}$P

February 2012
Peer Bundgaard, Henrik Skov Nielsen og Frederik Stjernfelt
Editors

1

H. Porter Abbott

Emeritus
English Department, UC Santa Barbara

---

1. Why were you initially drawn to narratology or narrative theory?

Like some of my older American colleagues, I was a narratologist before the word was invented,—that is, I was interested in answering questions that applied to more than one narrative instance. Rightly or wrongly, this is my current definition of narrative theory, though as a young scholar I would have called it theory of the novel, or of mimesis, had I used the word theory at all.

In those ancient days, when the old historicism and the New Criticism pretty well divided the landscape of American letters between them, what I wanted took the form more of a felt need than an understood absence. The New Criticism, of course, was not short on theory, but its appeal lay in a practice devoted to the complex beauty of particular achievements. It was great fun in the doing of it, but students like myself could get so immersed in the internal resonances of a single work, they would forget to come up for air. Had I at that time encountered the work of an actual narratologist in full structuralist regalia, I would have been horrified by how far it went in the opposite direction, powered by an omnivorous scientific vision, and wielding what to me would have been an icily abstract methodology.

I say all this to make it clear how at that time (the 60's) works like Erich Auerbach's *Mimesis*, Wayne Booth's *Rhetoric of Fiction*, and Frank Kermode's *Sense of an Ending* could shine like beacons—narrative-oriented versions of literary theory in the fullest sense. With them, one could travel over great swathes of narrative territory in the pursuit of general ideas without overlooking the originality of individual achievement. So, when I finally entered the main current of self-conscious narratology two or three decades later, I found I had leap-frogged the whole structuralist ferment that gave narratology its name along with its immensely useful toolkit and landed among friendly colleagues for whom Auerbach, Booth, and Kermode were as much a part of the pantheon as Greimas, Todorov, and Barthes.

The appeal of theory *per se*, of course, is rooted in a universal human appetite for general truths, but the appeal of narrative theory in particular is the power, flexibility, and importance of its subject, together with narrative's near universality in discourse and understanding. What also drew me to narrative theory, and continues to draw me, is the way it is practiced. In comparison to other spheres of literary discourse, there seems to be more discipline in the discipline. There is less of a sense of being blown about by the winds of fashion (always a problem in literary study) and more of a sense of being part of a common enterprise, with shared standards, and the possibility of real progress. Finally, "post-classical narratology" has opened up new ways to address the transaction that takes place between complex texts and the mind. This transaction is, I think, the defining difficulty in a field like literary study in which no text does what it is supposed to do without a mind to bring it to life. We have a long way to go in absorbing without distortion what is being learned in other fields about the way the mind works, but I think narratologists are getting more adept at this.

2. What do you consider your most important contribution(s) to the field?

This is a hard question to answer. I will handle it by touching down on four areas I've worked in, with varying degrees of influence. One is an idea I developed regarding diary fiction, which first appeared in *PMLA*("Letters to the Self ," 1980) and then in a book (*Diary Fiction: Writing as Action*, 1984). This was when I was a narratologist without knowing it. The idea was that intercalated single-writer narration—that is, narration in the diary or single letter-writer mode—provides a way to show how the manner in which events are rendered can quite literally determine what happens next. I found, from the late renaissance on, examples of this kind of "writing as action" or, in terms that I did not think in at the time, special instances of *discourse* driving *story*. The world has not exactly beaten a path to my door to talk about this issue, but it is an idea well worth developing given the problematic entanglements of the story-discourse model.

A second idea I have spent time on appeared notably in a 1988 article in *New Literary History* on discourse types ("Autobiography, Autography, Fiction,"), but also in other articles on various modernists as well as my second book on Beckett (*Beckett*

Writing Beckett, 1996). The concept is "autography" or more exactly "autographical reading"—an orientation toward self-writing (whether the writing was intended as such or not) as a form of self-making (or finding) at the time of writing. The force of the term lay in its opposition to framing the study of autobiography as a form of biography, that is, as a history of the autobiographer, and reframing it as a study of texts coded as autobiography but functioning as acts of rhetorical self-reflexivity, however historical they may appear to be in form. It is a kind of reading that requires considerable care since it can be an easy way to gain the illusion of ascendancy over the writer, especially when the evidence is thin.

More recently I have been writing a string of papers and articles on the limits of the narratable. There are two facets of this subject that I have been pursuing, one devoted to nonfictional efforts to convey modes of unnarratable behavior, the other devoted to efforts in fiction to forestall understanding. The first can be found notably in two essays, one in David Herman's *Narrative Theory and the Cognitive Sciences* ("Unnarratable Knowledge," 2003) that focuses on the unnarratable character of evolution by natural selection, the other more recently in *Poetics Today* ("Narrative and Emergent Behavior," 2008) on the problems of representing emergent behavior in general (of which natural selection is one example). The second facet responds to the excellent work by Lisa Zunshine, Alan Palmer, and others on the ways in which novels are designed at once to represent and to elicit mind-reading activity. My work is a response in that it deals with texts that require an immersion in states of unknowing, an experience that cannot be relieved without serious over- or under-reading. My work on this facet of the unnarratable has appeared in a number of essays and papers drawing on the work of authors like García Márquez, Melville, Stein, Coetzee, Alice Munro, and Beckett. Both of these lines of inquiry are on-going projects in which I also deal with the kinds of default modes of reader-response that allow the unnarratable to be naturalized. An important goal of my work, however, is to prevent these default modes from mitigating the experience of non-understanding, insofar as that is a demonstrable artistic intention. This, of course, requires an acknowledgment of the limits of what we can know—always a special challenge for academics.

One reason this question about my contributions has been hard to answer, aside from the humility for which I am famous, is that I seem to be more of a fox than a hedgehog, to use Isaiah Berlin's distinction. This has meant that many of the essays I write and the papers I give are stand-alone productions. Of course, I hope they, too, have had an influence, if only of provocation. But I should also mention *The Cambridge Introduction to Narrative* (second edition, 2008) because it seems to be pretty widely used. The influence above all others that I hope this book has made is an influence it had on me as I wrote it. On the one hand, it enlightened me regarding how much in narrative theory and practice I had been taking for granted, and on the other, it revealed to me how unsettled all the terms, distinctions, and models are that we deploy in narrative theory.

3. What is the proper role of narratology and narrative theory in relation to other academic disciplines?

I have two responses to this question. The first is that the field of narrative theory and interpretation should relate to other disciplines as a discipline. This sounds like a tautology, but with all the fervor about the value of being "interdisciplinary," it is easy to forget that we have a field with a special focus, a breadth of range, and years of practice and accumulated lore. This makes us different in that it gives us a complex understanding that informs the way we think about our subject. This is a point that Meir Sternberg has developed in several long articles. It means that whatever we absorb from other disciplines—and we must forever be doing this to keep our discipline alive—does not make our work interdisciplinary but, rather, enlarges our discipline. After all, it is of the nature of any discipline to be packed with material from other disciplines, but what makes it a discipline is that in the packing process the material undergoes a change. The work of David Herman, which has carried him deep into the arcana of many disciplines, is a shining example of how to do this.

The absorption of this material, of course, must be done properly, that is, with a clear undistorted understanding of what is absorbed as well as of the value it gives us. Which brings me to my second response: that we in our turn have a great deal to contribute to other disciplines, much as they may not know it. The psychologists Schank and Abelson, for example, labored for thirty years on their theory of the role of narrative in cognition all the while sublimely indifferent to most of what was being learned by narratologists. It left their work riddled with vulnerabilities. But we should also take care that what we do contribute is not distorted in the process by one or another form of reduction. Just as there is the danger for us of importing terms and concepts as a veneer of interdisciplinarity without any clear need for them, so there is the danger of our exporting material to serve as a garnish, amputated from key complexities that belong to it.

As for the specific disciplines that can help us and that we can help, there are some with which narratology is currently enjoying a lively interchange (sociology, developmental psychology, law, medicine, linguistics, the cognitive sciences). But, given the universality of narrative (as a deep structure, which would include narratives without anthropoidal characters or agency), there really should be no fields excluded from a potential exchange of influence in either direction.

4. What do you consider the most important topics and/or contributions in narratology?

There have been so many signal contributions in narratology, it is hard not to be arbitrary in making selections. What to include? Plato's distinction between *mimesis* and *diegesis*? Aristotle's absorption of that distinction into the broad category of mimesis (thereby paving the way for a broad concept of narrative)? The Russian formalist distinction between *fabula* and *sjuzet*? Propp's and Todorov's versions of causal sequence in narrative? Bakhtin's concepts of dialogism and the chronotope? Booth's promotion of an ethical/rhetorical narrative analytics? Sternberg's triad of suspense, curiosity, and surprise? The list goes on. So I will limit my focus to two areas of research within which these and other discrete contributions have played a part.

If I were to pick a moment inaugurating the first of these, it would be Sternberg's and Menachem Perry's 1968 article, "The King through Ironic Eyes," which initiated a view of narrative as a dynamic process in which formal properties are processed as effects by the reader. An interesting historical note is that the article appeared at the same time as the basis of so-called classical narratology was being laid (a year on each side separates it from foundational structuralist texts on narrative by Barthes and Todorov). Moreover, in the following decade, when the structure of classical narratology was being filled out by Genette, Prince, Bremond, Chatman, Culler, Bal, Greimas, et al., this thread of theory with its perspective on the reader's role in processing narrative was also being elaborated. Sternberg (1978), of course, went on to lay the groundwork for his theory of narrative exposition in that decade. Wolfgang Iser (1978) developed his own quite different theory of narrative in terms of "reader response." Labov (1972a) introduced the influential concept of "reportability" or "tellability", which he had developed by listening to inner-city youths shape their storytelling with a view to reader-effect. And in 1982, Robert Scholes developed the concept of "narrative competence" in direct opposition to the text-based orthodoxy of classical film theory. For all their differences, then, these latter scholars were expanding narrative study from its classical base up into the hearts and minds of reader/viewers, even as the structure of classical narratology was still being worked out.

In effect, then, classical and post-classical narratology grew up together. For me, there is a direct line from Sternberg and Perry's early article to the "cognitivist" blossoming in the 90s with landmark publications like Monica Fludernik's re-centering of narrative theory on an experiential basis in her *Towards a "Natural" Narratology* (1996), Ellen Spolsky's application of insights drawn from cognitive neuroscience in *Gaps in Nature* (1993), and David Herman's 1997 *PMLA* essay announcing the consolidation of a "postclassical narratology." In the following decade (now just ending) there has been an explosion of this kind of stuff by Herman, Zunshine, Palmer, Patrick Colm Hogan, Nancy Easterling, Frederick Aldama, Suzanne Keen, Alan Richardson, and others, plus excellent anthologies just out or in press.

The second development I want to feature goes way back. You can find it in the biblical typology of the early Christian church in which Old Testament stories are seen to prefigure their "antitypes" in the New Testament (e.g., Jonah's expulsion from the whale prefiguring Christ's resurrection). I lump this with Frazier's theory of the shared structure of fertility myths; Freud's theory of primal sequences replicated in myths, dreams, and literature; Jung's archetypes; Northrop Frye's major plots; Jean-François Lyotard's master narratives. These are all different conceptions, conceived at different levels of generality, but they are all examples of what I loosely call "masterplots"—recurrent skeletal stories that are either culturally specific or universal.

I'm not telling anybody anything new here. As an analytical device, explicitly or implicitly, the idea of a repeatable story structure or meta-narrative has given leverage to almost any namable approach you can find under the broad canopy of cultural studies—feminist, Marxist, queer, environmental, psychoanalytic, Foucauldian—most of which are now easily accommodated under the even broader canopy of post-classical narrative theory. The important thing is that the repetition of these embedded stories is a sign of need, fear, or desire that gives them enormous rhetorical power. It gives them a determinative force that operates everywhere in our economic, political, educational, religious, and domestic lives. And this I think makes them, as a subject of narrative theory, especially important.

5. What are the most important open problems in this field and what are the prospects for progress?

My first response to this last question extends my discussion of both lines of inquiry I featured immediately above. The open problem is the task of bringing them together. Without a neurobiology of the masterplot, we will remain at the level of continually exposing the covert power of these deep stories and reiterating attitudes of condemnation, allegation, exhortation, repudiation, and all the other ways we have of claiming the moral high ground. We need to understand more clearly how these deep narrative structures acquire their power, how they override the intelligence, and how they can be displaced, altered or replaced. There has been significant work on the way they operate at the level of self-narrativization (Bruner, Sacks, Keen, Eaken) and some at the social/cultural level (see especially Hogan). But there is a lot more room for valuable, productive work with real benefits.

The second problem I want to feature, and for which I hope there will be progress, can be broken down into a set of interlocking issues, each problematic in itself, yet all of them facets of the value we continue to place on singular achievement in the arts, itself a subject that we have come to neglect. The appreciation of one-of-a-kind works of art, of course, used to be the primary object of the study of arts and letters. This set the field off from the pursuit of general truth, which was the primary object of the sciences: physical, social, and psychological. The fascination with original achievement still abides, but the rise of "theory" within the gates of humanistic study is a sign of the increasing embarrassment that comes with our riches—that is, the subjective character of "success" in the arts, the absence of accepted standards, and the impossibility of proof, not to mention the taints of elitism, aestheticism, and exclusivity.

Here are a few of the interlocking issues that, in my view, we would need to address if we were fully to absorb into narrative theory the subject of the aesthetic value of original art. Qualia: understanding the generation, variety, layered character, subtlety, and variability of strength of qualia (how things seem to us) in the narrative experience. The narrative experience is saturated in complex braids of qualia (used broadly here to include both the sense-based experiences of characters as imagined within the storyworld and those of ourselves as we respond to the characters and events of that world). The intricate attunement of qualia to character and action is not only a measure of narrative achievement but also lies at the heart of narrative's ethical work. Yet we lack calipers of sufficient precision for dealing with them. Beauty: a word rarely used anymore in our field except as a kind of loose expression of liking. And for good reason, since it is one of our embarrassments—indefinable, immeasurable, subjective, and widely variable, person by person. Yet there is this *je-ne-sais-quoi* that refuses to go away, despite strenuous efforts to reduce it, along with the idea of a canon, to an instrument of cultural control. The literary: here empirical work has begun on the ways in which audiences use the concept (Bortolussi and Dixon, Miall and Kuiken), but we still have a long way to go, before we can apply the term with confidence that we mean something we can agree upon. Rhythm and musicality: qualities of lyric poetry and music would seem on the face of it to be antithetical to that which makes narrative narrative. Yet Forster (1927) wrote over 80 years ago of "rhythm" in the novel, defining it as "repetition plus variation," while elucidating such repetitions became a staple of the New Criticism. More recently, there has been work on narrativity as an aspect of music and, more recently still, on poetic meter as an important component of narrative in poetry.

Finally, I should note the recent enthusiasm for an expansion of narrative theory to accommodate the widening river of radical departures from narrative norms. This would include the continuing niche market for extreme subversions of narrative expectations in prose, poetry, and drama that arose a hundred years ago with the modernists, extended shortly thereafter into film, and now is finding its way into new electronic media. Over the last five years, a friendly band of narratological outlaws has sprung up, calling for an "unnatural narratology." They are doing a great job of gathering examples of the unnatural, isolating "unnatural" effects, and fielding lively sessions at annual meetings of the ISSN and other venues.

I am not, however, clear who they are opposing. In fact, I doubt that there is an opposition, since narratology (and certainly postclassical narratology) has often capitalized on radical departures from the norm as a source of limit-cases (one reason Beckett's highly "unnatural" works have so often been used in evidence). Unnatural narratives depend for their effects on natural expectations, a point that Scholes made almost 30 years ago and that Brian McHale (2001) echoed in his analysis of what he called "weak Narrativity." After all, the word "natural" is contained in the word "unnatural." So, though the band of Unnaturals will continue to come up with valuable limit cases of form and effect, I doubt that their efforts will result in an unnatural narratology if by that is meant a narrative theory of unnatural narrative.

I've made roughly the same argument ("The Future of All Narrative Futures," 2005) in response to calls for a fundamentally revised narratology to accommodate new narrative forms in digital and other electronic media (Gibson, Murray). Briefly, I've argued, a) that narratives with the look and feel of what we know as narrative (including the "subversions" of expectation that are the staple of any successful narratives) will continue to dominate the electronic market even as they continue to dominate the market for narrative in other media, and b) that those that don't have that look and feel will rely for their effects on the expectations that are natural to the narrative experience. That said, the really fascinating development has been on-line gaming, a huge expansion of the "fantasy role-playing games" of the 70s and 80s. In so far as the *sjuzet* of such games, and at times the *fabula*, are a product of the actual playing, they are what Espen Aarseth has called "ergotic." Marie-Laure Ryan, who has done wonderful work in this area, considers these still to be narratives. My own view is that they are hybrids, and that it is important to designate them as such. To the extent that, like games, they unfold for the first time as they happen they lack an essential feature of narrativity—the feeling of a story being related. In this they are more like theatrical improv, deriving their look and feel from the quality of instantaneity that characterizes life itself. But they are no less worth close theoretical attention on this account.

2

Jan Alber

Assistant Professor

English Department of the University of Freiburg, Germany

1. Why were you initially drawn to narratology or narrative theory?

In the summer of 1997, I attended a seminar by Monika Fludernik on Samuel Beckett's plays and short prose. In my final thesis about Beckett's "Residua," his later prose texts, I compared the work of structuralist narratologists (such as Mieke Bal, Gérard Genette, Franz K. Stanzel, Seymour Chatman, Shlomith Rimmon-Kenan) to Fludernik's 'natural' (or cognitive) narratology (1996) with regard to the question of whether these approaches can help to make strange and incomprehensible texts (such as the ones by Beckett) more readable. I argued that the identification of experientiality ("the quasi-mimetic evocation of real-life experience" (Fludernik 1996: 12)) may help us naturalize or narrativize odd texts but I also felt that an approach which is primarily based on real-world experience cannot really do justice to texts (like Beckett's "Lessness") which openly foreground their artificiality and seek to transcend real-world experience (Alber 2002 and 2005). I thought that a poststructuralist approach might be better suited for texts by Beckett and other avant-garde literature. However, I soon came to realize that poststructuralist critics have an odd habit of repeating the same ideas ('the text can never be mastered' or 'all texts deconstruct themselves') again and again, and I thought that after a while, this nihilist approach was no longer productive—in particular because, to my mind, it did not lead to provocative new readings or ideas. And in the poststructuralist awareness of the ultimate meaninglessness of our desperate human attempts to create significance (which I still appreciate as a necessary footnote to everything we do), I began to reconsider the meaning-making tools of cognitive narratology.

2. What do you consider your most important contribution(s) to the field?

In my Habilitation ("Unnatural Narrative: Impossible Worlds in Fiction and Drama"), which has a narratological outlook, I focus on unnatural narratives that transcend our real-world knowledge by projecting physical or logical impossibilities (see also Alber 2009: 80; Alber, Iversen, Nielsen and Richardson 2010).[1] I measure the unnatural against the foil of the 'natural,' which in my usage denotes our knowledge of natural laws, logical principles, and other cognitive parameters (about human agents, time, and space) derived from our real-world experience (Fludernik 1996: 10-11). From my perspective, it is the specificity of fictional narratives to project physically or logically impossible scenarios and events; I argue that the unnatural is what makes fiction interesting.

Furthermore, I look at the unnatural from a cognitive perspective in order to explain why the unnatural speaks to us and how we can make sense of represented impossibilities. I am primarily interested in the question of how the mind tries to cope with representations of the impossible (for example, by rearranging or recombining pre-existing cognitive parameters). Thus, on the basis of cognitive frames and scripts,[2] I have developed eight reading strategies which are designed to help readers come to terms with the unnatural: (1) I argue that the processes of blending (Fauconnier/Turner 2002 and Fludernik 2010) and frame enrichment play a role in all unnatural scenarios; the unnatural always urges us to create new (and initially unnatural) frames (such as 'the unborn character' or 'the dead narrator') by recombining, extending, or otherwise altering pre-existing cognitive parameters. (2) We can account for some unnatural scenarios through the conventions of literary genres (for example, we all know that animals can speak in beast fables or that time travel is possible in science fiction). (3) Other impossible elements can simply be explained as dreams, fantasies, or hallucinations ("reading events as internal states"); this reading strategy obviously unmasks the seemingly

---

[1] The retrogressive temporality in Martin Amis's novel *Time's Arrow* (1991), where time actually and objectively moves backward at the level of the story, is an example of physical impossibility, while the simultaneous projection of logically incompatible events in Robert Coover's short story "The Babysitter" (1969) is an example of logical impossibility.

[2] "Frames basically deal with situations such as seeing a room or making a promise while scripts cover standard action sequences such as playing a game of football, going to a birthday party, or eating in a restaurant" (Jahn 2005: 69).

unnatural as something distinctly natural (namely somebody's interiority). (4) Some examples of unnaturalness become more readable when we relate them to our literary knowledge and see them as thematic components rather than mimetically motivated occurrences ("foregrounding the thematic"). For instance, the impossible changes in weather and furnishing in Harold Pinter's The Basement (1967) can be recuperated thematically as a pointless yet inescapable struggle for power. (5) In a more specific variant of (4), readers see impossible elements as parts of allegories that say something about the world in general rather than particular individuals ("reading allegorically"). For example, we can deal with the disconcerting transformation of Grace into her beloved Graham in Sarah Kane's play Cleansed (1998) when we read the play as an allegory on the universal merits and dangers of love: on the one hand, Grace, who can be seen as Everywoman, finds tenderness and affirmation in the unity with Graham, but on the other hand, she also erases her identity. (6) Narratives may also use impossibilities to satirize, parody, or mock an entity. The most important feature of satire is critique through exaggeration, and the grotesque images of humiliation or ridicule may clearly merge with the unnatural. (7) Marie-Laure Ryan has shown that we can explain some logical impossibilities by assuming that "the contradictory passages in the text are offered to the readers as material for creating their own stories" (2006: 671). In such cases, the text serves as some kind of construction kit that invites free play with its elements ("do it yourself"). (8) Finally, as a radical alternative to my more or less intrepid moves of sense-making, all of which follow the human urge to create significance, I offer what one might call "the Zen way of reading." This way of reading presupposes an attentive and stoic reader who repudiates the above mentioned explanations, and simultaneously accepts both the strangeness of the unnatural and the feelings of discomfort, fear, worry, and panic that they might evoke in her or him.

My narratological work also has a historical dimension. In a first step, I argue that the postmodernist project primarily consists in the systematic undermining of our 'natural' cognition of the world (Alber 2009). In a second step, I try to unearth the history of this insurgence. In Alber (forthcoming), I qualify the argument about the playful extravagance of postmodernism by showing that narratives have always involved the unnatural. In comparison to earlier narratives, postmodernist texts acquire their specificity through the concentration and radicalization of unnaturalness. However, it is worth noting that the unnatural scenarios of postmodernism are not brand new phenomena. Rather, they have been anticipated in various different ways.³ Second, I show that during the course of literary history, many physically or logically impossible scenarios have already been conventionalized and turned into a cognitive category (Fludernik 2003b: 256).⁴ Third, I illustrate that the unnatural is a hitherto neglected driving force behind the development of new genres: new genres typically develop as an unnatural scenario becomes conventionalized (an example would be the development of the beast fable—starting with the ancient Greek Aesop—which went hand in hand with the conventionalization of the speaking animal).

My other work in narrative theory concerns cinematic narration and belongs to the area of transmedial narratology, which seeks to develop narrative theory so that it can handle new storytelling practices across a wide variety of media (Herman 2004). An interesting issue in this context is the question of how narrative practices are shaped by the capacities of the medium in which a story is presented. I am primarily interested in the question of how films narrate—and whether it makes sense to assume the existence of a cinematic narrator (Alber 2010), and in the (hitherto neglected) metaphoric potential of film (Alber, 2011).

I think that my work is postclassical (Herman 1997, 1999a: 2-3; Alber and Fludernik 2010b) because I have a reader- (or viewer-) oriented focus, am interested in various different narrative genres, and try to put narratology's "analytical toolbox to interpretative use" (Nünning 2003: 243-44). Also, I have a diachronic orientation and look at different manifestations of narrative throughout literary history. In *Postclassical Narratology: Approaches and Analyses* (2010b), Monika Fludernik and I show that postclassical narratology has now reached a new phase of consolidation but also continued diversification. Today's narratologists see the object of

---

³For example, the differential temporality in Caryl Churchill's play *Cloud Nine* (1979), where society jumps a century ahead, while the characters age only 25 years, finds its anticipation in science-fiction narratives such as Robert A. Heinlein's *Time for the Stars* (1956) or Joe Haldeman's *The Forever War* (1974), where characters age at different rates because one of them travels near light speed.

⁴Examples are the speaking animal in beast fables, supernatural creatures or events, the speaking objects in eighteenth-century circulation novels, time travel in science-fiction narratives, the 'omniscient' narrator in realist novels, and so forth.

their research as more variegated than was the case twenty years ago. Also, they resort to various different methodologies in combination when approaching a narrative, and they tend to ground their analyses in a rich contextual framework (Alber and Fludernik 2010a: 15-23).

Finally, I would like to stress that I think it is better if others judge whether my work is important or not. At least the unnatural is currently a rather controversial topic (which is a good thing, I think).

3. What is the proper role of narratology and narrative theory in relation to other academic disciplines?

I do not conceive of the relationship between narratology and other disciplines as a hierarchical one. From my perspective, narratology is simply one discipline among numerous other (and equally important) disciplines. Narratology's descriptive focus on the question of what a narrative is and how narratives function has resulted in the development of numerous analytical tools or concepts—such as plot typologies (Vladimir Propp), the story-discourse distinction (Boris Tomashevsky, Tzvetan Todorov, Chatman), the relationship between story time and discourse time (Müller, Genette, Chatman), the implied author (Wayne Booth, James Phelan, Peter Rabinowitz), Genette's concept of focalization, narrative embeddings and narrative levels (Genette, Bal), Stanzel's narrative situations, experientiality (Fludernik), the storyworld (David Herman), ways of rendering character interiority (Dorrit Cohn), character components (James Phelan), the continuing-consciousness frame (Alan Palmer), polychronic narration (Herman) and other unnatural temporalities (Brian Richardson), and so on and so forth.

From my perspective, there is no reason why these tools should not engage in fruitful dialogues with the concepts in other literary theories (such as feminism, queer theory, neo-Marxism, new historicism, postcolonialism, ethnic criticism, or reader-response theory) or other academic disciplines—if these fusions help to explain or analyze the object of study in a better way (I am particularly thinking of philosophy, psychology, sociology, law, and political science). As a matter of fact, numerous examples of such interactions do already exist. For example, feminist narratologists (such as Susan Lanser, Robyn Warhol, Kathy Mezei, or Ruth Page) study elements of both story and discourse against the foil of gender differences. Also, one can investigate the question of how narratives negotiate ideologies in the sense of Louis Althusser and determine whether certain plot types, character constellations, or narrative situations critique or reproduce these ideologies. This is, for instance, done by postcolonial narratologists who discuss the narrative negotiation of the colonial project (see, e.g., Marie Louise Pratt, David Spurr, and Frederick Aldama).[5] In such fusions of narrative theory and other disciplines, it is perhaps important to reflect upon the neutrality of narratological tools and concepts in order not to reach simplistic conclusions about the alleged links between narrative structures and certain ideologies (see, e.g. John Bender and D.A. Miller, who posit a link between the 'omniscient' narrator and Jeremy Bentham's *Panopticon*). Unless I am very much mistaken, narrative structures in and of themselves are ethically neutral (they do not have a Western bias), and can be used for a wide variety of different purposes (depending upon the context within which they are used). At the same time, I would like to argue that detailed knowledge about these narrative structures in their respective contexts is vitally important because it can make all analyses of stories more concise.

4. What do you consider to be the most important topics and/or contributions in narratology?

From my perspective, the most important contributions in narratology stress the specificity of fictional narratives by highlighting the ways in which they deviate from our real-world experience. Already in 1916, the Russian formalist Viktor Shklovsky came up with the notion of estrangement (*ostranenie*), i.e., the argument that art 'makes strange.' Shklovsky argues that

> [...] the technique of art is to make objects 'unfamiliar,' to make forms difficult, to increase the difficulty and length of perception because the process of perception is an aesthetic end in itself and must be prolonged. Art is a way of experiencing the artfulness of an object; the object is not important. [...] Art removes objects from the automatism of perception in several ways (1965: 12-13; italics in the original).[6]

---

[5] I would also like to mention Jarmila Mildorf who follows David Herman's suggestions concerning the development of a 'socionarratology' (Herman 1999c) and shows very convincingly that narratological categories can also be useful in social-science contexts.

[6] The unnatural in the sense in which I am using the term (Alber 2009) is a radical subcase of Shklovsky's notion of defamiliarization.

In this context, I would of course also like to mention Brian Richardson's profound analyses (1997, 2000, 2002, and 2006), in which he shows how anti-mimetic narratives transcend real-world notions of time, character, and voice (for further important work on impossible temporalities, see Ryan (2009); on the 'omniscient' first-person narrator, see Nielsen (2004) and Heinze (2008); on anti-mimeticism in general, see Tammi (2006 and 2008)). Furthermore, Brian McHale (1987, 1992) and Werner Wolf (1993) devoted themselves to the specific techniques used in postmodernist and other anti-illusionist narrative texts. McHale lists a substantial number of metafictional strategies, all of which are designed to foreground what he calls the ontological dominant, i.e., the inventedness of the narrative discourse. Wolf's study, on the other hand, presents an exhaustive description of anti-illusionist techniques which covers all anti-illusionist writing, not just the specific kind of anti-illusionism practised in postmodernist texts.

Since I feel that we as readers are ultimately bound by our cognitive architecture (even when we try to make sense of the unnatural), the only way in which we can respond to narratives is on the basis of cognitive frames, scripts, and schemata.[7] Therefore, I would like to argue that some of the most enlightening work in narratology was produced in the area of cognitive narratology on the basis of experiential frames, scripts, and schemata. In particular, I would like to stress two ground-breaking studies, namely Fludernik's *Towards a 'Natural' Narratology* (1996) and Herman's *Story Logic: Problems and Possibilities of Narrative* (2002). Fludernik's redefinition of narrativity in terms of experientiality has opened up an entirely new way of looking at narratives across the centuries and also in various different media. I would also like to stress that her flexible four-level model[8] al-

---

[7] Lubomír Doležel aptly describes this process of responding to fictional worlds as follows: "In order to reconstruct and interpret a fictional world, the reader has to *reorient his cognitive stance* to agree with the world's encyclopedia. In other words, knowledge of the fictional encyclopedia is absolutely necessary for the reader to comprehend a fictional world. *The actual-world encyclopedia might be useful, but it is by no means universally sufficient; for many fictional worlds it is misleading, it provides not comprehension but misreading*" (Doležel 1998: 177; 181; my italics).

[8] According to Fludernik, the process of narrativization (at level IV) is based on the following types of cognitive frames: pretextual schemata that involve our real-world knowledge and parameters used to parse events as intentional acts (level I); frames of narrative mediation such as "telling" (narratives focusing on a teller figure), "experiencing" (narratives that are focal-

lows for the integration of numerous new frames and scripts that relate to experimental texts or new media (see Fludernik 2003b). For Herman, narratives are tools for the organization of human experience. On the basis of countless stories (which are oral, written, fictional, and non-fictional), Herman looks at the world-creating power of narratives, and he also frequently analyzes challenging experimental narratives. I particularly admire Herman's study for the development of complex higher order modelling systems such as polychronic narration (see also Herman 1998), hypothetical focalization, and double deixis.

I would also like to mention Herman's *Narratologies: New Perspectives on Narrative Analysis* (1999b), where he introduced the term 'postclassical narratology'[9] and defined it as follows:

> Postclassical narratology (which should not be conflated with poststructuralist theories of narrative) contains classical narratology as one of its 'moments' but is marked by a profusion of new methodologies and research hypotheses: the result is a host of new perspectives on the forms and functions of narrative itself. Further, in its postclassical phase, research on narrative does not just expose the limits but also exploits the possibilities of the older, structuralist models. In much the same way, postclassical physics does not simply discard classical Newtonian models, but rather rethinks their conceptual underpinnings and reassesses their scope of applicability (Herman 1999a: 2-3).

Herman's *Narratologies* is an important publication because it documents the paradigm shift from the classical structuralist treatment of narrative as a langue to the pragmatic focus on the parole of individual (or concrete) narratives in postclassical approaches. As Luc Herman and Bart Vervaeck put it, the differences between the structuralist and the new postclassical paradigm can be characterized as follows: "Whereas structuralism was intent on coming

---

ized through the consciousness of a protagonist), "viewing" (the witnessing of events), and "reflecting" (the projection of a reflecting consciousness in the process of rumination) (level II); and criteria pertaining to genre as well as to narrative as a general mode of discourse (level III) (Fludernik 1996: 43-46).

[9] David Herman originally coined the term 'postclassical narratology' in an essay called "Scripts, Sequences, and Stories: Elements of a Postclassical Narratology" (1997).

up with a general theory of narrative, postclassical narratology prefers to consider the circumstances that make every act of reading different. [...] From cognition to ethics to ideology: all aspects related to reading assume pride of place in the research on narrative" (2005: 450). Furthermore, the term 'postclassical narratology' subsumes numerous new approaches such as cognitive narratology, feminist narratology, postcolonial narratology, the rhetorical theory of narrative, socionarratology, transmedial narratology, diachronic narratology (Fludernik 2003a), unnatural narratology, and so forth (see also Alber and Fludernik 2010b).

At the same time, I do not wish to disregard the pioneering work of structuralist narratologists without which postclassical narratology would not exist. In particular, I would like to mention Propp's *Morphology of the Folktale* (1927), Todorov's article "Les catégories du récit littéraire" (1966)[10]; Genette's *Discours du récit* (1972) as well as his *Nouveau discours du récit* (1983); Stanzel's *Theorie des Erzählens* (1979); Chatman's *Story and Discourse* (1978) as well as his *Coming to Terms* (1990a); and Gerald Prince's *Narratology* (1982).

5. What are the most important open problems in this field and what are the prospects for progress?

Most of the important open problems in the field of narratology have to be placed on the overlap between different postclassical narratologies and demand further fusions of analytical tools and concepts. I can see a number of open problems that relate to unnatural narratology, cognitive narratology, and transmedial narratology. For instance, one open problem concerns the inductive development of new cognitive frames on the basis of the analyses of experimental narratives as well as new media (such as hypertext narratives, computer games, new social networks, and so forth) and media that have traditionally not been analyzed as narratives (such as music and painting). As far as experimental narratives are concerned, I am particularly thinking of frames that pertain to unnatural or impossible narrators, characters, time, and space (such as 'the unborn narrator,' 'the character that displays mutually exclusive features,' 'reversed causality,' 'the impossible geography,' and so forth) and their potential functions (Alber 2009;

---

[10] The term *narratology* was coined by Todorov in *Grammaire du Décaméron* (1969), where he writes: "Cet ouvrage relève d'une science qui n'existe pas encore, disons la NARRATOLOGIE, la science du récit" (1969: 10).

Alber, Iversen, Nielsen and Richardson 2010). As far as new media are concerned, narratologists seek to determine whether the traditional tools are applicable or whether these have to be modified to match the new object of study (see Wolf 1999 and 2003; Ryan 2004; Bell 2010).

Another open problem concerns the question of narrative mediation, i.e., the question of whether it makes sense to assume that all narratives are mediated by a first-degree narrative instance or not (see also Alber and Fludernik 2009). For example, Manfred Jahn (2001) posits such a narrative instance for all plays,[11] while Irina O. Rajewsky (2007) is clearly opposed to this idea. Similarly, Seymour Chatman assumes the existence of a cinematic narrator (1990a: 127), while David Bordwell argues that cinematic narration is created by the viewer, who uses cognitive schemata to transform the film's visual images and sounds into a series of perceptible configurations (1985: 61). Richard Walsh even suggests eradicating extra- and heterodiegetic narrators in general: "Extradiegetic heterodiegetic narrators (that is, 'impersonal' and 'authorial' narrators), who cannot be represented without thereby being rendered homodiegetic or intradiegetic, are in no way distinguishable from authors." He therefore concludes that "the narrator is always either a character who narrates, or the author" (2007: 8,4; 78). From my perspective, one should look at the usefulness of these assumptions and categories for the actual analyses of narratives. Does it help to make our readings of narratives better if we assume that they are narrated by a first-degree narrative agency or not?

---

[11] Jahn argues that "all narrative genres are structurally mediated by a first-degree narrative agency which, in a performance, may either take the totally unmetaphorical shape of a vocally and bodily present narrator figure (a scenario that is unavailable in written epic narrative), or be a disembodied 'voice' in a printed text, or remain an anonymous and impersonal narrative function in charge of selection, arrangement, and focalization" (2001: 674).

3
Mieke Bal

Emeritus Professor of Cultural analysis
University of Amsterdam; independent scholar and video artist

---

1. Why were you initially drawn to narratology or narrative theory?

From early on, I considered the theory of narrative a relevant area of study because it is not confined to one specific academic discipline. This is so because narrative is a mode, not a genre. It is alive and active as a cultural force, not just as a kind of literature. The narratives that circulate constitute a major reservoir of the cultural baggage that enables us to make meaning out of a chaotic world and the sometimes incomprehensible events taking place in it. And, not to be forgotten, narrative can be used to manipulate. In short, it is a cultural force to be reckoned with. It was my fascination with narrative as a cultural force rather than as a literary genre that gave me the motivation to work on narrative theory at the time. At some point I realised that the reason I saw narrative in this way had to do with the concept of narrative that I had unreflectively endorsed. It was through the diffuse, self-evident yet powerfully specific concept of narrative that I began to consider culture at large as object of analysis.

2. What do you consider your most important contribution(s) to the field?

I suppose my work is best known for the revision—or better, reconceptualization—of the concept of focalization. This concept has allowed me to make several related moves. First, within (literary) narratology, it has helped me to transform the theory from a typology to a set of analytical tools. My argument with Gérard Genette turns around this distinction. For me, the primary point of narratology is to facilitate detailed analysis, not to divide the corpus of stories into types. (The elements of this discussion are in Bal (1991a); Genette(1972 and 1988).)

Second, between disciplines, it made it possible to articulate the relationship between linguistic and visual narrative with greater precision. Third, in methodological reflection it helped me articulate the distinction between transdisciplinarity, multidisciplinarity, and interdisciplinarity. Transdisciplinary approaches and concepts tend to be thematic, e.g. "adultery in Victorian culture." Multidisciplinary approaches, usually performed by groups, tend to be defined by periods, e.g. the Golden Age, where every group member contributes studies from single disciplines. Together, these provide an image of the era studied. Interdisciplinary approaches and concepts, the most challenging of these three, "borrow" necessary concepts from different disciplines. The trick is to not distort the concept or tear it out of its field of origin, but to deploy it in the new setting in responsible ways (to this, see the forthcoming volume Allan Repko (ed.), *Case Studies in Interdisciplinary Research*. London: Sage).

Focalization is a typically interdisciplinary concept. As I have come to see it later, focalization is part of a cluster of neighboring concepts such as the "gaze" in visual and psychoanalytic theory, and "iconicity" in semiotics. These concepts are different but affiliated. They are often conflated, with disastrous results, or, alternatively, kept separate, with impoverishing results.

The concept of the gaze has a variety of backgrounds. It is sometimes used as an equivalent of the "look," indicating the position of the subject doing the looking. As such, it points to a position, real or represented. It is also used in distinction from the look, as a fixed and fixating, colonising mode of looking—a look that objectifies, appropriates, disempowers, and possibly even violates. In its Lacanian sense (see Kaja Silverman. *The Threshold of the Visible World*. New York: Routledge, 1996) .It is most certainly very different from—if not opposed to—the more common use made of it as the equivalent of the look or a specific version of it. The Lacanian gaze is, most succinctly, the visual order (equivalent to the symbolic order, or the visual part of that order) in which the subject is caught. In this sense it is an indispensable concept through which to understand all cultural domains, including text-based ones. The gaze is the world looking (back) at the subject.[1]

In its more common use, the gaze is the look that the subject casts on other people, and other things. Feminism initiated the

---

[1] Ernst van Alphen's analysis of Charlotte Delbo's writings is suggestively titled "Caught by Images." See his *Art in Mind: How Contemporary Images Shape Thought*. Chicago: University of Chicago Press, 2005.

scrutiny of the gaze's objectifying thrust, especially in film studies, where the specific Lacanian sense remains important. Cultural critics, including anthropologists, have recently become interested in the use of photography in historical and ethnographic research. More broadly, the meaning-producing effects of images, including textual-rhetorical ones, have been recognised. In this type of analysis, the gaze is also obviously central. The objectification and the disempowering exotization of others further flesh out the issues of power inequity that the concept helps to lay bare. Indeed, the affiliated concepts of the other and alterity have been scrutinized for their own collusion with the imperialist forces that hold the gaze in this photographic and cinematic material.

Enabling the analysis of non-canonical objects, such as snapshots, the concept is also helpful in allowing the boundaries between elite and larger culture to be overcome. Between all these usages, an examination of the concept itself is appropriate. Not to police it, or to prescribe a purified use for it, but to gauge its possibilities.

So far, the concept of the gaze has demonstrated its flexibility and inclination to social criticism. But, for the issue of interdisciplinary methodology, it also has a more hands-on kind of relevance. It has an affiliation with—although it is not identical to—the concept of focalization in narratology. This is where I became involved. In fact, in narrative theory, the concept of focalization, although clearly visual in background, has been deployed to overcome visual strictures and the subsequent metaphorical floundering of concepts such as "perspective" and "point of view."

It is precisely because the concept of focalization is not identical to that of the gaze or the look (although persistently affiliated with both) that it can help to clarify a vexed issue in the relationship between looking and language, between art history and literary studies. The common question for all three of these concepts is what the look of a represented (narrated or depicted) figure does to the imagination of the reader or the look of the viewer.

Focalization was the object of my first academic passion when I became a narratologist in the 1970s. Retrospectively, my interest in developing a concept more workable than the usual ones was rooted in an idea about the cultural importance of vision, even in the most language-based of the arts. But vision must not be understood exclusively in the technical-visual sense. In the slightly metaphorical but indispensable sense of imaginary—akin but not identical to imagination—vision tends to involve both actual looking and interpreting, including in literary reading. While this is a reason to recommend the verb "reading" for the analysis of visual images, it is also a reason not to cast the visual out of the concept of focalization. The danger of dilution must be carefully balanced here against the impoverishment caused by conceptual essentialism.

The term "focalization" also helped overcome the limitations of the linguistically inspired tools inherited from structuralism. As these were based on the structure of the sentence, they failed to help me account for what happens between characters in narrative, figures in image, and the readers of both. The great emphasis on conveyable and generalizable content in structuralist semantics hampered my attempts to understand how such contents were conveyed—to what effects and ends—through what can be termed "subjectivity networks" (For more on subjectivity networks, I must refer to my book *On Story-Telling* (Bal 1991a). The hypothesis that says readers envision, that is, create, images from textual stimuli, cuts right through semantic theory, grammar, and rhetoric, to foreground the presence and crucial importance of images in reading.[2] When I managed to solve a long-standing problem of biblical philology "simply" by envisioning, instead of deciphering the text, I savoured the great pleasure and excitement that comes with discovery. Let me call the provisional result of this first phase of the concept-in-use dynamic the "gaze-as-focalizor."[3]

The second phase goes in the opposite direction. Take "Rembrandt," for example. The name stands for a text—"Rembrandt" as the cultural ensemble of images that are dis- and re-attributed according to an expansive or purifying cultural mood—and for the discourses about the real and imaginary figure indicated by the name. The images called "Rembrandt" are notoriously disinterested in linear perspective but also highly narrative. Moreover, many of these images are replete with issues relevant for a gender perspective such as the nude, scenes related to rape, and myth-based history paintings in which women are being framed. For

---

[2] A key text remains W.J.T. Mitchell's opening chapter "What is an Image?" from *Iconology: Image, Text, Ideology*. Chicago: University of Chicago Press, 1986. The word "envision" yields a tentative concept from Peter Schwenger's *Fantasm and Fiction: On Textual Envisioning*. Stanford, CA: Stanford University Press, 1999.

[3] Several examples of this can be found in Bal (1988) and (1997). Both books are devoted to literary texts. Offering an example here would lengthen my text beyond the format of this book.

these reasons combined, focalization imposes itself as an operative concept. In contrast, "perspective" can only spell disaster. But while narrativity may be medium-independent, the transfer of a specific concept from narrative theory to visual texts requires the probing of its realm, its productivity, and its potential.

This probing is all the more important because of the double ambiguity that threatens to occur here. Firstly, focalization is a narrative inflection of imagining, interpreting, and perception that can, but need not be visual imaging. To conflate focalization with the gaze would be to return to square one, thus undoing the work of differentiation between two different modes of semiotic expression. Secondly, and conversely, the projection of narrativity on visual images is an analytic move that has great potential but is also highly specific. To put it simply: images are not more narrative than narrative acts of focalization are visual. Yet narratives and images have envisioning as their common form of reception. The differences and the common elements are equally important.

In my own work, the examination of the concept of focalization for use in the analysis of visual images was all the more urgent because the new area of visual imagery appears to carry traces of the same word by which the concept is known. This was a moment of truth: is focalization in narratology only a metaphor borrowed from the visual? If so, does its deployment in visual analysis fall back on its literal meaning?

No. Instead, the concept of focalization helps to articulate the look precisely through its movement. After travelling, first from the visual domain to narratology, then to the more specific analysis of visual images, focalization, having arrived at its new destination, visual analysis, has received a meaning that overlaps neither with the old visual one—focusing with a lens—nor with the new narratological one—the cluster of perception and interpretation that guides the attention through the narrative. It now indicates neither a location of the gaze on the picture plane, nor a subject of it, such as either the figure or the viewer. Instead, what becomes visible is the movement of the look. In that movement, the look encounters the limitations imposed by the gaze, the visual order. The gaze dictates the limits of the figure's respective positions as holder of the objectifying and colonizing look, and the disempowered object of that look. The tension between the focalizor's movement and these limitations is the true object of analysis. For it is here that structural, formal aspects of the object become meaningful, dynamic, and culturally operative: through the time-bound, changing effect of the culture that frames them.

Focalization is an instance of a concept travelling from one discipline to another and back again. The itinerary is to be termed inter-disciplinary in this specific sense. To call it transdisciplinary would be to presuppose its immutable rigidity, a travelling without changing; to call it multidisciplinary would be to subject the fields of the two disciplines to a common analytic tool. Neither option is viable. Instead, a negotiation, a transformation, a re-assessment is needed at each stage. Thanks to its narratological background, the concept of focalization imports a mobility into the visual domain that usefully and productively complements the potential to structure envisioning that had been carried over from visual to narrative in the first phase. This answers already in practice the next question.

3. What is the proper role of narratology and narrative theory in relation to other academic disciplines?

According to my answer to question 1, "narrative" is a transdisciplinary concept, while "narratology," the systematic study of the phenomenon that this concept names, has been developed within the disciplinary niche of literary studies. But narratology itself is an interdiscipline precisely because it defines an object, a discursive modality that occurs in many different fields.

As a result of the move toward greater interdisciplinarity, others, such as narrativists in historiography, have alleged narrative as important see Hayden White (1973), Kellner (1989), Ankersmit (2001) for examples. But as long as such movements remain efforts within one discipline, very few of its participants can take the time needed to study the theoretical work from another discipline, even if it provides them with a key concept. Simply borrowing a loose term here and there does not make for true interdisciplinary practice. Narrativism for example has had little exposure to narratology. Conversely, the narratology that came to the attention of narrativists was so narrowly based on fiction that they saw little point in it for their historiographic project. This was a major setback for both.

Nowadays, narrative is more important than ever, not only in literary studies but also in history, where the awareness of narrative construction has grown tremendously; in cultural analysis, where cultural memory (documented in mostly narrative form) is a popular subject of study; and in film studies, which has itself bloomed over the past twenty years, with its inevitably narrative subject matter. Peter Verstraten's recent book *Film Narratology*

(2009), largely based on my own narratology, demonstrates the genuine interdisciplinarity that can result from such integrations.

4. What do you consider the most important topics in and/or contributions to narratology?

For me, there are three important areas in cultural analysis where narratology has a lot to contribute. First, the topics centered on vision and envisioning, outlined above, remain crucial. They are so important because in cultural practice, people process information through an integration of envisioning and the narrative imagination; image and story go hand in hand. Second, I find the focus on action, the agents involved, and the temporality inherent in action uniquely relevant for a dynamic cultural analysis. Here, both cultural artefacts and theoretical texts themselves are subject to such analysis. It is even possible to make a narratological analysis of abstract paintings, once the analysis focuses on the interaction between painting and viewer. This approach undermines the idea that pictures can be processed in a single, quick glance (see the chapter "Second Person Narrative" in Bal 1999).

Third, the insertion of narrative within argumentative discourse and descriptions accounts for the manipulation of cultural "speakers" or agents. This process deserves closer scrutiny. Just think of the role played by the devilish image of Saddam Hussein and his alleged secret weapons of mass destruction in setting the world on a disastrous course of war. I would argue that it is the narrative imagination rather than the arguments in themselves that decides on consensus. This cultural logic goes against the grain of argumentation as a privileged practice. Political scientists can potentially benefit immensely from a narratological analysis of political practice (see "Love Story," my analysis of a gossip story, in Bal 1994).

5. What are the most important open problems in this field and what are the prospects for progress?

First, there remains a tenacious discrepancy between text-based narratology and other, related developments. The lack of integration renders the former overspecialized and the latter more or less vague. Second, a tendency to either get stuck in, or reject altogether, a "formalist" approach to narrative makes the theories either rigid and blind to ideology, or else inoperable and conducive to a simplistic sense of political analysis. This opposition ignores the political value of teachability, intersubjectivity, and the kind of hands-on analytical skills that a balanced narratology can offer.

Intersubjectivity is a concern that binds procedure with power and empowerment, with pedagogy and the transmittability of knowledge, and with inclusion and exclusion. Thus it connects heuristic with methodological grounding. The power of concepts to facilitate invention cannot be thought of without the intersubjectivity of which power is a factor. My interest is in developing concepts we can all agree on and use, or at the very least disagree on, in order to make what has become labeled "theory" accessible to every participant in cultural analysis, both within and outside the academy. Agreeing does not mean agreeing on content, but agreeing on the basic rules of the game: if you use a concept at all, you use it in a particular way, so that you can meaningfully disagree on content. It is important to realize that such use does not go without saying. Intersubjectivity in this sense remains the most important standard for teaching and writing. Whatever else it does, cultural analysis owes it to its principles of anti-elitism, to its firm position against exclusion of everything that is non-canonical and everyone who is not mainstream, to take this standard seriously. A narratology geared toward this principle can have a democratic impact on teaching practice.

4
Ann Banfield

Professor of English
University of California, Berkeley

1. Why were you initially drawn to narratology or narrative theory?

What inintially drew me to narrative theory was an interest in the formal properties of literature and most particularly of the language of literature. That interest first led me to linguistics, rather than, linguistics leading me to literature, as it is often assumed. My Ph.D. is in literature and not linguistics. My doctoral dissertation was on the formal notion of a stylistic transformation, introduced by Noam Chomsky in *Aspects of the Theory of Syntax* (1965). The thesis took as its main body of data Milton's *Paradise Lost*; the two major stylistic phenomena I treated were so-called "free word order" in poetry and configurations (constructions) where an element in coordinate conjoined structures appears as null "under identity" with another (including the rhetorical figure called "zeugma"). Some of these constructions had been treated as the result of straightforward grammatical transformations within generative linguistics (e.g., "gapping" or verb deletion in coordinate conjoined structure). I argued that many problems with the assumption that all coordinate conjoined structures could be accounted for in the same way were solved if one assumed stylistic transformations were distinct from grammatical ones and applied to the output of the latter. I attempted to set down the formal operations that gave rise to these constructions.

It was the happy accident of S.-Y. Kuroda asking me to read the manuscript of what became his article "Where Style, Grammar and Epistemology Meet" (Kuroda 1973) that opened up a new direction for my interests in the language of literature. What Kuroda discovered in the behavior of sensation adjectives and verbs in the Japanese novel I felt had counterparts in English and French in the grammar of direct and indirect speech. (I recognized aspects of D. H. Lawrence's style I had speculated on in a 1963 Master's Thesis.) Seldom since has an intellectual discovery led me so quickly to set down my hypotheses in writing. My first draft was a bit premature, however. At the time (this was 1972), neither Kuroda nor I knew the literature on *style indirect libre* or *erlebte Rede*. Further reading led me to the early literature on that style. Initially I felt disappointed in finding myself anticipated, but eventually it pushed me to formulate hypotheses that went beyond a description of the data, hypotheses which remain controversial but that I still feel stand without convincing alternatives.

My interests in the formal properties of literature also include an interest in genre theory, something that, paradoxically, is rarely addressed in narrative theory. I say "paradoxically" because the question of what distinguishes narrative forms from others—e.g., the lyric or the drama—enters little into what has come to be known as "narratology", although it certainly interested the ancients, particularly Plato and Aristotle, and early twentieth-century theorists of narrative such as the Russian Formalists, Vladimir Propp or Mikhail Bakhtin. Unfortunately, the category of narrative has become a kind of "big, baggy monster," to borrow Henry James's term for *War and Peace*, into which almost any form can be stuffed, usually under the vague term "story", an entity not even necessarily treated as linguistic. Even ordinary language reserves the phrases "to tell or to recount a story" and "to narrate" for linguistic processes. A drama does not "tell" or "recount" but represents an event or series of events. It is, I think, legitimate to ask whether different literary genres can be defined, i.e., distinguished, whether they can be done so linguistically and whether one can distinguish sub-genres of narrative. Oral narratives differ in important ways from written narratives. The novel is not an epic, yet it shares properties with it. On the other hand, the novel shares properties with the short story that set both apart from the epic. "If we can't keep our genres more or less distinct, or extricate them from the confusion that has them where they are, we might as well go home and lie down", Samuel Beckett wrote (Letter to Barney Rosset, 27 August 1957, cited in *The Complete Short Prose: 1929—1989*, S. E. Gontarski (ed.), New York: Grove Press, 1995. n. 22, xxxii.). Stating precisely what the differences are is admittedly an often difficult task—why, for instance, did Beckett insist that his text "neither" was not poetry but prose? But invoking undecidability or the merging of forms is an easy way out. We might as well go home and lie down.

I continue to be drawn to considerations of the language of literature. Hence, I am currently writing on Samuel Beckett's style.

2. What do you consider your most important contribution(s) to the field?

"Narrative Style and the Grammar of Direct and Indirect Speech" (Banfield 1973), which initiated my interests in narrative style, already contains the core of the arguments about what I call, after Jespersen, "represented speech and thought", along with those bearing on the narrative tenses, developed in greater detail in *Unspeakable Sentences*. "Describing the Unobserved: Events Grouped Around an Empty Center" (1987) and "The Name of the Subject: the 'il'" (1998) connect my earlier treatment of pronouns in the novel to philosophical treatments of subjectivity, and "Grammar and Memory" (1985) and a section of "Tragic Time: The Problem of the Future in Cambridge Philosophy and *To the Lighthouse*" (2000) relate my earlier treatment of time and tense to philosophical treatments of time. More recently, I returned to the question of the origins of represented speech and thought in a paper examining examples from medieval through seventeenth-century literature that I gave in July, 2010, at the Congrès Mondial de Linguistique Française organized by the Institut de Linguistique Française (CNRS) in New Orleans.

5. What are the most important open problems in this field and what are the prospects for progress?

I think the specific role and contribution of narratology and narrative theory to disciplines such as literary theory in general and genre theory in particular, as well as to history, aesthetic theory and linguistics is to draw attention to the different forms narrative can assume and to describe those forms. This means that narrative should not be defined so widely that there is almost nothing that is not narrative. Moreover, I mistrust the collapsing of the terms "narrative" and "story", as I indicated above, particularly when the latter is taken as synonymous with fiction and when it is extended to scientific and historical theories. There are historical events that actually happened, and it is important to establish that they did, even if the truth value of a proposition in an important sense depends on the possibility of its being either true or false. Moreover, the truth or falsity of a statement in no way depends on who holds it; it is independent of the subject. I have also been long fascinated by what distinguishes a scientific proposition from one that is not and feel it is legitimate to raise the question.

This in no way is equivalent to holding that what is not a scientific statement is of lesser value. (Of course, it should be added that a scientific proposition can be falsified.) It is only by keeping these different categories distinct that each has conferred on it the value proper to it. Certainly literature will not hold its own if it is subsumed along with the others under a single category.

Finally, the claims of narrative theory should be supported by evidence. Sometimes the discovery of new evidence can be as significant as the formulation of a new theory. At the same time, one must negotiate the Scylla and Charybdis of the total absence of data and the list of counter-examples mistakenly assumed to falsify a theory, in the absence of any attempt to provide a counter-theory that explains all the original data as well as the counter-examples. The evidence for the claims of narrative theory can be of various kinds. I persist in thinking that language provides some of its most crucial evidence and that that source is far from exhausted. I think a return to language and to what linguistics has to tell us about language could revitalize narrative theory and open up new horizons.

5
Marisa Bortolussi & Peter Dixon

Modern Languages and Cultural Studies/Department of Psychology
University of Alberta

Beyond Post-Classical Narratology: The Next Stage

In the present essay, we describe an apparent impasse in the field of narratology in which the application of narratology "tools" has failed to create a real advance in the field. We argue that although classical narratology can provide an adequate analysis of the text, it does not lead to suitable methods for understanding reading in context. On the other hand, empirical methods, such as those developed by Bortolussi and Dixon (2003), generate evidence on contextual factors and form the basis for advances in narratology.

The Narratology "Toolbox"

Classical narratology has been referred to as a toolbox available for the analysis of narrative. It provides a repertoire of discursive strategies and formal, stylistic features established through rigorous dissection, analysis, and, ultimately, a high level of professional consensus, as well as a sophisticated technical vocabulary that can be put at the service of any analytical and/or interpretative goal. Its greatest strength is that for example it can be applied to any narrative, including literary sources, oral *stories,* or narratives in film or television (Nünning 2003). For example, it can be used to describe the specificity of genres and sub-genres or of a given author's style, it can support thematic readings or ideological interpretations, and, more generally, it can be used to ground assumptions, inferences, and conclusions in textual evidence, thereby minimizing the risk of idiosyncratic impositions on the text.

Given this functionality and flexibility, it is hardly surprising that these tools have been co-opted by a host of approaches to literary studies that were previously inimical to it. This has led to a host of "post-classical" subfields that include "narratology" in their hyphenated titles. We have, so far, counted 22 of these narratologies. (In alphabetical order, these are: contextualist, constructivist, cultural and historical, corporeal, communicational, cyberage, comparative, dyachronic, ethno, feminist, intercultural, natural, post-colonial, pragmatic, psycho, queer, rhetorical and ethical, sociological, thematic, transgressive, and visual narratologies.) Clearly, narratology's chameleon adaptability has safeguarded its continuity. However, we doubt whether the extension of narratology into these numerous subfields has solved any of its most basic, perennial problems. Indeed, Nünning (2003) argued that most of these developments are applications rather than novel methods. As a consequence, they are still fraught with the very problem that they criticized in narratology and sought to surpass, namely, the problem of how to ground the analysis of literary texts in their social, historical, and cultural context.

We argue in this essay that narratology, in both its classical and post-classical varieties, has reached an impasse or dead end. However, we also believe that a solution to the "contextual conundrum" is available to those who are willing to take the necessary plunge. We end our paper with a description of what this "plunge" entails.

The Contextual Critique

As many have argued, the core limitation of classical narratology is that it provides merely an analysis of the text (cf. Chatman 1999, Herman 1997, Fludernik 2005). However, texts are associated with meaning, and meaning is not located exclusively in the text. Rather, it emerges as a function of the interaction between the author, the text, the reader, and the context of both the author and reader. Because authors do not write in a vacuum, it is argued, they are conduits through which the norms and values of their age, society, class, and so on pass, so that the text must necessarily bear the marks of this preexisting structure. With respect to the context of reception, it is argued, it is the reader who makes sense of the text; since readers are also embedded in a context, they bring their contextual experience, knowledge, and expectations to bear on the texts they read, hear, or view. Thus, a deeper and more pertinent analysis of narratives requires that the analysis of texts be wedded to a suitable analysis of the context.

The revisions that narratology has undergone since the 80's as a response to this contextual critique all share the basic premise that a formal analysis of the text is only a point of departure. However, a survey of the hyphenated narratological paradigms suggests little in the way of rigorous methods for moving beyond that point. In particular, conclusions about context are often based on speculative or idiosyncratic interpretations that are unlikely to form the basis of general knowledge. Because there is no counterpart to the rigorous analysis of the text, causal inferences concerning context are too often based on intuition and a haphazard selection of instances. As examples, we describe below the investigation of context from three perspectives, feminist, rhetorical, and cognitive narratology.

Context from the Feminist Perspective

Feminist narratology provides an example of how literary scholars have responded to the contextual critique. In her state-of-the-art assessment of feminist narratology, Page (2006) exposes the fallacious nature of the causal attributions that were made early in the development of this perspective. For example, two contextual variables related to the author are sex and gender. Driven by the assumption that extratextual ideologies influence production, earlier feminist agendas mandated the search for causal connections between the sex of an author and such elements as writing style and narrative plot. However, consistent correlations of this sort were difficult to find (Warhol 1999; Page 2006). To counter this lack of a deterministic relation, author gender is no longer conceived as fixed but rather varying across individual readers and readings. Furthermore, it is now seen as only one variable among many others, equally as fluid. Although this flexibility seems required by the variation in texts and readings, it leads to a conceptual and methodological impasse. On the one hand, a conceptual impasse arises because the approach implies that the relationships between gender and writing and between gender and reception are tenuous. Thus, it is difficult to account for the intuition that gender is somehow important. On the other hand, a methodological impasse arises because it becomes clear that intuition and argumentation are not sufficient to prove causality. In particular, it is not apparent how to isolate relevant contextual variables nor how to study the interrelation of gender and other variables.

Feminist narratologists propose two specific ways around this impasse. The first is the argument that gender does not create texts but that rather, texts create gender (Warhol 1999; Page 2006). More than a solution, however, this acknowledgment implies a retreat from the investigation of context. If gender is in the text, then only careful textual analysis can reveal the mechanisms whereby gender is constructed. From this perspective, gender becomes a theme that is most profitably studied using the toolbox of classical narratology. The other is the notion of "subject positioning" in which individual behaviour is determined not only by any specific social group but also by individual subjectivity and "agency." But the argument that gender is experienced differently according to individual "subject positionings" has cornered feminist narratology into a dilemma in which their critical activity can only consist of either describing their own individual readings or hypothetically speculating on those of other women. Such an approach is reminiscent of reception or reader response theories of the 80's and provides little leverage in understanding the role of context in general.

Communication in Context

A second example of the difficulty in drawing inferences regarding the role of context lies in rhetorical narratology in which a communication model is used to understand how texts are constructed and interpreted. In this analysis, the text entails an extension of the intratextual communicative relationship between the narrator and a narratee (Chatman 1990; Kearns 1999) to the real authors and readers. Thus, authors construct texts in order to communicate with readers, and a literary text can be regarded as a speech act that allows the reader to identify the author's intended message. Context is critical in this conceptualization because communication between the author and the reader presupposes that they share a common context. Without such a common context, many of the mechanisms involved in oral communication cannot operate with any accuracy. For example, true communication would require referential mechanisms that enable referring expressions in the text to be associated with entities in the world. However, without a common context, such mechanisms may not operate reliably, and there is little guarantee that the reader understands that to which the author refers.

However, a serious weakness in this conceptualization is that literary reception is a fundamentally decontextualized activity and that consequently the assumption of a common context is unfounded. Sell's concept of the "contextual fallacy" captures this idea (Sell 1999). Even when the temporal, geographic, social, and ideological differences between author and reader are minimal, and even when the reader belongs to the same society, the same class, and the same age and gender as the author, a host of other reader-related variables bear on the act of reading and render the decoding model of literary communication naive and misguided. Some of these include educational level, familiarity with fictional literature, political ideology, profession, reading preferences, motivation for reading, and so on. (For an elaboration of this idea see Dixon and Bortolussi 2001.)

The Context of Cognitive Processing

Of all the new narratological applications, the one that makes the greatest effort to account for textual processing issues is cognitive narratology. This approach is inspired by a range of fields under the umbrella area of cognitive science, such as cognitive psychology, cognitive development, and philosophy of mind, as well as some specific applications, such as cognitive poetics. Apart from the shared interest in the functioning of human minds, these fields are concerned with different issues, based on distinct theoretical concepts, and typically employ unique methodologies. For example, theory of mind is largely based on empirical evidence in developmental psychology, and has been applied to children and animals. Both cognitive and theory of mind psychology incorporate experimental research, whereas philosophy of mind and cognitive poetics do not. More than than a well-defined, coherent approach or set of approaches, cognitive narratology is a collection of theoretical reflections on the workings of fictional minds both internal to the work (those of characters) and external to it (those of readers).

As an example, cognitive narratologists have borrowed the concepts of scripts and schemas (inspired by the seminal work of Schank and Abelson in the 70s) from cognitive psychology to describe how readers' knowledge is used in making sense of narrative texts. These ideas have a certain amount of empirical support in cognitive science. However, cognitive narratology remains exclusively theoretical. And while its musings on the extensive extratextual knowledge that readers bring to bear on texts are often plausible, the concepts of scripts and schemas are too limited and inflexible to account for the wide range of knowledge-based inferences that readers commonly make. Today psychologists recognize that not all knowledge can be packaged in terms of structured representations of stereotypical situations, and that readers have a wealth of memory and experience that can be applied dynamically and flexibly depending on the situation and their goals. Scripts and schemas provide little insight into how this is done.

Cognitive narratologists have also borrowed the concept of "theory of mind" – that is, a mental representation of other's cognitive and perceptual capacities—from cognitive science. While the origins of theory of mind are philosophical, recent empirical work on the concept has focused on cognitive development and on the cognitive abilities of animals. When used in conjunction with an analysis of literary texts, theory of mind raises the interesting question of the extent to which readers represent the cognitive capacities of characters in the story world who, after all, are not real individuals. Similarly, one may ask whether readers develop a theory of mind for authors and narrators; in other words, do they really treat authors and narrators as real people who may or may not know things about the story world? We believe that these are interesting empirical questions that can be answered by distinguishing between what is actually in the text and the inferences that readers draw under various circumstances. In contrast, cognitive narratologists have rarely pursued such an evidential approach, but rather have applied ideas such as theory of mind in speculative and intuitive analyses.

More generally, in the cognitive narratology framework, readers continue to be conceptualized in universal, homogenous, hypothetical terms. Many of the theories evoked by cognitive narratologists derived from empirical studies that had nothing to do with literary processing. Interesting as the theories may be, alone they cannot account for how real readers process real, and very different texts. The theories borrowed from the cognitive sciences can be used to support hypotheses about what mental model is evoked by readers, but only empirical studies can validate the conclusions drawn. The next stage of cognitive narratology needs to be founded in empirical methods. Nevertheless, in spite of these limitations, by recognizing that there is more to reading than a text-prescribed decoding of the text, cognitive narratology has dealt a decisive blow to purely text-based analyses.

Beyond reminding us of some of the contextual variables involved in literary response, however, cognitive narratology is ill-equipped to address the contextual critique. At one level of analysis, it complements classical narratology: One lays out the textual conditions, and the other lays out the cognitive conditions that enable meaning construction. Thus, cognitive narratology can also be considered a toolbox of sorts. However, like its counterpart, it does not by itself get us beyond the impasse of the contextual critique. Because cognitive narratology adopts the theoretical ideas of cognitive science but not its methods, it cannot delineate which of several possible analyses of cognitive processing is appropriate. Ultimately, all it can provide is minute dissections of textual passages and the critics' speculations about what schemas can be applied to them. Like other narratologies, while paying tribute to the need to understand the reading process, it ends up providing more of the close readings that proliferated during the reader reception and response theory stage of literary studies. Neither a catalogue of textual features nor a catalogue of known and potential scripts can show us what real readers actually do with real texts.

In all of these example, despite the emphasis on the role of context, the analysis of texts remains rooted in the earlier reader response stage of development. In particular, there is an exclusive reliance on either abstract notions of ideal readers or personal interpretations of professional critics, neither of which necessarily apply to real readers (cf. Bortolussi and Dixon 2003). Thus, the meticulous analysis of textual details that ensues reveals not so much how readers process texts as the skill and interpretational preferences of the professional analyst.

An Empirical Approach to Context

Literary critics no longer believe that literature simply imitates reality; they argue rather that it constructs its own reality and shapes readers' attitudes and ideas. If we are to truly understand how literature functions in society, we must start by investigating what ordinary, non-specialized, real readers do with texts and what texts do to them. To accomplish this, we must move on, beyond post-classical narratology's naive embracing of all things contextual, beyond its merely theoretical, speculative, professional-critic centered interpretations and justifications, and adopt truly interdisciplinary methods of investigation. And this means accepting the fact that literary studies needs a strong empirical basis.

In 2003, we outlined an empirical approach to the problems of classical narratology that we termed psychonarratology. Psychonarratology uses the methods and epistemology of cognitive psychology and discourse processing to understand how readers process the elements of the textual analysis developed by narratologists. We argue here that the same tools can be extended in order to develop a response to the contextual critique. There are two essential components to that approach. First, one must carefully distinguish textual features from reader constructions. Features are objectively defined aspects of the text that informed analysis can identify. They do not vary with the reader and the reading public because they are inscribed in the text. In contrast, reader constructions are mental representations generated in the course of interacting with the text. Constructions are potentially idiosyncratic and vary with the knowledge, background, and goals of the reader. Second, we proposed the notion of the "statistical reader" in order to incorporate both aggregate and individual responses to a text. The statistical reader is based on the idea of reader populations for which we can describe both the central tendency (how readers are alike) and variation (how readers differ).

These two methodological cornerstones allow us to build a framework for the investigation of context. For example, reader constructions are generally a function of the reading context. They are determined not only by the features of the text, but by the reader's knowledge, his or her culture, the circumstances in which the reading takes place, and the particular goals of the reader at the time. All of these contextual factors contribute to the nature of the mental representations generated during reading. Further, populations of readers can be defined by context. For example, one may distinguish male and female readers, readers from various cultural and ethnic backgrounds, readers from different historical periods, and so on. Using the technical tools of the statistical reader, one can conceptualize how such populations differ in aggregate without obscuring the individual variation among readers within each population. For example, one may be able to ascertain that female readers on average are more likely to prefer a given type of narrative than male readers. However, a description of this general tendency does not entail that all female readers will react to narratives of that type in the same way. That is, the general tendency may apply to the group as a whole, while individuals within that group may partake of the tendency to varying degrees. Both the general tendency and this individual variation can be measured empirically. Nünning (2004) pointed to the importance of demonstrating how values communicated by texts connect with those of reader groups; the notion of the statistical reader could help determine the specific groups.

More than developing such a framework, though, an empirical approach to context requires evidence. In order to disentangle the many possible conjectures and hypotheses concerning the role of context in reading, one must conduct carefully controlled experiments that provide evidence for or against possible interpretations. As a simple example, one might conjecture, based on extant feminist analyses of reading, that female readers should prefer stories with female protagonists while male readers should prefer stories with male protagonists. However, when the stories themselves are controlled and only the protagonist gender varies, we found that both male and female readers preferred a version with a male protagonist (Bortolussi, Dixon, and Sopcak 2010). Although this result does not necessarily invalidate the foundations of feminist criticism, it underscores the problem with using intuition to predict the behaviour of actual readers.

Indeed, the investigation of context effects on reading is well suited to experimental investigation in many cases. For example, several studies have examined the effect of genre expectation on reader constructions (e.g., Zwaan 1994). The results from these investigations indicate that those expectations can affect the nature of readers' memory for the material. The classic results of Pichert and Anderson (1977) demonstrate that reading goals can be readily biased and has strong effects on memory for text. The role of cultural context on reading is readily apparent in the results of Bartlett (1932; see also Kintsch and Green 1978). Explicitly instructed reading goals affect the manner in which readers think about story protagonists (Cupchik, Oatley, Vorderer 1998). In classroom setting, we have demonstrated that training in genre conventions affects how readers interpret stories and literary devices (Dixon and Bortolussi 1996). More recently, we have demonstrated that extratextual sources such as critical reviews have effects on reader' evaluations of stories (Dixon and Bortolussi 2010). More generally, a wide range of possible variables and issues are amenable to empirical investigation in this framework. These include the role of extratextual information concerning the author and the text, the impact of readers' culture, reading skill and literary expertise, to name a few.

Conclusion

Unfortunately, in the humanities there is still much resistance to the very thought of empirical studies of literature. For example, in her latest book, Ruth Page admits that the use of "empirically oriented methods... may be of use to feminist narratology." However, she objects that such methods may not be superior to close readings and may be used "to oversimplify and reach abstract generalizations" (Page 2006:14). Although caveats and a healthy skepticism are always warranted in interpreting empirical results, our response is that evidence concerning the behaviour of real readers is always helpful. Indeed, it is difficult to imagine that arguments based on empirical evidence could underperform the oversimplifications about reading and contextual influences produced by the post-classical narratologies to date.

One may argue that post-classical narratology derives much of its impetus from post-structural theory and a distrust of broad, unifying "meta-narratives." In fact, the empirical enterprise is much better suited to this post-structural spirit than the post-classical narratologies. The need to isolate specific variables, its rigor in establishing correlations, caution in drawing unwarranted causal inferences, and its humility in establishing achievable goals are aspects of science that map onto the poststructuralist view that absolute knowledge is illusory. In spite of the potent impact of poststructuralism and postmodernism, the postclassical narratologies still display a nostalgia for meta-narratives and their sweeping theoretical generalizations about readers and contextual causes. As Prince aptly put it: "La narratologie classique essayait d'écarter certaines questions. La narratologie post-classique cède peut-être trop facilement à la tentation de les poser toutes" (2006:3; that is: "Classical narratology tried to discard certain questions. Post-classical narratology yields perhaps too easily to the temptation of asking of all").

The empirical challenge that must constitute the next stage of narrative studies should not be seen as a rejection of other forms of scholarly inquiry; it does not diminish the importance of historical investigation, for example. But as Robert Darnton (1995) has shown, even historical investigation can be grounded in empirical observation. If we are to rise to the challenge of demonstrating the social relevance and value of literature in society, we must reorient literary studies towards an empirical path. To repeat what we wrote more than a decade ago, "To meet the challenges of the future, we must begin by acknowledging the need of the methods and approaches found in the natural sciences. How to formulate problems, how to collect and analyze data, how to distinguish between valid and invalid inferences, how to determine what counts as objective evidence are valuable lessons we can no longer refuse to learn." However, to capitalize on the advances made to date, this approach must build on the foundations of textual analysis as developed by classical narrative theorists.

6
Claude Bremond

Former Directeur d'études
l'Ecole des Hautes Etudes en Sciences Sociales, Paris

I don't consider myself a universal narratologist, but rather a researcher who, because of his work on certain types of narratives, has been led to submit a specific narratological problem to more thorough scrutiny. Consequently, I don't feel qualified to answer the questions which concern narratology as a whole (questions 3, 4, and 5), but only those which concern the origin of my interest for narratology (question 1) and my personal contribution to the field (question 2). Let me just make clear that my research has made me pay particular attention to authors who worked along lines cognate to mine or who otherwise helped me better define the extension of the research field; I am among others thinking of Roland Barthes, Gérard Genette, Tzvetan Todorov, Umberto Eco, Algirdas Julien Greimas, Paul Ricoeur, Thomas Pavel, Gerald Pince.

My interest in narratology is rooted in an ambition, which already guided my very first works: to develop procedures which may further the comparative analysis of stories. Thus, by the end of the 1950s, at the Institut de filmologie de Paris, I elaborated a protocol for recording stories told by people who had just seen an experimental movie; or later, under Edgar Morin's supervision, I refined a sociological questionnaire which should serve as the basis for an international study of movie heros. I felt rather uncomfortable about these works and I therefore asked Roland Barthes for advice. He oriented me toward Vladimir Propp whose *Morphology of the Folk Tale* had just been translated into English. Initially I was fascinated by this book, only to discover its limits at a later point. Claude Lévi-Strauss' critical reading of Propp confirmed my hesitations, but it seemed nevertheless to me that Lévi-Strauss was himself too absorbed by his own analysis of the structure of myths to be sufficiently sensitive to the paths Propp was likely to open for a study of the narrative in its very largest sense, that is, takenacross specific narrative genres such as tales or myths.

We were in the 1960s. At the Ecole des Hautes en Sciences Sociales, where I was working and had established a strong network with other researchers, the field of narrative theory was divided into Gérard Genette's and Algirdas Julien Greimas' works: two masters between whom the rookie I was had trouble navigating. I have not had much difficulty in situating my research relative to Genette's: his aim was to structure the *discourse* of the story, while mine was to structure the *event* of the story, or, to put it differently, he was concerned by the *narrating narrative*, I by the *narrated narrative*. On the other side of the barrier, as regards Greimas and his disciples, the situation was less clear. Like me, he and his disciples had departed from a reflection on Propp's Morphology and gradually constructed a doctrinal system which extends beyond the study of the narrative strictly speaking and toward an elucidation of textual signification at large; the text being construed in an exorbitantly extended sense. Being far more modest and circumspect, I couldn't follow Greimas in what seemed to me a dilution of the real issues in the study of the narrative: I restricted—and still restrict—myself to developing a hypothetic-deductive elaboration of the principal events and roles in a story, with the intention of making this construction further the inventory and comparative study of the themes and motifs manifested in different corpora of narratives. The fruit of that work was the article"Le message narratif "(1964), and a doctoral thesis, *Logique du récit* (1973). I still acknowledge the general principles laid out in these works, but I don't I think I then succeeded in defining all the consequences and possible applications I hoped to make of them: since I underestimated the difficulty of moving from theory to practice, I didn't succeed in establishing an indexation procedure which could concretely have made it possible to attain my final goal—the comparative study of different narrative corpora.

For the following twenty or thirty years, I therefore went on working with scholars from other disciplines (anthropologists, historians, literary critics) on the analysis of stories, but from other perspectives that were by no means narratological proper: they could be folklorist or anthropological when the object was African tales, or historical when it came to medieval exemples ... At least these investigations have made me familiar with the problems raised by narratives for specialists from a host of different disciplines.

Since I have been retired for the last dozen of years, I have had time to continue my work on the narrative from the point where I left it in my *Logique du récit*. I grasp the occasion you give me to sum up some of the main tenets of my present research in the field.

The events in the story are articulated in (relatively fixed) states and (basically mobile) processes. These states and processes most often concern persons (human beings or anthropomorphous creatures) who are either the patients affected by these states or processes or the agents who have initiated these states or processes.

Processes divide into two categories: the modifications that tends to cause a change in the state of the subject; the conservation that, on the contrary, tend to maintain the subject in his initial state. Modification and conservation are thus opposed just like action and reaction.

Insofar as the subjects are human or anthropomorphous beings, the processes they are affected by are likely to be assessed positively or negatively: modification being specified as either improvement or degradation, conservation as either protection (reaction which tends to block a process of degradation) or as frustration (reaction which tends to block a process of improvement). It is furthermore possible to predict two reaction processes against reaction, either in the form of a protection against frustration or as a frustration of protection.

At the frontier between agents and patients, it seems sensible to consider the possibility of a blended category: "the eventual-agent patients"; the patient may indeed be affected by, either persuasive or dissuasive, influences which will make it behave as an agent, either in order to act or in order to refrain from acting.

If we group in a table the series of states or processes just specified as likely to characterize the patient role at its most general level, we obtain something I would like to call the "elementary narrative cell":

state of X

satisfying state of X

unsatisfying state of X

modification of X

improvement of X (positively assessed modification)

degradation of X (negatively assessed modification)

conservation of X

protection of X (positively assessed conservation)
protection of X against degradation of X
protection of X against frustration of X

frustration of X (negatively assessed conservation)
frustration of improvement of X
frustration of protection of X

persuasion of X (triggering motivation)
dissuasion of X (inhibitory motivation)

The assessed states or processes, whether positively (satisfying state, improvement, protection, persuasion) or negatively (unsatisfying stated, degradation, frustration, dissuasion), can be grouped in three categories: affective, ethical, practical. Affective improvement can be identified as pleasure, affective degradation as suffering; ethical improvement as merit, ethical degradation as demerit; practical improvement as success, practical degradation as failure.

The (persuasive or dissuasive) influences exerted on the "eventual-agent patients" in order to make them act or refrain from acting are likely to be classified in the same three groups: affective influences are concretely the triggering of desire or aversion (or seduction vs. intimidation); the ethical influences are obligation or interdiction; practical influences are advice or inadvice.

Correlated to the patient roles, whether they are beneficients or victims, we find the roles of agents who intervene either as modificators (improvers or degraders), or as conservators (protectors or frustrators) of the agents' state. Likewise, correlated to the blended roles of "eventual-agent patients", we find the roles of influencing agents (seducers or intimidators, obligators or interdictors, advisors or inadvisors).

In so far as patients and agents are anthropomorphous beings who are conscious of either the states or processes they are affected by, or of the actions they initiate and control, they can be affected by information related to these states or processes. This information can itself be assessed, relative to its object, as either true (revelation) or false (misguiding).

The acknowledgement of the categories derived from the affective experience (pleasure, suffering, desire, aversion, ...), ethical experience (merit, demerit, obligation, interdiction, ...) practical experience (success, failure, advice, inadvice, ...), cognitive experience (revelation, misguiding, dissimulation, ...) rests on the hypothetic-deductive procedure which is the foundation of our logic of the narrative: the passions, motivations, and actions constructed by that logic are the universal and necessary conditions for the narrative.

However, this sort of logical scaffolding does not exhaust the thematic matter of the narrative. Other parcels of human experience, which are not logically deductible, display an all as evident anthropological quasi universality: physically, the patient has a body and interacts with his surroundings; economically, he is conditioned by the goods he possesses, acquires or loses; sociologically, he depends or may depend on the action exerted on him by his partners (sexual, working, social, political partners or family); he may, eventually, establish a relation to a supernatural or religious agent.

The encoding matrix that I have elaborated in order to lay down an index of the passions, actions and motivations in *Thousand and One Nights* is a result of the combination of both these approaches: the former is deductive and logical, the latter inductive and empirical. Narrative matter is thus carved out in a series of fields of which the first four are universal, and the following are quasi universal. The list of these fields can be extended so as to capture the specificities of certain corpora:

- affective
- ethical
- practical
- cognitive
- bodily
- spatial
- economical
- sexual
- family related
- social
- political
- supernatural
- religious

If we systematically combine the elementary narrative cell (states, processes, motivations) with the above thematic fields, we obtain a first classification of the narrative processes.

For example, the combination of states, processes, and motivation from the elementary cell with the affective field will engender the following classificatory tags:

- affective state of X
- satisfying affective state of X
- unsatisfying affective state of X

- affective modification of X
- affective improvement of X
- affective degradation of X

- affective conservation of X
- protection of X against affective degradation of X
- frustration of X for affective improvement of X
- protection of X against frustration of X for affective improvement of X
- frustration of X for protection of X against affective degradation of X

When applying the same formal model (states, processes, motivations) on each of the thematic fields (the ethical, practical, cognitive, ... fields), we obtain a list of categories in terms of which the matter of our narratives can be classified, just to mention some of them: satisfying ethical state of X, unsatisfying practical state of X, cognitive improvement of X, bodily degradation of X, protection of X against spatial degradation, frustration of X for economical improvement of X, protection of X against sexual frustration of X, frustration of X, frustration of X for protection of X against family degradation of X ...

Up to now, only one person has been mentioned in our classification, that is, the one designated by the letter X, and, moreover, he has only intervened in the role of the patient.

Now, the process that affects the patient X may remain impersonal and not involve any other agent's responsibility. Yet, most often this is not the case. If the responsibility of an agent is involved, this agent may be X himself, or another person Y. This difference should be employed systematically with a view to refining our classification: we will, for example, distinguish between the affective improvement of X by X (X comforts himself) and the affective improvement of X by Y (Y comforts X).

The classification of narrative processes (passions, actions, and motivations) pertains to different (affective, ethical, practical, cognitive, ...) fields. Granted this, is it then possible to further refine it? It is indeed, if the classification is supplied with an inventory of syntactic relations resulting from the combination of two processes.

I'll distinguish between two types of syntactic combinations which can serve to classify narrative states and processes:
- achronic combinations (modalisator/modalized relation)
- chronologized combinations: simultaneity, anteriority, posteriority.

1. Classification of states and processes in terms of the modalisator/modalized relation between two of them.

Let's consider the affective improvement, "pleasure": such a pleasure in X may be the pleasure felt by X because of an ethic improvement of X, i.e., pride or self-esteem; it can also be a pleasure felt by X because of an ethic improvement of Y, i.e. pride over someone else; yet another pleasure felt by X may be a pleasure caused by an affective degradation of X, i.e., masochism, or pleasure felt by X because of the affective degradation (suffering) of Y, i.e., sadism. By way of systematically combining the process "X's pleasure" with the whole list of already established processes, we can lay down an inventory of the different ways the process "X's pleasure" can be specified relative to its object.

This manner of classification is likely to hold for all cases in which one narrative process stands in a modalisator to modalized relation to another narrative process: pleasure vs. suffering, desire vs. aversion, merit vs. demerit, obligation, interdiction vs. permission, advantage vs. inconvenience, advice vs. inadvice, revelation, dissimulation, misguiding ...

For example, the combination of the modalizing process "affective improvement of X", in other words: "pleasure", with the series of modalized processes combining "elementary narrative cell" and "ethic valorization" yields the following list of possibilities:

- pleasure produced in X because of an ethic state
- pleasure produced in X because of a satisfying ethic state
- pleasure produced in X because of an unsatisfying ethic state
- pleasure produced in X because of an ethic modification
- pleasure produced in X because of an ethic improvement
- pleasure produced in X because of an ethic degradation

- pleasure produced in X because of ethic conservation
- pleasure produced in X because of protection against ethic degradation
- pleasure produced in X because of protection against ethic frustration
- pleasure produced in X because of frustration of ethic improvement
- pleasure produced in X because of frustration of ethic protection
- pleasure produced in X because of obligation
- pleasure produced in X because of interdiction
- pleasure produced in X because of permission

From this list, let's now pick up, still as a mere example, the item "pleasure produced in X because of ethic improvement". This formulation should be completed in different ways:

1. We should do so, firstly, in order to specify the identity of the patient who benefits from the affective improvement in contradistinction to the patient who benefits from the ethic improvement. This patient may indeed be X who enjoys the merit or honor attributed to him. But it may also be another person Y who enjoys the merit or honor attributed to X. We should therefore distinguish between:

- pleasure produced in X because of ethic improvement of X
- pleasure produced in X because of ethic improvement of Y

2. Secondly, in order to determine the identity of the agents involved in the complex process which results from the combination of two elementary processes (pleasure, on the one hand, and ethic improvement, on the other). We then obtain a series of possible specifications, among which we'll take a closer look at the following:

- pleasure produced in X because of ethic improvement of X by X
- pleasure produced in X because of ethic improvement of X by Y
- pleasure produced in X because of ethic improvement of Y by X
- pleasure produced in X because of ethic improvement of Y by Y
- pleasure produced in X because of ethic improvement of Y by Z
- pleasure produced in X by X because of ethic improvement of X by X

(...)

- pleasure produced in X by Y because of ethic improvement of Z by Y
- pleasure produced in X by Y because of ethic improvement of Z by Z

Without going into any further details, let's simply remark that supplementary determinations may occasionally be necessary to obtain a more precise specification: notably the modal distinction between possible process and effective process, or the temporal determination (state or past, present, future process).

2. Classification of states and processes in terms of the chronological relation (simultaneity, anteriority, posteriority) between two of them:

The first classification we looked at was one that rested on the specification of one process by another process which stands to the former in an achronic relation of modalizer to modalized. Now, there exist other syntactic relations, and consequently other types of classification could and should be made. In order to stay within the narrative domain, we could here mention a classification which rests on the chronological relation (simultaneity, anteriority, posteriority) between one state or process and another in the chain of narrated events. The importance of such a classification is obvious in two inverse and complementary cases:
- firstly, the case where the temporal relation of anteriority/posteriority between two processes is also a causal relation according to the principle *post hoc, ergo propter hoc*. In this case, it is indeed possible to specify either the conditioned elements, the effects, the ends relative to the conditioning elements, the causes, and means on which they depend, or, on the contrary, consider the conditioning elements, the causes, and the means relative to the conditioned elements, effects and ends which are their outcome.
- secondly, the case where the temporal anteriority/posteriority relation between the two processes is not a "normal" causal relation, but rather a paradox anti-causal relation (typically specified in the story by an expression such as "despite of" or a conjunction such as "although").

To illustrate this type of classification, consider the following sentence from a summary of a tale from *Thousand and One Nights*:
 - Ali Nur ruins himself in debaucheries with false friends without considering his steward's remonstrances.

This text could figure in our index with various tags, notably the following:

- economical degradation of X by X, caused by affective improvement of X by X (a young man ruins himself striving for costly pleasures)

- economical degradation of X by X despite of economical protection of X by Y (a young man ruins himself despite his steward's efforts to protect the young man's fortune)

- economical protection of X by Y, caused by practical dissuasion ("inadvice") of X by Y (a steward painstakingly tries to prevent a young man from ruining himself)

- economical degradation of X by X despite of practical dissuasion ("inadvice") of X by Y (a young man ruins himself despite his steward's warnings)

As is clear now, my contribution to the narratological studies is thus limited to the (still) unfulfilled effort to construct a formal model, in terms of an Index of passions, actions and motivations, which is likely to further the identification, conceptualization, formulation and rational classification of the various states and processes which may make out the matter of a narrative. In order to put this model to the test, I use a corpus of summaries of the tales from *Thousand and One Nights*. As regards the question how the construction of such indexes could help scholars in other disciplines (literary critics, historians, anthropologists, ...), this is something I definitely don't care too much about. A taxonomical work is always quite useful when it has attained a certain degree of rational order. It might be the case that the classification I propose does not meet the demands of scholars who, on empirical grounds, try to construct catalogues of motifs captured in terms of the problems they are familiar with, but it cannot be excluded that the narratological index I propose may open new paths for research, exactly because it approaches the story from the perspective of its logical structure.

7

Wallace Chafe

Professor Emeritus and Research Professor of Linguistics
Department of Linguistics, University of California, Santa Barbara

I have have always thought of myself as a linguist, not a narratologist. Linguistics is the field in which I was trained, and it is where most of my work has been conducted. It is true that I have sometimes diverged from the linguistic mainstream, and in fact some of those departures from standard linguistic practice have brought me closer to narratology. If narratology is defined broadly as the systematic study of narratives, much of what I have done over the years fits that definition well.

How, then, do we define narrative (cf. Labov and Waletzky 1967). Definitions are not always helpful, and I believe you know a narrative when you see one (or hear one), but it does seem correct to say that all narratives share an organization into a coherent sequence of events. The events may be fictional or nonfictional, and the sequence may vary in length from very brief to very long, as with a novel or autobiography. Events are things that happen, and a sequence of events achieves coherence through a common relationship to some topic. To the extent that ideas of events are expressed in language, narratology might readily be seen as contained within linguistics, although of course its concerns have also extended to drama and film.

My own earliest work in linguistics involved the recording of narratives in a Native American language called Seneca, which is spoken by a small number of people in the western part of New York State. In the summer of 1956 I made my first visit to one of the three Seneca reservations, where I began looking for speakers of the language with whom I could work. At that time it was not difficult to find Seneca speakers who were willing to sit in front of a tape recorder and, without further guidance, proceed to tell a narrative in their language. The first Seneca speaker I met was a man named Roy Jimerson, who recorded a fascinating semi-historical account of confrontations between the Senecas and people who lived to the west of them called the Gakwas. His narrative described how the Senecas defeated the Gakwas, both in athletic games and in battle, and how ultimately a number of the Gakwas were absorbed into the Seneca population, where until recently their Gakwa ancestry was still recognized.

Linguists record conversations as well as narratives, but I found that extended conversations nearly always included narratives within them. In those days it was still a favorite activity to meet in the evening and exchange stories and songs. There were stories of personal experiences, folktales and myths, and jokes (Chafe 2007). I had been taught to treat such recordings as primary data, and to work through them painstakingly in attempts to analyze each word and phrase, gradually constructing a picture of the language's structure: phonological, morphological, syntactic, semantic, prosodic, and, yes, narratological, although that term was unfamiliar to me at the time. Narratives like Mr. Jimerson's along with other types I collected all provided rich data for analyses that would now, in some respects, qualify as narratological.

Later I extended my work in a different direction with the so-called Pear Stories project, in which we based our research on a short film produced in Berkeley in the mid-1970s (Chafe 1980). We showed the film to people in various countries, asking them, after they had seen it, to relate what happened in the film in their own language. Our primary goal was to compare the ways speakers of different languages talked about more or less the same content. At the same time, however, I had a lively interest in the nature of remembering and the effects of memory on language (Chafe 1973). There had been a revival of interest in Frederic Bartlett's work in that area (Bartlett 1932), and I saw the Pear Stories project as in part an extension of Bartlett's work (Chafe 1986). It was around that time that I began to pay special attention to consciousness and its relation to such obviously linguistic phenomena as prosody and the use of pronouns.

Soon after that I became involved in a project to study differences between speaking and writing. As data for that purpose we recorded dinnertable conversations along with more formal styles of speaking, and we compared the language in those two spoken formats with personal letters (in the days before e-mail), and with academic papers. The two unplanned uses of language (conversations and personal letters) were also replete with narratives (Chafe and Danielewicz 1987).

All those activities came together in my book *Discourse, Consciousness, and Time* (Chafe 1994). The first half of that book focused on spoken language and how it is shaped by the flow of conscious thought. Especially relevant to narratology were Chapters 10 and 11, which discussed the organization of speech into topics, subtopics, and supertopics; how language signals topic boundaries; and how a speaker navigates through a topic, sometimes guided by a narrative schema, sometimes by interaction with one or more interlocutors. The final portion of the book focused on written language and the ways in which writers capture conscious thought. I became especially interested in the portrayal of a "displaced" consciousness, where the language dealt with phenomena that were absent from the immediate environment of the telling.

Chapters 17 through 20 all dealt squarely with narratological concerns, but at the end of Chapter 20, which was titled "Written Fiction That (Partially) Lacks a Represented Consciousness," I included a section titled "A Brief Comparison with Narratological Studies," where I described narratology as the area of scholarship that related most closely to what I was discussing. I noted, nevertheless, that the motives of narratologists seemed to diverge to some extent from mine. Whereas I "aimed at understanding the nature of the mind as determinable through consciousness and language," I described the concerns of narratologists as "categorizing or typologizing written fiction in terms of criteria that are applicable either to whole works or to their parts." I suggested "that a perspective on linguistic products that views them within a larger frame of reference, embracing mental life in its entirety, can only enrich our understanding of the devices by which authors illuminate the complexities of human experience." I compared my discussion specifically with ideas that had been set forth by Franz K. Stanzel (1984) and Gérard Genette (1980, 1988). Perhaps I came closest to Dorrit Cohn's distinction between psycho-narration, narrated monologue, and quoted monologue (Cohn 1978, 1999). I believe I added something useful to the discussion by recognizing a style of writing I called "displaced immediacy," in which the quality of immediate experience is conveyed by continuity, rich detail, and the use of spatiotemporal adverbs like "here" and "now," while at the same time there is an expression of displacement with the use of past tense and third person.

It has been my impression that narratology, which evidently coalesced as a distinct discipline in Europe in the 1970s, never achieved wide recognition in the United States. I was surprised recently when a linguist friend whose work, I thought, overlapped considerably with narratological studies, told me he had never heard of such a field. My guess is that if someone surveyed members of the Linguistic Society of America, asking them what they knew of narratology, expressions of ignorance would far outweigh any evidence of familiarity. The American narratologists that do exist are likely to find their homes in literature departments, but even there they constitute a small minority. When I published *Discourse, Consciousness, and Time* I was told that members of (American) English departments were no longer interested in topics of that nature. I find that unfortunate. Understanding more about the ways in which both oral storytellers and writers create beauty, enjoyment, and insight should be a topic of primary concern. Sadly, comments on such matters are for the most part left to critics, whose judgments are by definition highly personal and subjective.

Evidently the situation in Europe is quite different. I was pleased to be invited to a conference on Linguistics and Poetics in Denmark at the beginning of 2008, where narratology appeared to be quite at home. My presentation there expanded upon Roman Jakobson's challenge to make "poetics" an integral part of linguistics. "Poetics deals with problems of verbal structure, just as the analysis of painting is concerned with pictorial structure. Since linguistics is the global science of verbal structure, poetics may be regarded as an integral part of linguistics" (Jakobson 1990: 70). Perhaps the term "poetics" suggested a limitation to the study of poetry, but Jakobson had something broader in mind. One might interpret his statement as a call for making narratology, or something like it, a recognized and active branch of linguistics.

In my own contribution to the 2008 conference (Chafe 2010) I suggested three ways in which fiction writers capture the consciousness of their characters, ways that narratologists have recognized in one form or another. First, a writer may choose between direct or mediated access to a character's consciousness. This is the distinction that has often been characterized as mimesis versus diegesis, or showing versus telling. With mimesis the narrator has minimal involvement, while with mediated access the narrator plays a more interpretive role, reporting what omniscience has made it possible for him or her to know regarding the inner workings of the character's mind (cf. Cohn 1978: 46). A second choice available to a writer is whether the character's attention is focused on the immediate environment or is displaced from it, as in remembering or imagining. I showed in Chafe (1994) how immediacy is signaled by continuity of the conscious experience as opposed to the island-like nature of remembering, by the inclusion of rich detail, and by the use of proximal deixis. A third available choice recognizes varieties of conscious experience. Raw experience (direct perceptions, emotions, and actions) contrast with more fully processed propositional thoughts, which in turn may be either preverbal (not committed to specific wordings) or verbatim (fully verbalized). I noted also how the process of translating into another language illuminates the preverbal versus verbal distinction, showing that different languages can be joined only at the preverbal level.

Although I have no talent for predicting the future, my present guess is that scholars in the United States will not catch up with narratology any time soon. It is unfortunate that linguists with a professional interest in written literature constitute a small minority here. Unfortunately, too, most work in literature departments ignores narratological concerns.

As open issues for narratology itself, my continuing search for the psychological underpinnings of linguistic phenomena leads me to wish for an increased focus on ways in which memory, consciousness, and imagination affect and are expressed in narratives, and on ways in which, in the other direction, narratives themselves can be exploited to shed a brighter light on the workings of the human mind. Ideally, I believe, it would be desirable and productive if separate areas of scholarship, including narratology but also including the better known fields of linguistics, psychology, and literary studies, could be encouraged to combine their separate insights in order to achieve a deeper understanding of everything that makes us human

8
Seymour Chatman

Professor Emeritus of Rhetoric
University of California, Berkeley

---

1. Why were you initially drawn to narratology or narrative theory?

It was because of Barthes' 1966 article starting the discussion of the structure of narrative. I was on my way to Mexico and decided to prove/disprove his thesis with the shortest story I could find, Joyce's "Eveline."

2. What do you consider your most important contribution(s) to the field?

Story and Discourse (Chatman 1978)

3. What is the proper role of a narratology and narrative theory in relation to other academic disciplines?

I don't think about "Proper Roles."

4. Whose do you consider the most important contributions in narratology?

Gerard Genette's

5. What are the most important open problems in this field and what are the prospects for progress?

I'm not sure. Time relations between story and discourse are pretty well discussed. Perhaps what I raised in the last eleven chapters of *Narrative Discourse Revisited* (Genette 1988)

9
Jonathan Culler

Class of 1916 Professor of English and Comparative Litterature
Cornell University

---

1. Why were you initially drawn to narratology or narrative theory?

When I began graduate study I had developed a major interest in literary theory because it seemed to me crucial to attempt to understand what one was trying to do, and why, when writing about literary works. I wrote a short thesis for what was then called the B. Phil. in Comparative Literature at Oxford on phenomenology and literary criticism (this was the heyday of the Geneva School), focusing on the work of Maurice Merleau-Ponty and its potential critical implications. During the process, I became especially interested in theories of language and their implications for criticism, and decided to undertake a Ph.D. dissertation on structuralism, which in the late 1960s seemed likely to eclipse phenomenology and which explicitly announced its dependence on a linguistic model. In that context, I could not help but encounter narratology, which was central to the structuralist project. Narrative was one of the primary examples of a cultural phenomenon based on an underlying set of rules or norms that ought to be elucidated. Since literary and non-literary narratives seemed structured in similar ways, narratology was one of the domains where analysis broke down ordinary disciplinary boundaries and heralded the possibility of a general semiotics of culture. The chapter on Poetics of the Novel in my dissertation (which became *Structuralist Poetics*) surveyed structuralist contributions to narratology and served as the fullest illustration of possible structuralist contributions to poetics (Culler 1975).

When I completed my dissertation, I went to work on a book on Flaubert, where narrative theory played a different but equally central role. In analyzing Flaubert's novels, I focused on the various ways in which they disrupt readers' (and critics') expectations for narrative (Culler 1974). Though I was not doing formal narratological analysis, this work was deeply involved with narrative theory.

2. What do you consider your most important contribution(s) to the field?

In my early work on narratology I wrote a paper on the opposition between story and discourse (which of course also goes by other names) that was in effect a deconstruction of this opposition.[1] In "Story and Discourse in the Analysis of Narrative" I argue that that narratological analysis depends upon a distinction between story and discourse and requires a relation of dependency—either events are conceived as prior to their discursive representation or events are seen as the product of discursive (e.g. thematic) requirements. But this necessary distinction and dependency is often subverted by the complex functioning of narratives themselves. Examining *Oedipus Rex*, Freud's theorization of Nachträglichkeit, and Labov's analysis of "evaluation" in narratives, I argue that "this identification of a certain self-deconstructive force within narrative and the theory of narrative should not lead to a rejection of the analytical enterprise that drives one to this discovery," but that one must be willing to shift back and forth between the priority of story and the priority of discourse (ibid., p. 187).

The second contribution that seems to me significant comes more than 20 years later. I was prompted to take up the problem of so-called "omniscient narrative" by Nicholas Royle, who remarked that despite my call for literary studies to take a critical attitude towards religious themes and presuppositions, I seemed to accept without question, in my *Literary Theory: A Very Short Introduction*, a notion of "omniscient narration" modeled on a conception of divine omniscience (see Royle 2003). As I looked into this problem I discovered that, with a few exceptions, narratologists take this notion for granted but do not explicitly defend or define it. How strange to take as a model in the critical analysis of literature God's knowledge of the universe, since even if there is a God we know nothing about what he, she, or it might actually know! In fact, the notion of omniscience obfuscates rather than clarifies the functioning of narrative because, as it is used, it lumps together several different sorts of authority, which have quite different im-

---

[1] The first version of this paper, "Fabula and Sjuzhet in the Analysis of Narrative: Some American Discussions," (Culler 1980), was substantially revised for publication as "Story and Discourse in the Analysis of Narrative," in my collection of essays, *The Pursuit of Signs* (Culler 1981).

plications and effects. I distinguish four different phenomena that lead to the ascription of omniscience (Culler 2004, 2007):

(1) The conventional narrative authority which makes various facts true by definition: if a narrative tells us that a character is young and handsome this is true not because some all-knowing individual knows it but because the story stipulates it.

(2) The imaginative or telepathic transmission of inner thoughts, which could not realistically be known to a human storyteller. This is a distinctive narrative effect; quite different from the others, and it usually involves knowing only some private things, not everyone's private thoughts.

(3) The playful and self-reflexive foregrounding of an authorial or narratorial power to determine the course of events—again, a quite distinct literary effect.

(4) The production of wisdom through the synthesizing of different perspectives. This is quite different from authorial stipulation.

I argue that for a proper understanding of narrative and narrative technique we need to abandon the notion of omniscience and discriminate among different kinds of effects that have been lazily attributed to a consciousness modeled on notions of the divine.

3. What is the proper role of a narratology and narrative theory in relation to other academic disciplines?

The study of narrative seems to me central to the humanities and humanistic social sciences. Since narrative is one of the major ways of structuring human experience, no discipline that deals with these matters should ignore narratology.

4. What are the most important open problems in this field and what are the prospects for progress?

Certainly one major issue at present is the question of how far the categories of cognitive science help illuminate the functioning of narrative or whether they simply provide a different vocabulary for the description of structures that might be better grasped in more specifically rhetorical or narratological categories. Is "blending" more perspicuous than "metaphor"? I also believe that we need to pursue more vigorously the question of whether description of narrative does require, as narratologists have often suggested, the positing of a narrator. The focus on narratives in other media, such as film and television, and in periods other than the 18th-20th centuries, should help to show that the positing of a narrator for every narrative is an unnecessary fiction.

10

Monika Fludernik

Professor of English
University of Freiburg

1. Why were you initially drawn to narratology or narrative theory?

I cannot easily answer this question. I suppose a number of different reasons could be cited. For one, I was lucky to study at the University of Graz in Austria, where Professor Franz Karl Stanzel was teaching. He was a superb teacher, lively, witty, extremely knowledgable and yet lucid in his presentation, providing a clear structure for each lecture, and presenting us with in-depth readings of the texts besides noting aspects of narrative art and other theoretical matters. He always spoke freely from notes, never read out his lecture. He also had a way of always introducing theoretical issues, concepts and concerns. He would bring in Viktor Shklovsky's defamiliarisation, or Roland Jakobson's aphasia study, or Roland Harweg's distinction between emic and etic texts. What I learned from him was a superb combination of theory and practice. He had a strong interest in literary history and the texts themselves; and this has remained an important model for my own work.

So, after being swayed by Professor Stanzel towards narratology, I suppose another reason for opting for narrative theory in my postdoctoral work was that I moved from Graz to Vienna and from British to American literature. It made great sense, seeing I had not had much exposure to American texts before, to shift my research interests from James Joyce and Modernism (my thesis topic) to postmodern American fiction and to continue my narratological framework. This helped to ease my transition from British to American literature.

A third major impact came through the work of Dorrit Cohn and through her kindness in hosting me at Harvard in 1987-88. Her *Transparent Minds* (1978) and her model were extremely important in encouraging me to continue with a narratological topic.

Finally, at least during my days as a student, I found that narratology—like linguistics—was a "safe" subject because it did not involve one's personal views or require much facility at interpreting texts. As a student I was scared to utter my own personal beliefs about texts; I mistrusted my ability to say anything really worthwhile. Narratology was a way of allowing me to say something interesting by doing an empirical analysis of the text and drawing conclusions from that; it did not force me to talk about emotions and moral beliefs, etc. Since I also studied linguistics and, briefly, mathematics, I had no problems with logics and formalism.

2. What do you consider your most important contribution(s) to the field?

To my own mind, I have contributed a series of studies to narratology that have shifted through a number of stages of interest. I started out with free indirect discourse and representations of speech and thought (Fludernik 1993a). Doing that, I got interested in constructivism and cognitive issues, resulting later in work that is now labelled "cognitive narratology" (Fludernik 1996, 2003b). At the same time, my work on speech and thought representation opened my eyes to the importance of natural narrative in the Labovian sense and prepared the way for my analyses of conversational narratives and the historical present tense (1991; Chapter 2 in Fludernik 1996). In conjunction with the analysis of conversational narrative, the diachronic development of narrative, especially before the rise of the novel, became my concern (Fludernik 1996: chapters 3-5; 2003a), resulting in a new field: diachronic narratology.

Looking at postmodernist narratives, I also came across texts in the second person, and started to collect the material. When it became apparent how many texts there were, I realized one needed to systematize these and attempt to align them with the narrative typologies of Gérard Genette and Stanzel (Fludernik 1993b, 1994a,b).

More recently, I have been interested in metaphor theory and blending (Fludernik 2011), which has taken me back to cognitive poetics and narratology (Fludernik 2010).

However, since my appointment as a professor of English literature at the University of Freiburg, I have been teaching British and postcolonial literature from the Middle Ages to the present. As a result, I have been studying many other topics and have acquired a reputation in eighteenth-century studies (particularly on the concept of the sublime), in postcolonial theory, Indian fiction, law and literature studies (see Brooks 2006 and Sternberg 2008), and in early modern drama. Major work in these areas has little to do with narratology in its narrow sense (Fludernik 1998, 2003c, Fludernik and Olson 2004)

3. What is the proper role of a narratology and narrative theory in relation to other academic disciplines?

This is a very difficult question to answer, particularly because it is not quite clear what is meant here by "other academic disciplines" (ethnology, physics; or deconstruction, reader response theory, etc.?). I think for me the most important question today is to what extent narratology remains part of the philological departments or becomes a discipline in its own right. On the one hand, it would make a great deal of sense for narratology to be conducted in a purely interdisciplinary manner, with linguists, literary scholars, psychologists and historians participating in the dialogue. On the other hand, narratology still has an important role to play in the analysis of fiction, and therefore continues to be a requirement for students in the philologies (at least in Europe).

4. What do you consider the most important topics and/or contributions in narratology?

Possibly, Alan Palmer's work on the social mind (Palmer 2010) is the most important recent contribution to narratology because it persuasively links with cognitive studies but also points up a real blind spot in traditional narratology. I would also like to highlight Meir Sternberg's work and underline its patient and probing emphasis on textuality. The most prolific and innovative narratologist of the past two decades is probably David Herman.

5. What are the most important open problems in this field and what are the prospects for progress?

What I would like to see more of is narratology being conducted in application to Spanish and Russian literature—for instance, I would love to know reliably what there is and is not in Spanish and Russian second-person narrative. In the same vein, intercultural narratology should become a flourishing field. We know too little about how narrative works in, say, Igbo or Zulu or Kannada or Vietnamese. Are narratives different in other, non-European languages, do they function differently, and if so, how? Training scholars from different cultures in narratology might help spread the knowhow and result in such work.

11
Dorothy J. Hale

Professor of Philosophy
Department of English, University of California, Berkeley

1. Why were you initially drawn to narratology or narrative theory?

The Anglo-American modernist novel didn't just draw me to narratology—it drove me to it. I was engaged particularly with the novels of William Faulkner and determined to make sense of his relentless narrative experimentation both within individual novels and over his career. The Faulkner criticism of the time gave me interesting ways to think about the social and literary investments that motivated Faulkner's commitment to narrative innovation, but no one did justice to what I felt was the full oddity of Faulkner's narrative management. Both on the micro-level of diction and syntax and on the macro-level of emplotment and character formation, Faulkner's narrative practice is more complicated and just plain weirder than the criticism of the time allowed. I found that narratology provided categories and terms that enabled me to account for Faulkner's narrative effects. But I also then became equally interested in the way that narratology imported into my description of Faulkner a theory of value. Voice; free indirect discourse; overt vs. covert narration; psycho-narration; quoted monologue—to employ this vocabulary was to invoke a certain normative understanding of personhood, language, culture, and, of course, the novel. What started as my need for a simple definition—what exactly is narrative voice?—to explicate a specific aspect of Faulkner's narrative technique thus grew into *Social Formalism: The Novel in Theory from Henry James to the Present*, a theoretical examination of the concept of narrative voice in twentieth-century theory.

2. What do you consider your most important contribution(s) to the field?

My abiding scholarly interest has been in understanding the novel as a literary form. To be engaged in such a project is to take none of the key terms (novel, literary, form) for granted. My own ideas about each of these categories, and how these categories modify one another, have been formed by reading widely in theoretical approaches that are often regarded as mutually exclusive: narratology, cultural studies, identity politics, deconstruction, and moral and aesthetic philosophy. I have attempted to contribute to narratology by accounting for its formative influence to the theory of the novel in the twentieth century. This is an endeavor that requires the assessment of not just the positive contribution narratology has made to novel studies but also its disciplinary blind spots. My current book project, *The Novel and the New Ethics*, seeks to show how the implied social values that attend narratological analysis are part of a larger public discourse about the novel's ethical capacity and artistic worth. Narratology has played an important role in shaping what I argue is the dominant contemporary understanding of the novel's distinguishing generic feature: its representation of the social good of diversity and alterity in relation to the problem of epistemological relativism in the modern world.

3. What is the proper role of narratology and narrative theory in relation to other academic disciplines?

This question might be taken to imply that narratology is a homogeneous pursuit and that narratologists are those who have come to a shared agreement about its purpose and objectives. But today most would agree that narratology continues to thrive, after its structuralist heyday, precisely because it sponsors a family of investigations. The valuable work of classification and nomenclature being conducted by scholars such as Gerald Prince, Peter Rabinowitz, and Brian Richardson is both different from and related to political projects pursued by theorists like Homi Bhabha, Eve Sedgwick, Fredric Jameson and Gayatri Spivak whose work theorizes the power of narrative in its ideological aspects.

At the moment of my writing, the burgeoning multidisciplinary interest in narrative has led some narratologists to applaud what they call the "narrative turn" in academic studies. But I would also note that this turn is reciprocal: narratology has moved forward by moving outward through its alliance with different fields. What especially interests me is how each discipline harvests particular aspects of narratological theory. The Theory of Mind scholar or cognitive psychologist, for example, is interested to develop the ideas of story and story-telling into an universal structure of mind. The scholar of law examines the way the cultural construction of narrative coherence influences a jury's verdict about the innocence or guilt of the accused. The moral philosopher posits the task of composing a narratable life to be the source of ethical value in the modern world. The field of narrative medicine seeks to redress the hierarchies of social position and knowledge that medicine has traditionally been based upon by developing the physician's ability to comprehend the patient's story of illness by attending to narrative structures such as focalization, elision, repetition, and temporal management.

The proper role of narratology in relation to other academic disciplines would thus be to explore how new narrative concepts and terms are generated through the study of narrative within particular disciplinary contexts; to study the way familiar narratological terms undergo modification or development; and to offer a synthetic overview of the systems of value that attach to the study of narrative—as a specific category and as a larger cluster of attributes—through travel to these new settings.

4. What do you consider the most important topics and/or contributions in narratology?

Because of my interest in the philosophical framework that informs theoretical approaches to literature, I find the most intellectual excitement in moments when narratology, in responding to wider intellectual and cultural developments of a given social moment, accomplishes a paradigm shift. The enthusiasm and sense of possibility with which Roland Barthes first pursued his structural analysis of narrative would be one such formative moment—as would be the deconstruction of this method and the alternative sense of possibilities that result in S/Z. Fredric Jameson's engagement with Northrop Frye and Vladimir Propp marks another transformational moment in the life of narrative theory. And Wayne Booth's embrace of Mikhail M. Bakhtin enacts the shift in Anglo-American formalist theory from closed rhetorical systems to the political and ideological aspects of narrative form.

5. What are the most important open problems in this field, and what are the prospects for progress?

I'm especially interested in how the development in other disciplines of terms that are key to the study of the novel—story, narrative, fiction, fictionality, plot, focalization, dialogism, free indirect discourse, and alterity–might help us better understand the novel as a cultural form. Here are some issues that are currently on my mind.

- Is the recent interest in narrative as a state of cognition an answer to problems raised by theoretical difficulties encountered in identity politics? Or is the move to cognition a new universalism that ignores or suppresses the role of social power in the production of actual minds?
- What exactly is being claimed when it is said that narrative is not just one mode of knowledge among many but a better mode of knowing?
- Does the definition of narrative change radically depending upon which discipline is employing the term?
- Is it true, as some ethicists have claimed, that fictional narratives are ethically valuable because they open up the possibility of the counterfactual? Or is narrative the term we use to suggest that knowledge itself is fictional, constructed by a partial or biased interpreter?
- Is it true, as some political theorists have claimed, that narrative understanding might be a means to cross-cultural accord?
- How does public discourse contribute to the social understanding of literary affect?
- Is the current multidisciplinary interest in narrative a social panacea? Is narrative a means of theorizing a paradigm of non-confrontational social diversity in keeping with the "yes, we can" racial strategy of the Obama campaign?

I would hope that collective reflection on the current state of narratology might lead to a meta-reflection on the tendency of the field to narrate its own development as a progress. The view that narratology can or should be an empirical science promotes the idea that the field can grow internally, as a closed-system. Concepts can be refined or emended; new categories of narrative practice can be added in. But as the examples of Barthes, Jameson, and Booth remind us, narratology also develops through the confrontation of its disciplinary limits, especially the limit of empirical science as a paradigm for the study of narrative. Throughout the last century and now into the new, narrative study has been vitalized through the cross-conversation and paradigm shifts enabled by a rich plurality of theoretical endeavor. This seems like a good way to continue.

12
David Herman

Arts and Humanities Distinguished Professor, Department of English
Ohio State University

Pathways to Narrative Theory

1. Why were you initially drawn to narratology or narrative theory? and 2. What do you consider your most important contribution(s) to the field?

Taking these first two questions together, I begin my reply with a rather odd narrative—an autobiographical tale that features a kind of backward chronology. When I was a doctoral student (in the late 1980s and early 1990s), poststructuralism was the dominant paradigm for critical theory. While studying poststructuralist theorists like Jacques Derrida, Jean-François Lyotard, and others, I thought that it might be important to go back and study the structuralists against whom the poststructuralists were reacting. In this way, I found out about narratology. At the same time, I began to read some of the scholarship of Gerald Prince, who helped introduce narratology to North America and with whom I eventually went on to study for my dissertation research. I was greatly impressed by Prince's work, which opened up for me whole vistas of research that I thought it might be productive to explore. Some 20 years later, I still feel as though I've only barely begun to scratch the surface of those areas of inquiry!

There's another part of the story, too. As I began to study structuralist narratology, which I came to with a background in philosophy and classics as well as literature and literary theory, I also developed an interest in linguistics—in part because the structuralists thought that they could use Saussurean linguistics as a pilot-science for the study of narrative, among other cultural phenomena. Fortuitously, shortly after being appointed to my first teaching position, I was asked to teach a graduate seminar in discourse analysis, and while studying linguistic pragmatics, Erving Goffman's interactional sociolinguistics, Conversation Analysis, the ethnography of communication, and other linguistic frameworks, I ran up against the limited applicability of Saussurean language theory for the analysis of narratively organized discourse—or discourse more generally, for that matter. (See, however, my response to question 4 below.) Recall that one of Ferdinand de Saussure's basic premises is that *parole*, or situated uses of language in particular communicative contexts, lies outside the domain of linguistic science, which for Saussure properly limits itself to *langue*—or the system underlying any specific utterance or communicative act. By contrast, the ideas on which the discourse analysis seminar focused—from the notion of turn-taking systems, to concepts of politeness, to the distribution of given and new information over a stretch of talk—brought into focus the systematicity of language in use (Herman 2001). This work also accentuated for me the need to enrich classical, structuralist understandings of "narrative langue" with more recent work in language theory (Herman 2001, 2002, 2009a, 2009b). I felt that the field of narratology could only benefit from greater convergence with sociolinguistic, discourse-analytic, and other work on narrative viewed as a contextually situated communicative practice.

What is more, research on discourse understanding has emerged as a subdomain within the sciences of mind, and points up how linguistics can be viewed as part of a larger constellation of disciplines concerned with the structure of intelligent behavior. Over time I came to recognize the importance of working to situate narratology within this same constellation of fields, in order to develop strategies for studying the nexus of narrative and mind. In sketching out strategies of this sort, I have drawn not just on language theory and discourse analysis but also areas such as cognitive and social psychology (Herman 2002, 2007, 2010a), cognitive linguistics (2009a), cognitive anthropology (e.g., work on folk taxonomies, or indigenous systems for classifying elements of experience) (Herman 2009b), and the philosophy of mind (Herman 2008, 2009c, 2011a, 2011b; Herman, Phelan, Rabinowitz, Richardson, and Warhol, 2012).

3) What is the proper role of narratology and narrative theory in relation to other academic disciplines?

In a broad perspective, narratology/narrative theory can be viewed as a kind of meta-discipline–or at least as a highly syncretic interdiscipline. To take the true measure of what stories are, how they work, and what they can be used to do, narratologists will need to interweave insights from a range of fields, including psychology, comparative media studies, linguistics, philosophy, literary theory, ethnography, and others. I would therefore resist characterizing narratology as a subfield within literary studies or critical theory, for example. For one thing, the proper scope of narrative inquiry extends beyond literary narratives, encompassing stories told in face-to-face interaction, graphic narratives, films, digital narratives, and so on. By the same token, narrative theorists cannot limit themselves to the analytic tools used by literary scholars if they are to develop a model capacious enough to characterize stories of all sorts.

I do not mean to suggest, however, that all scholars of narrative must obligatorily study all manifestations of narrative, across all possible communicative situations and storytelling media. Instead, a pathway to progress in the field (to anticipate part of question 5) is for scholars working with particular kinds or corpora of stories to collaborate with one another, so that medium-specific aspects of story corpora can be sorted out from generically narrative features of those corpora. For example, by collaborating with sociolinguists and literary scholars, experts on comics or cinema can explore commonalities and contrasts among the storytelling techniques used in these domains. Honing in on the contrasts, analysts can then determine which differences arise from the constraints and affordances associated with specific media. At the same time, joint work by theorists bringing different perspectives to bear on one and the same narrative corpus–say, literary narratologists adopting feminist versus diachronic approaches to printed fictional texts–can help illuminate the structures and functions of stories told in a given medium.

But I would like to respond to this question in another way as well–namely, with reference to my particular interest in developing models for studying the nexus of narrative and mind. Granted, narratologists can productively adapt ideas from the sciences of mind, including psychology, linguistics, philosophy, and other fields, to explore basic mental dispositions and abilities bound up with storytelling practices. Conversely, though, concepts developed by analysts of narrative can also benefit the sciences of mind themselves. Narrative theorists' work on techniques for representing the minds of characters, for instance, can inform discussions in the philosophy of mind about the status and functions of consciousness itself (Herman 2011a, 2011b). Likewise, convergent evidence now suggests that narrative not only triggers inferences about authors', narrators', and characters' mental states and dispositions, but also constitutes a key source of the commonsense models of mind that support everyday reasoning concerning one's own and others' actions (Bruner 1990; Hutto 2008; Herman 2009c). In short, researchers investigating the mind-narrative nexus should strive to avoid the unidirectional borrowing–i.e., the importation of ideas from the cognitive sciences into traditions of narrative study but not vice versa–that Sternberg (2003) rightly characterizes as problematic.

4. What do you consider the most important topics and/or contributions in narratology?

In my response to questions 1 and 2, I suggested that recent work in discourse analysis, the philosophy of language, and related fields points up some of the limitations of Saussure's ideas when it comes to studying narrative discourse. Yet the inadequacy of Saussurean models for narrative inquiry in no way impugns the original insight of the structuralists: namely, that language theory provides invaluable resources for analyzing stories. This key insight has proved to be the starting point for much of my own research on narrative–and in particular my ongoing attempts to help foster a "postclassical" narratology. In addressing the present question and the next, I will sketch how I arrived at the idea of postclassical narratology; discuss trends in the field that I interpret as manifestations of this ongoing reassessment, from multiple theoretical standpoints, of earlier, structuralist models of narrative; and then (in my response to question 5) pinpoint five open problems that have emerged along with this shift from classical to postclassical approaches.

As I use the term in my introduction to *Narratologies: New Perspectives on Narrative Analysis* (Herman 1999a), postclassical narratology refers to frameworks for narrative research that build on the work of classical, structuralist narratologists but supplement that earlier work with concepts and methods that were unavailable to story analysts such as Roland Barthes, Gérard Genette, Algirdas J. Greimas, and Tzvetan Todorov during the heyday of structuralism. My choice of the term was inspired in part by some of the work presented at a symposium on "Mathematics and Postclassical Theory" that I attended in 1993 at Duke University here in the U.S. After attending that symposium and reading published versions of some of the papers (Herrnstein Smith and Plotnitsky 1997)–especially the one by Arkady Plotnitsky, with whom I had also worked during my doctoral studies–I began to think of the contrast between classical and postclassical physics as a possible analogue for the contrast between structuralist narratology and approaches that focus on aspects of narrative that were not considered by structuralist theorists.[1]

To develop the analogy somewhat more fully: the classical physics of Newton is not "invalidated" by the postclassical physics of Einstein, Bohr, and others. Rather, what the postclassical frameworks clarify is the scope of applicability of the earlier, Newtonian models. Newtonian physics is very good at describing and predicting the behavior of mid-sized objects like chairs and bicycles. But it is not so good at describing and predicting the behavior of very large or very small (or very fast) things, such as the evolution of a galaxy or what goes on inside a particle accelerator. A theory with a wider scope of applicability is needed to account for such phenomena, and the classical Newtonian model can then be re-interpreted as a special case within the broader, postclassical account. By analogy, structuralist narratology is not invalidated by later developments in the study of narrative; instead, those developments suggest that, though scholars of story can build on the aspects of narrative discussed by the structuralists, the scope of narrative analysis–the range of narrative phenomena that need to be investigated by theorists–is more expansive than the structuralists envisioned.

Research concerned with storytelling in face-to-face interaction exemplifies the shift in question; this shift corresponds to a rethinking of the scope of applicability of models for narrative analysis. Precipitating the shift, in this case, is the recognition that the model pioneered by the linguist William Labov in studies such as "The Transformation of Experience in Narrative Syntax" (1972) captures one important sub-type of narrative told face to face–namely, stories elicited during interviews–but does not necessarily apply equally well to other storytelling situations, such as informal conversations between peers, he-said she-said gossip, or conversations among family members at the dinner table. Narratives do different things, and assume different forms, in different communicative environments (Ochs and Capps 2001). In conversations among peers, for example, participants may all be trying to capture the floor at once in order to tell their own version of a story under dispute. Such competition for the floor will drastically

---

[1] I should stress here that the classical/postclassical distinction is not exclusively a matter of chronology. The distinction reflects, rather, different understandings of the proper scope and methods of narrative inquiry.

alter the shape of the stories participants (try to) tell; given the communicative exigencies at work, storytellers are likely to truncate or omit all but the most essential orienting information, and conversely to bolster their efforts to signal the point of their narrative, or why they should be heard out rather than interrupted with a competing story. Meanwhile, the narratives told in this context are likely to bear on the social status or "face" of their tellers in ways that they might not in the context of interviews. Hence new, richer models of the structures and functions of storytelling in interaction need to be developed–with the Labovian account now acquiring the status of a model suited to a special case within a larger array of storytelling situations.

More generally, subfields within postclassical narratology have taken shape as theorists engage in different ways with the possibilities and limitations of prior models for studying stories. These earlier models can then be redescribed as capturing particular aspects of narrative–or specific kinds of narrative experiences– but not necessarily (the experience of) narrative tout court. Although it is not possible to provide an exhaustive list here, relevant strands of inquiry include the following:

- research on narrative and mind (Fludernik 1996; Herman 2002, 2007, 2008, 2009a, 2009b, 2009c, 2010a, 2010b, 2011a, 2011b; Herman, Phelan, Rabinowitz, Richardson, and Warhol, 2012; Hogan forthcoming; Jahn 1997, 1999a; Palmer 2004);
- feminist narratology, which explores how issues of gender bear on the production and interpretation of stories (Lanser 1992; Page 2006; Warhol 2003);
- corpus-based approaches, which draw on large, multimillion-word corpora to test out intuition-based hypotheses about stories and also to rethink foundational categories for narrative study (Mani 2010; Salway and Herman forthcoming);
- research seeking to come to terms with narrative traditions associated with non-Western cultures and also with the full range of narrative experimentation within Western traditions (Gu 2006; Alber, Iversen, Nielsen, Richardson 2010);
- and transmedial narratology, which I've already touched on in my response to question 3, and which is premised on the assumption that, although narrative practices in different media share common features insofar as they are all instances of the narrative text-type, stories are nonetheless inflected by the constraints and affordances associated with a given medium (Herman 2004, 2009b, 2010b; Ryan 2004).

In my response to the next question, I discuss some of this work, or rather the problems it has enabled narratologists to articulate and begin exploring, in more detail.

5. What are the most important open problems in this field and what are the prospects for progress?

I focus here on five open problems in the field–problems that not only grow out of postclassical approaches to narrative but also cut across multiple frameworks for research on stories. The five problems are (A) narrative worldmaking; (B) storytelling across media, as well as variable narrative practices within particular media; (C) diachronic narrative study; (D) large narrative corpora; and (E) the use of narratives to model the experiences of non-human animals. Although these problems by no means exhaust the scope of current-day research on stories, they do suggest something of the range and diversity of the work relevant for postclassical narratology. The five problems also span established as well as emergent areas of inquiry in the field.

A. Narrative worldmaking

A key open problem in the field is how best to characterize procedures of narrative worldmaking. At issue are practices whereby story creators cue interpreters to engage in the co-construction of narrative worlds, or "storyworlds," whether they are the imagined, autonomous worlds of fiction or the worlds about which nonfictional accounts make claims that are subject to falsification. Indeed, imaginative relocation to narrative worlds can be viewed as a core aspect of all narrative experiences–as an enabling condition for storytelling and story-interpreting practices as such (Herman 2009b: 105-36). Despite important contributions over the past two or three decades, researchers have only begun to characterize the nature and scope of narrative ways of worldmaking.

Major questions remain unresolved. How exactly is narrative worldmaking imbricated with–how does it at once support and get supported by–basic mental abilities and dispositions? How do communicative, aesthetic, and other norms bear on the design and interpretation of storyworlds? And, to anticipate the second open problem (or set of problems) to be discussed here, how do differences among storytelling media impinge on the process of building narrative worlds?

B. Storytelling across media and cultural traditions; the variability of narrative practices within a given medium or tradition

Another important research question is whether the narratological principles and methods developed to date–principles and methods extrapolated from a growing but still relatively limited corpus of narrative texts–are sensitive enough to capture differences in storytelling practices as they play out across different cultural and linguistic traditions (Gu 2006). Narrative scholars from all over the world will need to engage in a collaborative, cross-cultural as well as cross-disciplinary effort to refine the narratological toolkit, as necessary, in light of attested storytelling traditions. This work is a necessary complement to the research on narrative across media that is likewise emerging as a focal concern in the field. Unlike classical narratology, transmedial narratology disputes the notion that the story level of a narrative remains wholly invariant across shifts of medium. However, it also assumes that stories do have "gists" that can be remediated more or less fully and recognizably—depending in part on the semiotic properties of the source and target media (Herman 2004). In other words, since medium-specific differences among narratives are nontrivial, inter-translation among storytelling media will be more or less possible, depending on the particular formats involved. A key question is how the process of remediation plays out in a given instance, given the constraints and affordances associated with the media involved (Herman 2010b).

Complementing the cross-cultural and transmedial focus in contemporary narratological research is a focus on the variability of narrative practices within a given medium or tradition. A case in point is the emergent debate concerning the relation among subgenres of narrative fiction–and also among fictional narratives and other kinds of narrative texts. One of the issues under dispute is whether reflexive, avant-garde fictions require a different analytic framework than fictional narratives that do not comment as overtly on the procedures for worldmaking that they simultaneously cue interpreters to deploy. See Alber, Iversen, Nielsen, and Richardson (2010), Herman (2011b), and Herman, Phelan, Rabinowitz, Richardson, and Warhol (2012) for different positions in this debate.

C. Diachronic narrative study

The previous problem or set of problems concerns the variability of narrative practices at any given time. Another issue is how to study changes in storytelling practices over time. Here the distinction between synchronic and diachronic methods of analysis, outlined by Saussure in the context of linguistic study, can be brought to bear. This distinction is pertinent for all aspects of narrative–e.g., techniques of characterization, focalization, emplotment, and so forth. For the purposes of this brief remark, however, I will focus on the relevance of the synchronic-diachronic distinction vis-à-vis techniques for representing minds in narrative.

In the introduction to a recently published volume titled *The Emergence of Mind* (Herman 2011b), I build on work by Fludernik (2003) and Palmer (2004: 240-44) to suggest that, along with differences in methods for presenting minds that may obtain among different narratives (e.g., different narrative subgenres) produced during the same time-period, narrative theorists also need to consider changes in techniques for mind representation across texts written in different epochs. A diachronic perspective focuses on the evolution, or changing distribution, of the strategies for mind representation that are built into narrative viewed as a system for worldmaking. The question is how best to identify commonalities and contrasts among narratives from different periods and any trajectory of change that the narratives might reveal when examined together. Arguably, story analysts will need to employ–and ideally combine–many kinds of investigative tools to study patterns of change of this sort. One set of tools has emerged from qualitative approaches based on in-depth examinations of case studies. But another set of tools is emerging from quantitative, corpus-based methods of narrative study–methods enabled by the large narrative corpora that are now available via digitization. These methods for dealing with large narrative corpora–my next open problem–can be used either to test or to generate hypotheses about the structure of stories, including hypotheses about changing distributions of mind-evoking cues in stories written at different times.

D. Large narrative corpora

I have teamed up with computational linguist Andrew Salway to establish what we've christened as the Corpus Narratology Initiative, which centers on the following key question: will coming to terms with large narrative corpora—not single narratives or even groups of stories but rather multimillion-word collections of narratively organized texts—alter the foundational concepts of narrative theory? Or, to put the question in somewhat more specific terms, what methods for studying large amounts of textual data have been developed in other fields, e.g., corpus linguistics, and how might incorporating those methods into narrative inquiry afford new foundations for the study of stories, and perhaps also new applications for narratological research?

To assess how corpus-analytic methods bear on the core concepts and explanatory aims of narrative inquiry, Salway and Herman (forthcoming) situate their analysis vis-à-vis two broad approaches: top-down or hypothesis-driven approaches, and bottom-up or data-driven approaches. Top-down methods have been used in stylistics-based research (e.g., Semino and Short 2004) that begins with categories of structure proposed in advance by analysts and then seeks to (dis)confirm the existence of those structures—and study their patterns of distribution—in textual corpora.[2] Thus Semino and Short (2004) use top-down methods to test whether earlier work on modes of speech and thought representation is borne out by distributional patterns found in an actual corpus of narrative texts. By contrast, Salway and Herman (forthcoming) use bottom-up, data-driven methods. Corpus-enabled research of this second kind seeks to remain as much as possible at the surface level of the texts included in corpora, rather than assuming beforehand that some features will be more relevant than others for the analysis of those texts. Our bottom-up approach begins with textual features that are computationally tractable, aiming to work up from there to an account of the structures and functions of narrative. We suggest that a data-driven approach of this sort may provide new strategies for addressing one of the root problems of narratology—namely, what constitutes narrativity, or the property or set of properties that makes stories interpretable as narratives to begin with. Our suggestion is that narrativity can be defined, at least in part, as a distinctive mode of information packaging, which contrasts with how lists, syllogisms, and other kinds of representations structure the information that they convey. Corpus-driven methods may prove especially useful for research on narrativity from an information-theoretic perspective of this kind.

E. Non-human experiences

Recently (Herman 2009b) I proposed that a factor contributing to narrativity is a focus on human or human-like individuals experiencing events in storyworlds. However, I believe that this claim needs to be set against representations of the experiences of non-human animals in stories. To what extent can stories figure non-

---

[2] Likewise Herman (2005) draws on top-down or hypothesis-driven strategies for analysis. This study uses quantitative evidence to test hypotheses about genre-based preferences for representing actions and events—hypotheses that grew out of earlier qualitative work (Herman 2002).

human experiences, and what are the markers, structures, and effects of such experiences in narrative discourse?

In broaching this issue, I mean to suggest that narratology can be informed by as well as contribute to the emergent, interdisciplinary field of critical animal studies (Wolfe 2003). Practitioners in this field question assumptions about the primacy of the human—and call for a rethinking of institutions and practices based on such assumptions. By investigating how stories use methods of focalization (Nelles 2001) and consciousness representation to model non-human experiences, narratologists can contribute to this same far-reaching project. If narrative worldmaking affords a bridge between the human and the non-human, not merely through anthropomorphic projections but also by figuring the phenomenal worlds of creatures whose organismic structure differs from our own, then the study of narrative can in turn provide scaffolding for this important mode of ideology critique. By modeling the richness and complexity of "what it is like" for non-human others, narratives can underscore what is at stake in the trivialization–or outright destruction–of their experiences.

13
Manfred Jahn

Scientific Assistant (ret.)
Department of English, University of Cologne

---

1. Why were you initially drawn to narratology or narrative theory?

In the nineteen-sixties and early seventies, narrative theory at English Departments in Germany was mainly taught on the basis of Käte Hamburger's *Logik der Dichtung* (1957), Franz Stanzel's *Typische Formen des Romans* (1964) and Wayne Booth's *Rhetoric of Fiction* (1961). A prominent focus of attention in the German textbooks was the phenomenon called *erlebte Rede* - free indirect discourse - but we little anticipated what was to be gained by tackling it from a joint literary and linguistic perspective. (As students of literature we were required to take obligatory courses in linguistics.) A series of foundational essays of French structuralism had been published in Vol. 8 of the French periodical *Communications* in 1966, and Tzvetan Todorov had coined the term *narratology* in 1969, but I have to admit I did not pay any attention at the time, nor did I have the good sense to catch the impact of Gérard Genette's *Discours du récit* when it appeared in 1972. In 1979, however, Stanzel toured German universities in order to introduce his new study entitled *Theorie des Erzählens*. In Cologne, the main lecture hall was packed with an audience of five hundred plus, and I remember that we listened spellbound as he re-defined the three typical narrative situations, stressed the importance of intermediate types, demonstrated the technique of rewriting passages by switching narrators and points of view, and argued the case for the "typological circle", a design that arrays narratives past, present, and future along overlapping and sliding scales of perspective, identity, and distance. All this seemed fascinating and to open up vast vistas of exploration. *Typische Formen* had been a slim booklet of eighty or so pages, *Theorie des Erzählens*, soon translated as *A Theory of Narrative*, had grown to over three hundred. The index, I now notice, had been collated by somebody named Monika Fludernik; we were soon to hear more of her. Narrative theory had come of age, and even though it took a while for the term to catch on, narratology eventually came to stand for the study of the system and structure of narrative. When Ann Banfield published *Unspeakable Sentences* in 1982, a linguistic analysis of free indirect discourse in fiction, I wrote a critical review, more to clear matters in my own mind than with a view to possible publication. Banfield's approach - basically Chomskyan transformational grammar adapted to handle "subjective expressions" - was based on interesting pieces of evidence, and it produced a number of very useful concepts and distinctions. Yet for many narratologists the conclusions springing from the odd notion expressed in the book's title seemed to lead straightway into a dead end. Everybody began looking for counterexamples and alternate theoretical frameworks. For me, the controversy surrounding Banfield's book was a catalyst. Todorov, Roland Barthes and Genette finally swam into my ken, as did the work done by Chatman, Dorrit Cohn, Brian McHale, Meir Sternberg, Mieke Bal, Susan Lanser, Shlomith Rimmon-Kenan, and Marie-Laure Ryan. In Cologne I was lucky to have Helmut Bonheim, author of *Narrative Modes* (1982) and *Literary Systematics* (1990) as a sympathetic reader, and I also had the considerable pleasure of working with Ansgar Nünning, who had a gift for organizing collaborative projects and events. I also began corresponding with Monika Fludernik, the person who had been in charge of Stanzel's index, but in the meantime had gone on to publish *Fictions of Language* (1993) and was in the process of writing *Towards a 'Natural' Narratology* (1996). My own excursions into narratology began to focus on stretching the boundaries to reach beyond literary texts and to add insights from psychology (Sigmund Freud and Eric Berne), philosophy (John L. Austin, Stanley Fish), linguistics (Ray Jackendoff), pragmatics (Paul Grice, Dan Sperber and Deirdre Wilson), artificial intelligence (Marvin Minsky, Roger C. Schank), and cognitive stylistics (Menachem Perry, Meir Sternberg). All of these authors have exerted a strong influence on me, and their names tend to pop up regularly in my copy.

2. What do you consider your most important contribution(s) to the field?

My first extended piece of research (well, a 26-page essay) was originally entitled "Frames, Preferences and the Reading of Third-Person Narratives" (1997), but Ansgar Nünning with his sharp sense of all current "turns" immediately suggested adding the subtitle "Towards a Cognitive Narratology". The main point of the essay was to explain attribution of narrative situations to narrative passages and to explore what Perry and Sternberg had called "literary dynamics". The cognitive frames concept that was added to this was lifted from Marvin Minsky's frame theory (an Artificial Intelligence approach), and the notion of preferences was imported from Ray Jackendoff's *Semantics and Cognition* (1983).

My next project focused on the perceptional filtering of narrative information or "focalization" ("Windows of Focalization" 1996, "More Aspects of Focalization" 1999). The term itself and three main types had been distinguished by Genette, re-arranging and streamlining what had previously been covered under the labels of perspective and point of view. Bal and Chatman had come up with interesting proposals as to modifications and refinements, all more or less rejected by Genette, who now seemed to consider the topic exhausted as well as exhausting. I did not agree; Genette had successfully integrated focalization into the general framework of narratology, but focalization theory itself was fragmented and there was no consensus about its scope. Considering that no part of narratology is tied closer to cognition than focalization, re-assessment simply had to proceed from a cognitive grounding. I therefore began my treatment of the subject by outlining a simplified model of the perceiving eye. This model allowed me to graphically disentangle the two main meanings of *focus* as being (1) the perceptual zero point located within the perceiver, and (2) the perceived object itself, the object *in* focus. For what I thought would be a practical shorthand, I used the terms *focus-1* and *focus-2*, respectively, but for some unfathomable reason these never caught on. Much to my delight, a famous piece of author-theory, Henry James's metaphor of the million windows in the *House of Fiction*, fitted this model of focalization perfectly, as did Jackendoff's account of the reading process in *Consciousness and the Computational Mind* (1987).

In my continued assessment of what focalization is and does I find that one of the most helpful concepts is "apperception"— that is, understanding a perceived entity in terms of previous experience. The term stresses the fact that our necessarily indirect perception of reality is the product of a good deal of personal interpretive processing. Apperception is the mental construct that makes us see (or from an interestingly different perspective: *allows* us to see) the world and what's in it *as* something. Whether our seeing-as interpretation of the world is correct or distorted, ecologically viable or not, and how it agrees with other people's apperceptions is a question that is clearly as central to life as it is to literature. Regarding the problematic relationship between narration and focalization I came to conclude that narration and focalization are mutually dependent and mutually reinforcing powers. A narrator's narrative is shaped by his or her perspectival orientation both on the level of the how and the what, and deliberative storytelling will change a teller's outlook on the world. From this I proposed that narration and focalization, rather than being prized apart, are best placed in a common cognitive framework which includes all major players tagged with their respective space-time coordinates. In this general frame, the narrator is grounded in a discourse here-and-now, the recipient in a reception here-and-now and the characters in the story here-and-now. Shifts to second or third-order (make that n-order) time-space coordinates can happen anytime. Narrators may imaginatively transpose to the story here-and-now or adopt a character's view of the scene; characters may phase out to or return from daydreams or recollections; and readers may imaginatively hear the narrator speak and let themselves be transported into the world of action. I have found this scenario to be well suited to explaining a wide variety of forms and techniques, styles and effects.

In real life, perception is such a habitual mental activity that its true workload and achievement goes largely uncredited. Our routine processing of sensual input freely and easily generates representations that serve to interact with the world without bumping into the furniture. Most of the time, that is, for there are also incidents when one is brought up short because a perception conspicuously misconstrues its input. This is readily illustrated by "The horse raced past the barn fell", a famous "garden-path sentence" first submitted by cognitive linguist Thomas Bever. We usually need to be told that this is just as good a sentence as "The horse driven past the barn fell" - because it can clearly be construed identically and therefore makes perfect grammar and sense. However, it is precisely such cognitive hiccups that give us a glimpse into the mechanics of perception. Once alerted to the possibility of cognitive failure and its explanatory potential we can readily recognize similar but interestingly different cases. For instance, while we fail to make sense of the "raced past the barn fell" gibberish of Bever's sentence, we just as easily fail to detect the *nonsense* inherent in an otherwise well-formed string such as "The book fills a much-needed gap", an example invented by Philip Johnson-Laird. Because this time we do not notice the oddity - or did you notice that it is the *gap* that was said to be much-needed? - this second example is philosophically quite serious because it illustrates Wittgenstein's fly's way into the fly-bottle. Interestingly, pragmatic implicatures can be seen to kick in immediately, not resting content with what was actually said but freely producing an edited version that generates substance and sense where and when needed. Thus Bever's sentence is often mentally revised to be about a horse that raced past the barn "and" fell, and Johnson-Laird's sentence is mentally corrected to read what everybody expects it to read, namely that it is about a much-needed book that fills some gap. I have a theory that we do *anything* to read for maximal personal cognitive payoff. *De te fabula narratur*, the story is about you, the poet Horace said, and garden paths, which crucially involve the reader via the reading experience itself, can certainly be met in stories of all kinds, especially jokes and riddles, but also short stories, novels and films. In "Speak, Friend, and enter" (1999) (itself a garden path, naturally) I explore the narratological consequences arising from misunderstanding in garden-path stories and our attempts to learn the lessons coded via the reader's garden-path experience.

Still bent on testing the narratological system by feeding it unusual story data I turned to "internal stories" ("Awake! Open your eyes!" 2003) - stories without form or substance (unless mental representations can count as such), untold stories, stories in the mind, stories in the making, dreams, and visions - as opposed to external stories, stories written on paper, told to an audience or shown in a film. Psychologically-minded critics have always been interested in internal stories because they have seen them as constituting a person's "narrative identity". But because of the fleetingness of the "data" there is no easy route of access to them from a narratological vantage, in fact, many commentators believe a narratological approach is out of the question. Can one treat an internal story as a hyponarrative? Surely not, since there is no teller and it's virtually untold. Nevertheless, I stipulated that narratology can be let in by the back door by asking two questions: (1) *Where do internal stories come from?* (2) *How do internal stories turn into external stories?* They come, I argue, from online or offline perception (including the perception of external stories), and they are processed by procedures that enable us to store them in, and retrieve them from, memory. On these assumptions I drew a cyclical flowchart linking two input-output boxes called Internalization and Externalization. The Internalization box contains procedures such as emplotment and indexing, which prepare stories to be stored in memory, while Externalization procedures massage internal stories into an external form. For illustration I used Coleridge's account of the external source story that preceded the dream that preceded the writing of "Kubla Khan" that preceded Coleridge's own reading, re-reading, and assessment of the poem. In a second example I dissected Siegfried's account of how he met Brünnhilde in Act III of Wagner's *Götterdämmerung*, a case of retrospective storytelling, simultaneous narration and direct perception, all in one. While much of the flowchart model is tentative and speculative, the test cases are significant in their own right because they challenge some basic narratological tenets and do so without taking recourse to any self-conscious postmodernist playacting. (Okay, a magic drink is involved in Siegfried's story.) Even though I failed to comment on it at the time, an interesting by-product of the cyclical model is that it breaks the spell of focusing on input cognition - such as reading - to the exclusion of what I am now tempted to call output or *creative* cognition.

3. What is the proper role of a narratology and narrative theory in relation to other academic disciplines?

When publishers Routledge approached David Herman, Marie-Laure Ryan and myself to act as editors of the *Encyclopedia of Narrative Theory* (2005) we decided to pursue what Herman calls a "postclassical" orientation, a stories-in-all-disciplines approach rather than one that narrowly focuses on technical terms, genres and models. This led to the inclusion of many entries called "narrative in X" or "X and narrative", covering the treatment of stories in Xs as diverse as psychology, history, anthropology, law, medicine, religion, and so on. But as the entries arrived on our editorial computers we were often struck by two deficiencies. One was a lack of awareness of research done in neighboring disciplines, and the other was a lack of narratological basics. Even though the list of entries had been made public, contributors often left it to us to point out commonalities and parallels. In short, we found ourselves in the position of expert coordinators sitting at the center of a spider's web of cross-references apparently only known to us. What became obvious at this point was how much was to be gained if the disciplines could come together on a different basis - not stumbling about in a maze of encyclopedic entries but coming together in an organized interdisciplinary meet-up, held for the explicit purpose of exchanging views and approaches.

Indeed, suppose authors, critics, lawyers, journalists, teachers, historians, psychologists, doctors, cognitive scientists, and others were invited to discuss the role of storytelling in their specific areas of practice, teaching and research. Just as in the *Routledge Encyclopedia* a team of postclassical narratologists might well act as organizers and coordinators. It so happens that dividing the world into "spaces" is a common strategy in cognitive science. The real world can be assumed to be such a space, as can the world of percepts, as can the many worlds of specialist and theory-based descriptions. While cognitive science is mainly interested in the processes that link real-world input to percepts, interdisciplinary narrative research can go a step further and take account of specialist and theory-based descriptions. In fact, disciplines might meet as mental spaces in terms of Gilles Fauconnier's mental spaces theory. Once such modalities have been established and agreed on, it's all very simple and straightforward. All one has to do is ask, How are stories of (for instance) personal experience handled in your discipline? What kind of evidence are they assumed to provide? Which types of stories do you distinguish? Which interpretive tools do you have at your disposal? Which theoretical and practical consequences result from your work? And in my mind's eye I can virtually watch everybody sit up and take notice. Incidentally, encouraging the disciplines to talk about stories using their specialist descriptions does not mean that if one gets it right the other must have got it wrong. It *is* a possible outcome, certainly, but the far more likely outcome is that they both get it right, each on their specific focus of interest, or, indeed, that both get it wrong. But what better way to engage fruitful debate and research? I am happy to see that quite a number of university departments now encourage such meetings and that interdisciplinary symposia are becoming increasingly popular. In "Foundational Issues in Teaching Cognitive Narratology" (2004) my contribution to this was to sketch the organization of such an event—an interdisciplinary summer course - in some detail.

4. What do you consider the most important topics and/or contributions in narratology?

In my view the most important contribution of narratology lies in its ordering of a large body of significant data and its provision of a toolbox of terms, models and approaches. Narratology has always prided itself on being transparent and teachable, and there is a remarkable set of excellent textbooks which provide pleasant and instructive reading. Unfortunately, there is no state-of-the-art narratological bible in which all relevant basics are set in stone. Better make this "fortunately" - because if there is one thing that might stand as a necessary condition it is that narratology must remain open to new philosophical and cultural concerns and the paradigmatic stories that come with them. Very important, too, is narratology's emancipation from its rigid structuralist orientation, which greatly aided its initial success and equally greatly contributed to its near demise. Finally, the interdisciplinary diversification which marks narratology's move into the postclassical phase was a step that needed to be taken and has raised narratology to the level interdisciplinary importance that it currently has.

5. What are the most important open problems and what are the prospects for progress?

Obviously, the broader one sets the scope the more narratology is in danger of losing sight of core essentials that would merit closer in-depth exploration—including things that we are normally taking for granted, such as plot and character. Equally important are the political problems attending an ever-expanding narratology. Many people will have doubts about accepting narratology as a moderator discipline fearing it may be an underhanded move toward academic dominance - narratology welcoming other disciplines in with gently smiling jaws. I know that this threat is felt to be implicit in my own online guides to "Poems, Plays, and Prose" (2005), which began life as a student-oriented support system for the analysis of literary texts. Over time, the scripts grew in size and complexity to become a structured (i.e. non-alphabetical) dictionary of technical terms using standard divisions of the subject. But, narrative theory being my specialty, I also began importing items from the narratological toolbox into drama and poetry analysis on the well established scholarly principle of the more the merrier. A chapter on narratological film analysis was added to the package, and to make it all come together, I ended up by proposing a taxonomy of genres (modifying an original design by Chatman) in which the root division is not poems, drama, fiction, film, etc., but narrative genres vs non-narrative genres (the resulting taxonomical tree and the specific case for a narratological approach to drama was written up in "Narrative Voice and Agency in Drama" 2001). There are many commonalities that link novels, drama and film (the latter two classically considered non-narrative) - there is first-person narration in drama and film, stage directions and "action text" (in film) are narrative sentences, and the point-of-view shot in film is a plain case of focalization, to name just some of the most obvious correspondences. Of course, there are also many instances where genres deliberately meet and mix as in many internet-based forms of narrative. Any insistence on sticking to an ideal of pure narrative (narrative *stricto sensu*, Genette called it, excluding not only drama but nonverbally transmitted narratives as well) seems to let go of what we are all after - finding the rules and structures that impose order on endlessly diversified data. Admittedly, adapting narratology to suit all narrative genres is not plain sailing, and often it is difficult to adjust the narratological framework to the specificities required by a particular genre. But it needs to be done even if it means that narratology remains, after all these years, a site under construction. The challenge still is to make it succeed.

Surveying the history of narratology I have often been struck by the non-linear character of its progress - our going one step forward and then one step back. Whether this is progress by Echternach procession, or the baby thrown out with the bathwater, or double fallacy as in Stanley Fish's famous "affective fallacy fallacy" (which marks the birthplace of reader-oriented constructivism), the lesson is twofold: one, that one should not easily condemn anything as a fallacy, two, that some fallacies are well worth revisiting. I find it an encouraging thought that in recovering the baby, in revisiting a fallacy, we rarely go back in order to come to a final resting place but in order to go to places where we haven't been before.

14

Susan S. Lanser

Professor of Comparative Literature, English, and Women's and Gender Studies

Brandeis University

---

1. Why were you initially drawn to narratology or narrative theory?

What first drew me to narrative theory was narrative itself. Like many academics in the field of literature, I nourished early aspirations to become a novelist. After I received my bachelor's degree (in English and French with doses of comparative literature), I took time out to have children and try my hand at fiction. I loved experimenting with the formal capacities of narrative and found questions of method compelling. I had a couple of very minor successes publishing short fiction and got good enough to receive lovely personal rejection notes of the "we-almost-took-this-please-send-us-more" variety.

At this promising stage, I enrolled for a master's degree with the primary goal of deepening my knowledge of literature so that I could write better fiction. No more than two weeks into the first semester, I fell in love–again–with literary *studies* and decided to pursue a Ph.D. in Comparative Literature. I vowed that I would keep writing fiction, which has been true on and (mostly) off: in the end, I'm a better narratologist than I am a novelist. That's okay: turning my attention toward how fiction works has kept me gratifyingly close to the compositional, nuts-and-bolts side of narrative. And I had the serendipity to be in graduate school at a time when Gérard Genette's *Figures III*, Tzvetan Todorov's *Poétique de la prose*, and other works of structuralist narratology were offering an exciting new way to think about–and analyze– narrative.

During these same years, feminist theory was also emerging in the academy along with a new attention to women writers, many of whom had languished in unmerited obscurity. Studying the works of women offered me new perspectives on the relationship between ideology and form and new interests in forging a narratology that could accommodate attention both to gender and to the often unconventional writing I was encountering in an expanded and gender-integrated canon.

Indeed, the convergence of feminism and structuralism as intellectual commitments probably accounts for my tenacity as a narratologist. I found myself embracing a dual mission: to help forge a narratology that would, on the one hand, be supple enough to acknowledge the ramifications of gender and the issues of authority at work in the apprehension of fiction even at the level of form—and thus appeal to mainstream narratologists, and that would, on the other hand, seem useful enough to non-narratologist feminist literary scholars to warrant their integrating narratological questions into their study of women's writings both recovered and new. I made this double interest explicit in my first book, *The Narrative Act: Point of View in Prose Fiction*, when I wrote that "my training as deeply formalist and my perspective is deeply feminist. This uneasy union has led me beyond traditional formalism without diminishing my interest in form. I have come to conceive the notion of form more broadly, to understand form as content and ideology and form, and to recognize relationships between textual and extratextual structures" and I have sought to "initiate a merging of seemingly disparate inquiries by attempting a synthesis of feminist and poetic analysis" (pp. 7, 10).

One might rightly conclude, then, that my interest in narratology was overdetermined: by my passion for writing fiction, by my fascination with fictional form, and by the critical moment in which narratology and feminism were both emerging as academic projects. I was fortunate to have been in the right place at the right time.

2. What do you consider your most important contribution(s) to the field?

Ironically, and sometimes–though not in my case–poignantly, the contribution that the field considers most important is not always the contribution one considers most important oneself. It's been said that Sartre wished to be valued more for his literary works than for his philosophy. May Sarton wanted to be remembered as a poet rather than as a novelist. In the same way that the 'death of the author' means 'the birth of the reader,' to quote Barthes's famous claim, scholarship, once launched, gets evaluated and appropriated for other people's ends. And that is at it should be: what scholars take up is what is useful to the times and to the contexts of their work.

Clearly I am best known and probably best appreciated for coining the term, and helping to forge the practice of, feminist narratology. 'Toward a Feminist Narratology,' the then-controversial essay I wrote in 1986, and my book *Fictions of Authority: Women Writers and Narrative Voice* (1992; Chinese translation, 2002), are certainly the most cited and probably the best read of my writings on narrative.[1] I am grateful to have had the opportunity to contribute to the development of feminist narratology, which now celebrates its first quarter-century. Sexuality also has a newly recognized place in narrative theory, and my essay 'Queering Narratology' makes, I hope, a modest contribution to that field.

Within my writings that are explicitly framed as 'feminist narratology,' I hope readers will appreciate the distinctions I make between public and private voice, the historical trajectory of authorial, personal, and communal voice that I identify in women's writings, and of course my insistence that gender and sexuality are not only fit but critical matters for narratological inquiry. I'm also glad to be known for what got coined (first by David Richter and later by Manfred Jahn) as 'Lanser's Rule': that in the absence of textual clues to the contrary, readers will assume that the narrator of a male-authored fictional work is male, and of a female-authored work, female. This would apply particularly to heterodiegetic narrators who need to be identified with gendered pronouns when students and scholars discuss them. The 'rule' (their term, not mine) was motivated, as I recall, by my frustration that scholars spoke of the narrator of *Pride and Prejudice* as 'he,' defaulting to the generic masculine even in the case of Jane Austen's novels. Such a move simply keeps recodifying narrative authority as male.

At the same time, I like to think that some of my work, in *The Narrative Act* and in such essays as "The 'I' of the Beholder", has a conceptual utility that extends well beyond feminist concerns. I hope that four aspects of *The Narrative Act* will remain particularly useful. First is the argument that narrative form also entails questions of authority by virtue of the connections readers make

---

[1] I also write widely beyond the field of narrative theory, as is suggested by essays such as "Charlotte Perkins Gilman, *The Yellow Wallpaper*, and the Politics of Color in America," "Befriending the Body: Female Intimacies as Class Acts," and "Strategies of Coding in Women's Cultures," the latter co-authored with Joan Radner, as well as by other essays and edited books, and indeed by the book I am now completing, *The Sexuality of History*.

between fictional and extrafictional structures and knowledges.[2] Second is my claim that the fictional compact entails formations of what I called *status, contact,* and *stance* that are at once culturally conditioned and formally inscribed. Third is the laying out of *multiple* axes for understanding any single aspect of narrative voice or vision; a narrator's reliability, for example, embraces a range of quite different qualities including honesty, narrative competence, and trustworthy judgment; thus, as I say in *The Narrative Act,* Faulkner's Jason Compson (*The Sound and the Fury*) is a relatively competent reporter of external events but morally and psychologically untrustworthy, while Benjy has a limited capacity to construct or interpret a sequential narrative yet is more reliable than Jason in his intuitions about both people and truth. Last but not least, I hope readers find useful and will emulate the practice of recognizing aspects of narrative in terms of *spectrums* rather than of absolute and exclusive categories. Some narrative elements need not be either A or not-A, but may occupy a place along a continuum *between* A and not-A. Even heterodiegesis and homodiegesis can be understood to occupy such a spectrum; consider, for example, that *Madame Bovary,* despite having a mostly heterodiegetic narrator, opens with the eyewitness voice of a 'we.' I'd be gratified to think that some of these contributions to narratology 'proper' are still of use.

3. What is the proper role of narratology and narrative theory in relation to other academic disciplines?

I assume that 'other academic disciplines' means disciplines outside literature, but I do hope (as I suggest again below) that narratologists and literary historians will achieve a deeper *rapprochement* than has been the case thus far. My career is something of a hybrid insofar as I work in both narratology and in literary/cultural history (especially eighteenth-century studies and the history of gender and sexuality), and I often find myself in a minority in bringing narratological concerns to, for example, the history of the novel, even though so many important works in that field are themselves invested in formal analysis.[3] Yet a recent call for papers in eighteenth-century studies, for example, asked: "Is there

---

[2] I develop this idea in relation to specific genres in "The 'I' of the Beholder," which appeared in the *Blackwell Companion to Narrative Theory.*

[3] One need only think of Emil Auerbach's *Mimesis* or Watt's concept of 'formal realism' in *The Rise of the Novel* or the complex thought of Lukács to take my point.

a place for 'formalist' criticism in the study of the eighteenth century novel? Given the current dominance of historical, thematic, and cultural studies approaches to the eighteenth century novel, can we usefully speak of novelistic form?" As a narratologist, I find it hard to imagine that one could study the novel *without* speaking of 'novelistic form.' Yet literary historians are also right to lament the meager interest that narratology, as a field, has shown in the history of narrative. Surely literary studies as a whole would benefit from an imbricated attention to narrative form and narrative history.

As for fields outside of literature, the 'narrative turn' in the humanities and social sciences makes a transdisciplinary narratology imperative. Scholars in these fields can already benefit from the diverse work narrative theorists have been accomplishing in studying a range of genres far beyond prose fiction. At the same time, it behooves narrative theorists to turn more attention to non-literary genres and media, both because different commitments and practices are often entailed by these forms and because reaching scholars in fields beyond literature will happen far more readily once we can demonstrate the *direct* relevance of narratology to other disciplines. My own small contribution to this effort is a look at plotting strategies in the nonfictional and counterfactual narratives that have been foundational for feminist thought. I suspect that forays beyond literature also have something to teach us about literary narrative, but even if they don't, they are deeply worthwhile in themselves and should help to demonstrate the value of attending to all narrative not only as a historical, social, cultural, and political project but as a theoretical, formal, and cognitive one.

4. What do you consider the most important topics and/or contributions in narratology?

I would have to put Gérard Genette's *Figures III* at the top among single-book contributions to the field: it effectively *created* a narratology, and it has stood the test of time. Although even narratologists have been put off by its excess of 'lepses' and 'diegeses,'*Figures III* (in English, *Narrative Discourse*) has been crucial in giving the field a precise language for the distinctions narratology needs to make if it is to understand and explain the workings of both individual narratives and narrative conventions writ large. Yet even before Genette, Wayne Booth published his generative essay, "Distance and Point of View: An Essay in Classification," and of course his *Rhetoric of Fiction*, both which, while grounded in ethical commitments that not all narratologists share (as continuing controversy over the 'implied author' reminds us), offer path-breaking distinctions among narrative practices. Of course a number of Genette's distinctions stem from prior work of theorists such as Mendilow, Stanzel, Hamburger, and Uspenskii, who broke important new ground for narratology *avant la lettre*. Where would narratology be, for example, without such concepts that predate Genette as *style indirect libre* or the distinction between *Erzählzeit* and *erzählte Zeit*?

Considering narrative theory more beyond the contours of structural(ist) narratology, however, leads me to name Mikhail Bakhtin as probably the most influential theorist of narrative, and especially of the novel, to emerge into prominence during the past thirty years. Whether we are considering the idea of the chronotope, of heteroglossia, or of the 'speaking person and his [*sic*] discourse,' Bakhtin's thought, if far less systematic than Genette's, starts to bridge the distances between narratology and literary history, and between formal analysis and historicized interpretation, that I identified above.

But the conundrum of 'most important' is arguably a trap from which I now happily escape. The narrative theorists whose work I value, teach, and study are far too numerous to be named here, and I hope I have paid ample respects to them in other writings. Narratology has been a collaborative, far more than a competitive enterprise, and we are fortunate as a community of scholars that so many people have contributed so many insights, distinctions, hypotheses, terms, and divergent viewpoints to our field.

5. What are the most important open problems in this field and what are the prospects for progress?

I have already identified some of the challenges facing narrative theory, particularly in relationship to literary history and interdisciplinarity. In my view, the largest challenges are these:

(1) to develop a narratology that synthesizes the cognitive, the contextual, and the formal in ways that foster our understanding of narrative as at once a large human project spanning known time and earthly space, and a historically contextual and also formally specific set of practices serving myriad purposes within time and space. Rather than competing for explanatory power as they now sometimes do, these three different narrative approaches need, I think, to be approached in tandem. One recent work that begins to achieve such a synthesis is Hilary Dannenberg's *Coincidence and*

Counterfactuality: Plotting Time and Space in Narrative Fiction; its approach is at once historical, formal, and cognitive.

(2) to create fuller recognition, both within the broader field of literary studies and across the span of the human sciences, of the importance of form as content–a truism that is now mostly honored in the breach. To take an example from my own recent work on representations of same-sex relations: I have recognized certain practices of seventeenth- and eighteenth-century fiction that effectively constitute intimacy between female figures on the level of narrative form. We cannot apprehend this intimacy if we attend only to textual events; we must also look at the ways in which female intimacy operates in narration itself. In other words, we have something to learn about the history of sexuality from studying narrative form and about the history of narrative from studying sexual representation. To the extent that scholars eschew formal analysis, we impoverish our own ability to understand the texts we are studying.

(3) Finally and urgently, we need to expand the corpus from which we theorize. If narratologists were to come clean about the corpus on which most of our work is founded, we would have to recognize that it is still heavily European, white, canonical, and restricted primarily to the nineteenth and early twentieth centuries. That is, our narratological maps are not only Eurocentric, but heavily partial to two or three European literatures and heavily centered on the nineteenth century and/or modernist novel. This is true even of feminist narratology, which has been as heavily invested in Victorian fiction as Genette has been invested in Proust. As narratology moves more surely to grapple with the literatures of all peoples past and present, we may see some paradigm shifts in our current understandings that are as important for the next generation of theorists as Booth's and Genette's were for mine.

As for the prospects for progress, that depends on the young among us: the future of the field lies in your hands.

15
Uri Margolin

Professor Emeritus
Comparative Literature, University of Alberta

Three good reasons drew me to narratology in the late 1970s, having spent the previous decade working on general issues of methodology and meta-theory in literary studies. The first was the wide range of areas of enquiry and problems offered by a discipline concerned by definition with all issues of forms, of content, and of expression in narrative and the manifold of their possible interrelations. There will always be something exciting to explore here! The second, at least as important to me, was the inherently multi-disciplinary nature of any adequate theorizing in this field. Having been trained equally in literary studies and in formal philosophy, and having developed from early on a keen interest in linguistics and aesthetics, and believing furthermore that *all* literary theorizing needs to be multi-disciplinary, work in literary narratology was an obvious place to put this conviction into practice. The third reason is the challenge posed by Postmodernist narrative, especially in its French and Latin American varieties, of which I was, and remain, an avid reader. Classical narratology had inevitably to start by developing simple canonical models, which proved to be woefully inadequate for modeling the variety of these complex and apparently chaotic new forms. I felt that "segregationism", that is, developing two different kinds of narratological models, one for standard and one for Postmodern narratives, was methodologically wrong, since broadest possible scope and unity are the ideal goals of any theory. Even worse was the counsel of despair, claiming that Postmodernism was inherently transgressive and therefore incapable of manifesting any definite regularities. Could one then tame such texts? Could one extend or modify the classical model to account for such radical novelties? And if so, would this lead ultimately to the formulation of a more powerful narratological theory? Of course I did not know the answers in advance, but I felt it was meaningful and worthwhile to grapple with these issues and see what the outcome would be.

15. Uri Margolin

The major focus of my narratolgical work has been on individuals in story worlds—in the spheres of narration and the narrated alike—their basic or structural properties and their possible interrelations. This work can be divided into three segments, corresponding to the tripartite division of narration, narrated and text. The first deals with the person system and concentrates on homocommunicative instances (I, you, we) and on telling in the plural in general. The second deals with individuals in the narrated domain, exploring the basic constitutive aspects of individuals in fictional worlds: modal status, uniqueness, possession of attributes, category membership, temporal continuity amidst change and sameness across story worlds. The third segment focuses on the use of referring expressions and their interrelations in the discourses of narrator and characters alike, and how they reflect different cognitive mappings of the population of the narrated domain. As for wider frameworks, the first segment is based on the linguistic communication model, especially in its énoncé/énonciation version; the second on possible worlds semantics and theories of fictionality, as well as on a whole range of more specialized theories dealing with each of the constitutive conditions listed above; and the third on theories of reference and proper names in Anglo-American philosophy. In carrying out this work I have been constantly guided by three methodological norms:

–Find the most powerful linguistic, philosophical or aesthetic theory pertinent to your topic and draw on it to anchor your work
–Seek to set up a unified, systematic and exhaustive calculus or matrix of all possible varieties (options, combinations, choices) defined by your parameters
–Search high and low for actual instances which exemplify any and all theoretical possibilities, with special emphasis on those usually considered unlikely, deviant or non-occurring, since it is precisely such varieties which serve as a true test of the model's or theory's descriptive and explanatory powers.

Let me now provide some more details of my work in each area. Starting from Bühler's *Ich-Origo* or the I-Here-Now of the speaker/ narrator at speech time as the basic point of reference I proceeded to set up a calculus of all personal, temporal and spatial relations between the narrating and narrated individuals. This provided at least 18 possibilities: first, second and third person (each with the singular and plural varieties), each coupled with three possible temporal relations (narrated events as earlier than, simultaneous with or later than narration time) and two locative ones (narrated events with same or different location than narration site). Now in the cases of first and second person narration the individual(s) in question are members of both the narration and the narrated system: speaking, spoken of and possibly also self addressing in first person, and both addressed and spoken of in the second person case. The unity of speaker and topic, subject and object, is the standard case of first-person (autodiegetic) narratives. But there are cases when this unity is dissociated, when one 'speaks of oneself as of another' in Beckett's words. These are the cases of transferred personal deixis, of the narrator referring to himself or herself as character through the use of one or more of "you", "s/he", or "one." I examined each such variety and its possible thematic correlates. Even more radical are those cases where uses of the "I" no longer identify the one using this expression, when 'I seem to speak, it is not I' to quote Beckett once again. The two versions, both occurring in Postmodern narratives, are narrator regression, where the "I" tokens are just being quoted by a speaker who becomes mere conduit to the speech of another, and speech imputation, where the speaker speaks for and as another. The foregoing dissociation phenomena in both spheres define the extremes of the first person as narrated and narrating individual respectively. In the case of second person narratives I examined additionally their possible temporal varieties, thematic justifications for telling one one's own story, and the possibility of actual readers inserting themselves into the "you" role as narrated individual. "We" narratives are on the cusp between individual and collective propositions, posing a problem as regards the narrator's identity: a singular individual speaking for a group or collective speaker, and the narrated group's actions being viewed globally or distributively. I next extended the discussion to telling in the plural in all three persons and offered a definition of collective narrative as one in which narrated individuals are represented first and foremost as parts of a collectivity. This was followed by a discussion of the kinds of occasions on which actual world individuals or groups can insert themselves into collective narratives in the speaker and/or character roles. This segment of my work was rounded off with another extension of the narrative model, this time as regards time, aspect and modality. I proposed that the canonic form representing any narrated event or situation should consist of a nucleus (the event/situation) and of three operators defining its temporal position (past, concurrent, future), its aspect or inner temporal contour (completed or in progress), and its modal status (actual, hypothetical, indeterminate, counterfactual etc.).

Lubomír Doležel(1998) and Marie-Laure Ryan (1991) provided an ontology of fictional worlds. I felt that this work needed to be complemented by an ontology of the non-actual individual existents inhabiting these worlds, focusing on their most basic constitutive features as listed above. The results of my work in this area are compactly presented in my articles in the *Routledge Encyclopedia* and in *The Cambridge Companion to Narrative* (Margolin 2005, 2007), so I will forego any further presentation here.

The basic constitutive features of story world participants can also be presented in terms of a series of questions: What is the modal status of any individual in the story world e. g. "actually" existing vs. existing only in the belief world of one or more characters? How many different individuals are there in this world? Who's who in it, in terms of associating a proper name with one or more defining properties? What basic categories (such as natural or supernatural, human or animal) does each belong to? Is the individual we encounter in an early temporal phase of the narrative the same as the one we encounter in a later phase in spite of the change in his name or properties? Our answers to these questions form our epistemic map or set of beliefs concerning the basic features of the individuals constituting the population of the story world in question. But we are not the only ones asking such questions and providing answers (sometimes tentative, temporary, or mistaken) to these questions. Both narrator and the characters do so constantly, with respect to themselves and to others. As their versions change constantly and usually do not coincide, this creates an ever-changing interplay of perspectives, which is one basic feature of the dynamics of story worlds. These versions in their turn are textually embodied first and foremost in the narrator's and characters' use of referring expressions (proper names, definite descriptions and personal pronouns) with respect to themselves or to others, and the equations (co-reference) each of them establishes, or fails to establish, between such expressions. In my articles on reference and on proper names in narrative I explored the dynamics of the use of referring expressions by narrator and characters and the patterns of interplay of epistemic perspectives they set up.

Moving now from one individual practitioner to the discipline as a whole, one notices right away that narratology has been from the beginning a collective and cumulative enterprise, based on constant exchange between numerous participants who share basic methodological norms of rationality, explicitness and intersubjectivity. Now such exchanges are the most fruitful when they occur within a shared theoretical paradigm or theoretical language, and with each participant locating his work relative to what is available in it at the time. I think therefore that the most important contributions to narratology to date are to be defined in terms of the paradigm in which they occur and the historical succession of the latter. Classical, structuralist oriented narratology of the 1960s and 1970s shed much light on the questions of the way or "how," that is, the modes of narrative organization and transmission, systematized within a general linguistic communicative model. Many of these insights have by now become the disciplinary received view or orthodoxy, in that they are represented in the core chapters of every textbook in the field. These contributions encompass at least the following: the very distinction telling/told or narration/narrated, based on the linguistic énonciation/énoncé; relations of order, frequency and duration between told and telling; the narrator-narratee pair and their interrelations; levels of narration and speech; focalization or perspective; and thought and speech representation, especially relations between the discourses of narrator and characters. Prominent in this paradigm are the works of Mieke Bal, Seymour Chatman, Gérard Genette, Gerald Prince, Wolf Schmid and Franz K. Stanzel. But nothing in any paradigm is ever complete or concluded: every established model or claim is always open to challenge and modification, either because of the emergence of new literary practices or because of theoretical reformulation.

The next set of major contributions occurred with the shift of focus to questions of the "what" or macro-semantics, with the corresponding theoretical reorientation or paradigm shift from linguistics to philosophy, especially issues of the non-actual (possible worlds semantics, modal logic, the nature of the fictive and of fictionality). The major achievements here are the various typologies of fictional worlds according to their governing modalities; the inner structure of such worlds in terms of relations of embedding or "levels of reality"; the detailed description of the modal status of story worlds (what "actually" happens" vs. characters' pretend behaviour and beliefs or wishes); and the dynamics of action and interaction, based on notions such as alternative courses of events, goals, plans, wishes and norms. Of the major figures in this paradigm, Umberto Eco and Doležel stuck to philosophy, while Ryan introduced a whole series of computer analogies to describe both the hierarchical structure of story worlds and the dynamics of action within them. Even though the current discussion of event and eventfulness (Hühn, Schmid, Sternberg) has its origins elsewhere, it too clearly belongs to the modeling of the basic elements of the narrated, and has already introduced some much needed distinctions.

In the last few years a new paradigm, one associated with the cognitive sciences, has come to prominence in narratology. Since this one is still in progress one can only speak of achievements to date. Among them are David Herman's research programme for a cognitively oriented narratology and his reformulation of key concepts in such terms; Monika Fludernik's re-conceptualisation of (literary) narrative as the rendering of human experientiality, as a record of the working of a mind in a world and with respect to a world; and Alan Palmer's and Lisa Zunshine's descriptions of key aspects of characters' cognitive mental functioning in terms of simulation and collective or distributed cognition respectively. The future rise of new trans-disciplinary paradigms in the human sciences will inevitably bring to the fore new perspectives and new contributions to narratology. But we don't know when they will arise or what they will be like, since the growth of knowledge is not a predictable process.

Before discussing the proper relation between (literary) narratology and other disciplines, let me provide informal definitions of several key terms in this area. *Narrative* is minimally the representation in any medium of one or more events by means of semiotic procedures/devices. A theory occurring in any discipline and dealing with a domain of objects of any kind shall be considered *a narrative theory* if and only if its main concern—regardless of the theoretical language it employs– is with one or more aspects of the form or functioning of narrative as manifested in this domain of objects. *Literary narratology* in the narrowest and most conservative sense is a sub-discipline within literary theory concerned with developing general categories, models and theories regarding the forms and functioning of the telling and/or told primarily in those verbal, written narratives considered literary (artistic, aesthetic) in our time and culture. Such theories are developed for their own sake and not as sub-tasks for other, higher or different theoretical goals. *Narratology* tout court can thus refer to the institutional framework, the activity within it and the product(s) of such activity. The *relation between disciplines* needs to be defined in terms of at least two dimensions: their respective theoretical frameworks and their central domains of objects.

It is obvious that some pertinent disciplines such as philosophy, linguistics, cognitive science and philosophy of art are more fundamental than narratology in terms of the kinds of questions they ask and the entities they deal with. As a result, every narratological theory I am aware of is *anchored*, explicitly or implicitly, in theories in one or more of these fields, and it is they which have provided the major paradigms for our discipline. While being anchored does not mean being derivable from or reducible to, it does mean a hierarchical or vertical relation of theoretical *reliance* upon these disciplines for "inspiration," that is, general orientation, foundational work and conceptual underpinning. But work in our discipline can also feed back into these higher frameworks and lead to a modification of their own claims. Secondly, almost all disciplines in the study of culture and society have some kinds of verbal narratives in their domain of objects, and have developed models and theories of their own, using their own theoretical machinery, to deal with one or more aspects of these narratives, but not for their own sake, but rather as a function of their overall disciplinary goals or orientations (sociological, ethnographic, text-linguistic, theological, psychological etc.). It makes perfect sense for the literary narratologist to examine such theoretical projects and decide whether some of their concepts, categories, models etc are worth importing, that is, transferring with possible modifications (adopt and adapt) in order to become part of his own work. Such *borrowing* has always gone on, but there is so much narrative theorizing going on all over that no single scholar can survey it all, no matter what his individual focus is. Conversely, the practitioners of these other disciplines may treat literary narratology as a *lender,* a source of categories, models etc to be borrowed by them in order to enrich or modify the ways they deal with texts in their own domain of verbal narratives. One spectacular example is the change such borrowing has wrought in Biblical studies sine the 1960s. This transfer either way is a horizontal relation, a commerce among equals so to say. Some disciplines in the study of the arts (film studies, art history, theatre studies) have in their domain of objects either mixed media or non-verbal narratives. Such disciplines have developed, sometimes only incidentally, narrative models, which, like the literary ones, are formulated for their own sake, but which have been until recently at a much lower level of sophistication. Here literary narratology could serve –and often does– as stimulus, *point of departure* or 'pilot science', at least as far as procedure is concerned, for these disciplines to develop their own medium-specific narratologies, which may turn out to be quite different from the literary one in view of major differences in media affordances and constraints.

So far we have dealt with relations between disciplines on the inter-theoretic level. But there is also the issue of domains of objects. Literary narratologists can legitimately *expand* their domain of objects to any and all of those verbal domains standardly dealt with by some other disciplines, utilizing their own slant or lead questions, methods and models, which may eventually require modification in view of the nature of the new domain. This activity is obviously the mirror image of the importation of narratological perspectives by the practitioners of these other disciplines. Now some disciplines in the humanities, primarily the historiography of any and all phenomena, not only study narratives as givens but also produce narratives as an essential part of their disciplinary discourse. Both the practitioners of such disciplines (by theoretical borrowing) and the literary narratologist (by domain expansion) can use narratological models to study such narratives. One prominent example is Hayden White's meta-historiographic work. Some ambitious literary narratologists have gone even further and applied the narratological toolkit to the study of mixed-media (theatre, opera, film) and non-verbal (pictorial) narratives. Since many of the basic concepts of narratology are not language-specific this is prima facie legitimate. However, in this case (as in the mirror image of art historians etc. borrowing from narratology) domain cum medium expansion and the requirement of adequacy to the new domain may ultimately result in the formulation of theories which differ considerably from those of literary narratology. One striking example is the issue of narration and image in film vs. verbal narratives. Finally, I wouldn't know where to place it, but there is obviously room for a contrastive narratology, defining both the similarities and differences between the possible ways of story telling (and maybe also kinds of stories tellable) in different media. Examples are the numerous studies comparing the verbal and cinematic versions of a novel or the operations involved in such cross-medial transfer.

As for fundamental open problems in our field, I believe one can identify several. Because of their very nature I am not sure any of them is capable of a definitive solution, but any solution proposed to them will influence the direction of theoretical work, and any theoretically self-conscious narratologist must assume a definite position with respect to at least some of them. The first problem may be defined as the simultaneity vs. succession issue (or being vs. becoming, process vs. product). Should one describe any aspect of the telling or the told in retrospective terms, that is, in top-down terms of a global co-existing structure, a construct or static finished product, or rather in on-line terms of an unfolding sequence of phases, a dynamic process of coming into being, of continuous production with its ever changing pattern of relations between elements? Almost all existing narratological models are of the static, retrospective type which facilitates an overall view, but which runs counter to the dually sequential nature of verbal narrative, which is also the defining factor in the reader's successive formation and reformation of a mental representation of the narrated. Sternberg's studies on telling in time have been a major challenge in this respect. A second, related problem concerns the proper way of representing any plot or narration pattern: is it enough to do so in the descriptive terms of a dynamic structure (= features and relations) of some degree of complexity, or should one seek to provide an underlying set of operations, rules or procedures that bring this pattern into existence, from generative plot grammars to blend theories for perspective creation? Once again, the latter option seems to operate on a deeper level, but all attempts in this direction, from the text grammars of the 1970s to computer-generated stories, turned out to be inadequate.

A problem of a different nature is posed by the putative non-specificity of literary narratology and its models. It has been claimed by numerous scholars in several fields that the distinctions, categories models etc formulated in literary narratology on the basis of literary texts are not specific to text types considered literary and maybe not even to the text-type 'story' in general. Is narratology then (part of) a general text theory without realizing it? And if so does it still provide any specifically literary knowledge? Moreover, following the fruitless quest of the 1970s for textual features that are specifically or exclusively literary, the prevalent current opinion is that literature is not a textual category but rather a pragmatic and functional one, pertaining to cultural role and modes of reception. Is it useful then to go on looking for signposts of fictional-artistic narratives vs. factual ones? And if this search is doomed, what is the justification for a narratology whose corpus is limited to texts considered literary? No solution is forthcoming, but some good reasons for maintaining this practice could be put forth. One argument is that the texts we consider literary embody to the highest degree and explore most intensely all the potentialities of the telling, the told and their interrelations, and therefore it is methodologically justified to focus on them as preferred source material, even if we are after or end up with theories with wider scope of application. Another reason would be that many of the text types falling under the literary grouping have special value in our culture and this is why there should continue to be a (sub)discipline dealing with them primarily or even exclusively. And then there is also a methodological solution, separating between a general or theoretical narratology and a descriptive one which focuses on literature as a particular, culturally specified corpus, on the analogy of general linguistics and the linguistic description of specific languages, based on the general theory.

This leads us directly to the next problem: the possibility or desirability of a universal narratology. Such a discipline could be defined in one of two ways. It could concern itself with the quest for the universals of narrative, of what is common to all narratives in all media, probably mostly on the level of the told (narrativity, eventfulness), similar to the universals of language. Or it may concern itself with developing a sufficiently powerful universal theoretical language (concepts, categories, mechanisms) such that the narratologies formulated for different domains of objects or media will constitute their various, alternative specifications. Here the analogy would be Louis Hjelmslev's universal grammar as related to grammars of specific languages.

Finally, and maybe most crucially, where is narrative and what kind of a discipline is narratology? Quite simply put, when we identify and describe story world elements and structures, are these immanent to the text and discovered by us or are they all rather the product of readerly constructive operations to begin with and hence purely mental and cognitive in nature? Is narrative accordingly an object with an at least quasi mind-independent status or is it a mental representation produced by us from the words of the text as cues? In the first case narratology is a semiotic discipline dealing with sign structures, while in the second it is a cognitive science discipline dealing with text processing and text comprehension. I believe every narratologist must make a clear choice here, and a mix and match of elements from the two paradigms is theoretically as unsound and untenable here as it is in linguistics. Now choosing the cognitive interpretation will require right away a reformulation of most narratological descriptions in terms of the mental operations producing them. Another consequence would be the need to redefine the status of the discipline. Narratology is a rational, but not empirical discipline. Its cognitive variant could stay conceptual, like much speculation in philosophy on text processing, from Ingarden onwards. But there is also the strong current within cognitive psychology requiring experimentally testable models of text processing, representing what actual rather than hypothetical readers do. Should a cognitively oriented narratolgy, or at least some of it, follow this lead and become part of empirically oriented cognitive psychology? As I said before, the question is moot, but the consequences monumental.

16
Brian McHale

Arts and Humanities Distinguished Professor
Department of English, Ohio State University

1. Why were you initially drawn to narratology or narrative theory?

I blame first Roger Fowler, and then Jonathan Culler. I began my graduate education as a student of stylistics thanks to Fowler, the British stylistician and apologist for what he called "linguistic criticism," with whom I had taken a revelatory undergraduate seminar at Brown University when he was visiting there from the University of East Anglia. A scholarship made it possible for me to undertake graduate work at Oxford, where I studied with Stephen Ullmann, a Continental stylistician of the old school. It was through Ullmann that I discovered the perennial problem of speech representation in the novel, and in particular free indirect discourse, a topic about which he was one of the world's experts. But Ullmann died suddenly of heart disease, and the supervision of my doctoral project was taken over by his former student, Jonathan Culler.

Culler's *Structuralist Poetics* (1975)– to this day still the most comprehensive and reliable synthesis of literary structuralism— had just appeared, and under Culler's influence I began to reframe what I had initially conceived of as a problem of style in broader, more narratological terms. I recall that one of the first things Culler said to me was, "You've read Bakhtin, of course." I hadn't, of course, but I immediately went out and read everything by the Bakhtin school that was then (in the mid-Seventies) available in the languages I could read. The effort to reconcile the Bakhtinian approach to discourse in the novel with the classic stylistics approach to free indirect discourse profoundly reoriented my thinking. It was lucky for me that it did so, because the Bakhtin school turned out to be the common ground I found I shared with Benjamin Hrushovski (subsequently Harshav), one of the founders of the Tel Aviv school of poetics, who was visiting at Oxford, and to whom Culler introduced me. On the strength of my paper on free indirect discourse, Hrushovski invited me to come to Tel Aviv University as his research assistant, where I immediately became involved in arrangements for the landmark 1979 Porter Institute conference on Narrative Theory and Poetics of Fiction, and subsequently in helping to edit the three special issues of *Poetics Today* that resulted from that conference. That conference, and the publications that it generated, re-energized narrative theory. It also introduced me to the international community of narratologists (including a number who appear in the present volume), and inspired me to want to be one of them.

2. What do you consider your most important contribution(s) to the field?

If there is one contribution with which my name is associated, I suppose it is the distinction that I developed in *Postmodernist Fiction* (1987) between modernist and postmodernist fiction. Modernist fiction, I argued there, is dominated by questions of epistemology (theory of knowledge); its techniques and devices are generally geared toward investigating human perception and cognition, differences in perspective, the subjective experience of time, the circulation and (un)reliability of knowledge, and so on. Postmodernist fiction, by contrast, is dominated by questions of ontology (theory of being), and its characteristic techniques and devices are designed to explore issues of fictionality, modes of being and the differences among them, the nature and plurality of worlds, how such worlds are made and unmade, and so on. The transition from the modernist period style to postmodernism (like many other comparable literary-historical changes) involved not the wholesale replacement of one set of features and values by new ones but rather a reshuffling of existing features in the light of a new dominant function. Arguably, my distinction makes less of a contribution to narratology than it does to periodization and literary historiography, but I do think it has some narratological implications.

Apart from this contribution to the definition of postmodernism, I am most proud of my early work on free indirect discourse—though, to be honest, this mainly involved a synthesis of the contemporary state of knowledge in this area rather than any genuinely innovative breakthroughs. Somewhat outdated now, this work has over the years turned out to be useful as a starting point and springboard for later researchers whose scholarship I admire, so it has justified its existence, as far as I'm concerned. I could also mention one or two more minor contributions to the field: the notion of "weak narrativity," that is, the practice of telling stories "badly" in order simultaneously to evoke narrative forms of organization and to resist or discredit them; and more recently my proposal to investigate the interaction of segmentivity and narrativity in narrative poems. I am hopeful that this proposal, whether it is widely taken up or not, will have the effect of stimulating new research on narrative in poetry, until lately a relatively neglected area of narrative theory.

3. What is the proper role of a narratology and narrative theory in relation to other academic disciplines?

Narratology's relationship to other academic disciplines seems somewhat paradoxical. On the one hand, in view of how many disciplines in the humanities and social sciences concern themselves one way or another with narrative forms of knowledge—not only literature but history, philosophy, anthropology, media studies, cultural studies, some fields of psychology and sociology, etc.—narratology could rightly claim the status of a kind of *master-discipline*, or if that sounds too imperialist, then at least as a kind of "big tent" under which other disciplines and sub-disciplines could find a place. On the other hand, relative to these other fields it is in many respects a strictly *ancillary* discipline, a potential source of tools and insights capable of being applied in a range of disciplinary contexts, to a variety of different ends.

My phrasing just now was deliberate: narratology is only "a *potential* source of tools" for other disciplines, because in point of fact few scholars in adjacent disciplines who work on narrative—anthropology is perhaps an exception—actually make much use of current narratological knowledge. Even in literary studies, it is scandalous how few of our colleagues who are not themselves narrative theorists actually show much curiosity about the findings of narrative theory, even when those findings would directly benefit their own work (or indeed complicate it). Both within our own discipline and across the academic disciplines, most of our colleagues who work on narrative materials seem content with the narrative theory they learned in secondary school. One could imagine what disadvantages a research biologist would face who was content with secondary-school biology—or rather, one *couldn't* imagine such a thing; but secondary-school narrative theory? Good enough, apparently.

4. What do you consider the most important topics and/or contributions in narratology?

I especially value the foundational contributions of the early researchers in the formalist-structuralist tradition, on which all subsequent approaches build. Without the breakthroughs achieved by the Russian Formalists and the Bakhtin circle, there would be no Paris structuralist narratology and no Tel Aviv school, and for that matter no rhetorical narrative theory or feminist or queer narrative theory and no cognitive narratology—no narratology at all as such. (Given the *curriculum vitae* I sketched in my response to question one, I suppose I could hardly be expected to answer any other way; if I had been trained elsewhere, say in Germany or Chicago, I might see things differently.) I reread the Russian contributions often, whenever I am beginning to think about a new problem, or revisiting an old one. Back to basics.

If I were called on to specify particular contributions that were of the greatest importance to the field, there are a handful I could mention that seem absolutely fundamental—the corner-stones of narratology. The most fundamental corner-stone of all, arguably, is the Formalists' distinction between *fabula* and *syuzhet*—in other terminological systems, between *histoire* and *discours*, or story and discourse; in other words, between the story that is told and *how* it is told, including who tells it, from what perspective, in what order, and so on. Recognizing this basic disparity between the *what* and the *how* of narrative opens up the space within which narratology develops. It is narratology's inaugural gesture, and all subsequent distinctions and refinements of narrative theory are predicated on it.

Another corner-stone, comparable in impact to the Formalists' *fabula/syuzhet* opposition, is Gérard Genette's distinction, in *Discours du récit* (1972), between narration and focalization, that is, between who speaks and who sees (perceives) in narrative texts. Genette's proposal represented a marked advance over earlier, confused accounts of point of view and perspective, though it brought in its wake confusions of its own. Contentious and problematic though they are, Genette's notion of focalization, and his theoretical separation of the apparatus of narrating from the apparatus of perceiving, have proven to be invaluable to subsequent narrative theory.

Finally, I could also mention, coming from a different tradition, Wayne Booth's concept of the implied author, introduced in his *Rhetoric of Fiction* (1961). This concept is a corner-stone of all rhetorical approaches to narrative, and more particularly of all discussions of the reliability and unreliability of narrators, a major topic of narrative theory. Again, like Genette's focalization, the implied author has proven to be a source of contention, but productive contention, and the development of narrative theory is inconceivable without it.

5. What are the most important open problems in this field and what are the prospects for progress?

Interestingly, in recent years some of the problems of narratology that had seemed settled, or at any rate exhausted and no longer very promising, have been reopened and revisited. This is the case with both focalization and the implied author, which I named above as fundamental contributions to narrative theory. Both of these concepts have come under renewed scrutiny and pressure lately, and both have been threatened with Occam's razor. Is the full apparatus of "focalizers" and "focalizeds" (objects of focalization) and so on, developed by Mieke Bal in the wake of Genette's initial proposal, really necessary? Is it necessary in every case? Do we always need to include the implied author when describing the communicational structure of every text, or only of those where the narrator's reliability is at stake, and are there cases where the distinction between real and implied author is essentially nonfunctional and superfluous? Surprisingly, not just focalization and the implied author but even the omniscient narrator, safely taken for granted for decades, has come under pressure in recent years. However, here the issue is not the unnecessary multiplication of entities but the reverse, a suspicion that there is more than one kind of omniscience, that what we have been satisfied to treat as a unitary package of narratorial qualities labeled "omniscience" is actually a haphazard grab-bag of features that ought to be distinguished and that don't necessarily co-occur.

However, the most interesting and consequential challenges to narratology as we have understood and practiced it seem to be coming nowadays from the cognitive-science-oriented wing of narrative theory. While I am extremely skeptical about some of the cognitivists' bolder claims and speculations—their speculations about the neurological basis of narrative structures, for instance, or about narrative's evolutionary function—I can't deny that they have reinvigorated a number of areas of narrative theory, raising fresh questions and reopening others that seemed resolved. I am thinking, for instance, of Alan Palmer's proposal to decouple the study of consciousness in the novel from the problem of speech representation, with which it has for too long been conflated, and to reorient inquiry toward the much more diffuse and pervasive element of *mind* in fiction. I am thinking, too, of Monika Fludernik's cognitivist redefinition of narrativity in terms not of events or sequence or causality but of *experientiality*, the presence of an experiencing consciousness. These are problematic proposals, provoking contradictory responses: on the one hand, don't they just restate, in slightly different terms, familiar distinctions and approaches? and, on the other, aren't they too reductive, tending to flatten out and unduly homogenize phenomena whose variety and diversity the older narratologies were much better at capturing? Nevertheless, whatever misgivings one might have and whatever resistance one might be disposed to put up, there is no doubting the power of the cognitivist approaches to shake up settled assumptions.

17
David S. Miall

Professor of English & Film Studies
Department of English and Film Studies, University of Alberta

1. Why were you initially drawn to narratology or narrative theory?

My main interest is in the empirical study of readers' experiences of literary reading. Although I don't consider myself a narratologist I have been drawn into considering aspects of narrative theory as a way of framing empirical inquiries. These include examination of aspects such as situation models, episode structures, stylistic aspects, empathy, and reader emotions.

As a beginning student of literature in the 1970s I studied fiction, and was intrigued and frustrated by the way in which the instructor seemed able to derive an interpretation from the story or chapter we were studying while giving no account of the reading processes by which he arrived at it. He was unable to explain his method when challenged. It seemed to me that we should be able to describe our experience of a text and show how this leads us to our understanding of it. This was how I began to develop an interest in reading, and in empirical studies of reading in particular: what actual readers do and how they develop their understanding of a given text. Were there, for example, some processes elicited in common in readers by a literary text? Even though readers could arrive at different readings of a text, were there aspects of it to which all readers necessarily paid attention? Why did readers experience emotions in response to literature, and what role might the emotions play in facilitating or modifying readers' grasp of a text?

As I began to consider these questions I turned first to the mechanics of reading, and for this purpose started to read articles in the psycholinguistic journals. I quickly noticed that emotion played no role in the theories being developed; and that it was assumed that the readers involved in the empirical studies reached the same interpretations of the (usually) rather simple narratives they were asked to read. There was no attempt to accommodate literary texts in the field. If literary texts were mentioned at all, it was to assume that once we understood the basic cognitive processes of non-literary or sub-literary reading, the same processes would explain the literary. The question whether literary texts are distinctive continues to be a source of ambivalence in the theoretical literature (e.g., Kintsch 1998: 205; Bortolussi and Dixon 2003: 29). My working assumption has been that literary texts evoke, in part, reading processes that are unique to them (I review this issue in the next section).

My initial empirical studies were on metaphor comprehension, and on readers' responses to the formal structures of poetry. But I was then drawn back to narrative as a way of testing some ideas about response to literary texts: in particular, what aspects of the text tend to influence all readers. While it is clear that readers can arrive at quite different interpretations of a text, it remains possible for readers to share responses and often reach agreement. To allow for this common experience there must be a level of response to textual features prior to the development of the larger, interpretive ideas. I approached this issue from two directions: from the side of the text (analysing the text for features to which readers are likely to pay attention) and from the side of the reader (tracking responses that involved imagery, emotion, memory, etc.). I carried out several empirical studies which were published between 1988 and 1990, and these led to a series of further studies after I moved to the University of Alberta; these were conducted in collaboration with my colleague in Psychology, Don Kuiken (Miall and Kuiken 1994). The later studies showed that readers were, indeed, systematically influenced by stylistic features in literary narratives at the phonetic, syntactic, and semantic levels, features that we termed *foregrounding*, following the Czech theorist Mukařovský (1964).

2. What do you consider your most important contribution(s) to the field?

Much of my subsequent work in this field has been an exploration of the issues raised by these initial empirical findings. Although my primary focus has been on the question of literariness, we have continued to use narrative texts frequently as a vehicle for these inquiries, and this has involved engaging with debates about narrative that have occurred in two fields: discourse processing study, with its emphasis on empirical verification, and narratology for its theoretical insights into the nature of narrative.

The studies of foregrounding that we conducted were not the first to be empirical: we modeled our design in part on a prior study by Willie van Peer (1986). While we borrowed one of his measures, a rating for strikingness (applied by readers judging a segment of text, usually a sentence), we added several other measures. Our most promising findings included these: readers took measurably longer to read segments high in foregrounding; in addition, they gave higher ratings to such passages for intensity of feeling and for uncertainty. This combination of measures, including strikingness, seemed to us to confirm a long standing claim (e.g., by Coleridge, Shelley, Shklovsky, Mukařovský) that a major function of poetic language is to defamiliarize. For example, in Coleridge's terms, it evokes "the depth and height of the ideal world around forms, incidents, and situations, of which, for the common view, custom had bedimmed all the lustre, had dried up the sparkle and the dew drops" (1993, I:80).

In addition to helping confirm such insights, the findings were also important in another way: they provided evidence that the encounter with foregrounding was the inception of a sequence of processes undertaken to locate an interpretive framework for the defamiliarized passage. This was indicated not only by the elevated ratings for uncertainty, but more specifically by the ratings for feeling. We suggested that the latter ratings were an indication that feeling and its associated memories directed the search, creating the momentum to sustain it. This is not an easy process to demonstrate empirically, but the conception raises one of the central issues of narrative comprehension, how the reader develops and structures an interpretation, and the role of the response to foregrounded features in bringing this about.

We made a preliminary contribution to this issue in a chapter (Miall and Kuiken 2001) in which we developed a more formal phases model: that is, we proposed that the readers' encounter with foregrounding resulted in defamiliarization at phase 1; the search for recontextualization led by feeling occurred during phase 2; at phase 3 the search was concluded, marked by shifts in story understanding. This chapter offered some preliminary evidence for the model, drawing on readers' data from studies with three literary short stories. Currently we are carrying out a study directed specifically at understanding better what may be occurring during phase 2. Evidence so far suggests that the modifying process we envisage occurs some 15 seconds downstream from the encounter with foregrounding, and that a pattern of distinctive hemispheric differences may be a key part of the picture.

Feeling has played a central part from the outset in this research on narrative response. It has also been central in other contexts. For instance, in Miall (1989) I outlined an account of the constructive role of feeling in response to narrative, focusing on three functions. Feeling involves self-reference (it evokes a concern relating to the self), it is anticipatory (e.g., projecting the shape of the whole during reading), and it enables cross-domain linking (relating concepts across conventional conceptual boundaries). These functions have been elaborated with the help of empirical evidence in some of our later work (e.g., Kuiken, Miall, and Sikora 2004), and I have also since provided a further theoretical account of the roles of feeling during literary reading (Miall 2008), including a specific focus on empathy in the light of theories of feeling and emotion (Miall, forthcoming). This work has involved reference to several other disciplines, as I will mention in answering the next question.

3. What is the proper role of a narratology and narrative theory in relation to other academic disciplines?

My first published paper, entitled "Aesthetic Unity and the Role of the Brain" (Miall 1976), developed a model of the anticipatory powers of feeling that drew upon neuropsychology. The intention was to identify a response structure for which there was empirical scientific evidence and apply it to illuminating a little understood process in our aesthetic experience. This way of relating two disciplines has been my practice in several other contributions I have made to understanding the neuropsychology of literary reading. Given that my interest lies in accounting for the literariness of our experience of narrative, it is not appropriate to claim that the models of science can extend to including the literary phenomenon. For example, this approach by Walter Kintsch (1998) seems likely to eliminate what is distinctively literary: "My hypothesis is that the comprehension processes, the basic strategies, the role of knowledge and experience, as well as the memory products generated, are the same for literary texts as for the simple narratives and descriptive texts we have used in our research" (205). A study by Seilman and Larsen (1989), for instance, has shown that the memory products generated by a literary and a non-literary text differ systematically.

A more fruitful procedure, then, is to identify a feature of the response process that appears to be distinctively literary, and turn to neuropsychology for evidence of how such a process might be possible: what already known processes may be analogous to it, what neural circuits are implicated, under what conditions are they activated, etc. For instance, the nature of the response to foregrounding has been well established by a series of empirical studies, including the one I mentioned earlier (Miall and Kuiken 1994), but we know very little about the early temporal processes involved. In order to develop a perspective on what may be distinctive to foregrounding, I have reviewed brain-scanning (evoked response potentials, or ERP) and imaging (fMRI) studies that focus on response to various aspects of language during the first 500 milliseconds of response (Miall, submitted). Among other findings, this has helped demonstrate the primacy of feeling and prosodic aspects, and the early impact of deviant or unusual aspects of language—supporting the view of foregrounding that we have hypothesized. This research is thus enabling us to reveal, and substantiate empirically, what Reuven Tsur (2003: 66) has termed the precategorical dimensions of response, and to begin to demonstrate their role in the response to narrative. Eventually, too, this work is likely to lead to testable hypotheses about narrative response that will be evaluated through specific ERP studies of foregrounded features.

To gain insights about narrative in the light of response (however studied: whether ERP findings or think-aloud responses, etc.), the direction of approach thus runs from the formulation of an inquiry into a narrative or literary quality, then the turn to cognitive or neuropsychological findings for evidence of analogous processes, followed by the framing of an empirical inquiry with readers that may help verify the process in question. So we will find ourselves asking whether the proposed literary process is viable; is it likely to occur; under what (literary) conditions does it occur; whether it is appropriate, distinctive, or perhaps even unique to the literary context. While I turn to another discipline, such as cognition, to gain a wider perspective on an issue of narrative theory, my primary commitment is to the literary issues involved in my question.

4. What do you consider the most important topics and/or contributions in narratology?

Among those who have either significantly enlarged our sense of how we understand narrative or who have identified some of the sources of narrativity, I would include the following: Art Graesser and his colleagues, Wolfgang Iser, and Patrick Colm Hogan.

Graesser, who has frequently collaborated with other notable scholars in his field, is primarily known for his work in discourse processing. At the same time, he has also been attentive to literary issues and has laid out some of the criteria for empirical studies of response to literary narratives. For example, one chapter (Graesser, Person, and Scott Johnston 1996) challenges the empirical scholar by describing three obstacles to such research: first, that there is no single essence to the literary object or to our experience of it; second, that the components of aesthetic response appear to be relatively inaccessible to consciousness; and third, that the field so far lacks powerful theories or mini-theories (suggesting that it is in a pre-paradigmatic stage, in Kuhn's terms).

Unlike a number of other scholars (e.g., Kintsch, whom I cited earlier), Graesser has been alert to the distinctiveness of literary concepts such as defamiliarization, although this has not been a central concern of his research (e.g., Graesser et al., 1997: 168). He has also been influential in elaborating empirical approaches to the study of narrative. His "three-pronged method" proposes triangulating on research issues by employing three different but complementary methods: verbal protocols, produced by readers asked to think-aloud about their response while reading a text; theories of text comprehension that help model or account for some of the data in the protocols; then specific testing of a reading process by experimental designs that measure readers' behavior (Magliano and Graesser 1991).

But Graesser's most important contribution has been towards the elaboration of a detailed discourse processing model that demonstrates the components of narrative understanding. One of his major studies, for example, laid out definitively the inferences that readers generate online automatically while reading narrative (Graesser, Singer, and Trabasso 1994). This study evaluates the evidence for thirteen classes of knowledge-based inferences that map onto the representation of a narrative in working memory, and concludes that only six classes occur automatically during the first 650 msecs following passage onset (cf. Palmer 2004: 177). These include features such as resolving anaphoric reference, causal antecedents, the superordinate goal of a character, and a character's emotional reactions. The inferences enable the reader to construct a representation of the narrative that is both locally and globally coherent. This study thus lays down a baseline for what is essential to narrative response, including literary narrative, and what is optional. It challenges research on the literary aspects of narrative to show what additional processes (online or otherwise) are required for a narrative to be characterized or experienced as literary. An example of such research is provided by our study of foregrounding in a literary short story by Elizabeth Bowen. Graesser and his colleagues (Zwaan, Magliano, and Graesser 1995) analysed the story at the sentence level for the components of the situation model (time, place, character), and confirmed the model by empirical evidence from readers (reading times per sentence). We reanalysed the reading data and were able to show that the presence of foregrounding in Bowen's story accounted for readers' responses as effectively as the situation model components (Miall and Kuiken 1999). We can thus argue that foregrounding, which has not been a part of the discourse model, is a characteristic feature of literary reading.

Wolfgang Iser, to refer only to his early work, elaborated an influential theory of reading (based primarily on narrative), that demonstrated in detail the constructive processes involved in literary reading. In particular, as I will mention, Iser's work demonstrated a major commitment to identifying what is distinctive to the process of literary reading. While Iser took no interest in actual readers, his work suggested the possibility of empirical study at a number of points, as my own work has shown.

In his essay "The Reading Process," extracted from *The Implied Reader* and often anthologized (Iser 1980), Iser proposed that reading manifested two poles, the artistic (the text created by the author) and the aesthetic (the reader's realization). Like Donne's famous compass points, one (the artistic) is fixed while the other consistently varies in distance and location (i.e., readers differ in their realizations of the significance of the text), and—to stretch the analogy—the further apart the two poles the more challenged or imaginative the reader's understanding. Our think-aloud studies of response to literary narratives provide much evidence of the two poles: readers often repeat a phrase or sentence from the text as if to interrogate or to savour its artistic qualities (the phrases typically exhibit high levels of foregrounding, demonstrating the writer's artistry). At the other pole we find, although less often, comments that begin to thematize the text, i.e., realizations of its aesthetic implications (Miall and Kuiken 1999). Other readers' comments, such as observations on the setting, or on the character's or their own feelings, indicate points between the two poles, often motivated by the gaps and indeterminacies in the text that are central to Iser's account. Other empirical studies we have conducted seem to evoke Iser's comment, that "As we read, we oscillate to a greater or lesser degree between the building and the breaking of illusions" (62). That is, readers fluctuate between periods of absorption, immersed in the literary illusion, and awareness of their responses or of the reading process. As one of our readers put it, aware of the inadequacy of a previous response, "it makes me feel a bit insecure" (Miall 1990: 335). To borrow from Iser again (51), empirical evidence also helps confirm that the dynamics of literary reading draws upon a two-level process of schema recognition and invalidation that invokes the reader's effort and creativity (Miall 1990: 328).

Iser's approach also leads to the proposition that a literary text possesses an intrinsic structure to which all readers will respond; this arises from, but is independent of, the evaluative response which readers make (Miall 1990: 326). As Iser describes it, individual differences among readers are like seeing a pattern of stars differently: "The 'stars' in a literary text are fixed; the lines that join them are variable" (57). The imagination of the reader is thus dependent on the indeterminacy of the text, on supplying what is not there (58). As Iser also points out, the reader's realization can change during a given reading. He notes that alternative interpretations may occur to us that threaten our current understanding; "we sometimes find that characters, events, and backgrounds seem to change their significance"; there is a "shifting of perspectives" (62). This will also occur during a second reading. I was able to demonstrate this over the course of two readings by a study of readers' responses to the opening of a story by Virginia Woolf (Miall 1989): readers' evaluation of a number of key passages changed at a second reading after their reading of the whole story had invalidated their first schema.

In Iser's later work he turned to another issue: literary reading helps reveal something about us, our desires, dispositions, and proclivities. Is this why we still need literature (as we seem to do)? This question points to the need for what Iser called "a literary anthropology that is both an underpinning and an offshoot of reader-response criticism" (Iser 1989: vii). In this respect, Patrick Colm Hogan has put forward a comprehensive and valuable theory, primarily in his book *The Mind and Its Stories* (2003).

Although Hogan makes no claims to contribute to either discipline, his work can be seen as a contribution both to anthropology, since he treats of human universals in our extensive, world-wide creation of narratives, and to evolutionary psychology, given the basis of his work in the phylogeny of the emotions. While presenting the universals he identifies in literary culture he poses the central question, but does not pursue it: "the specifically literary universals should indicate what is at the origin of the development of literature, what defines the human urge to make and experience verbal art" (Hogan, 1997: 234). Nor does Hogan's work engage in or require empirical study, although he refers to it at times. But his work is remarkable for its cross-cultural comprehensiveness, which enables him to make persuasive claims about the universal presence of the literary experience. Among the universal aspects he discusses, foregrounding and other stylistic features are shown to pervade literary texts from every culture.

Hogan's most far reaching claim, however, is that most literature in the world is based on three emotional situations: love, power, and sacrifice which give rise to romantic tragi-comedy, heroic tragi-comedy, and a third type involving sacrificial tragi-comedy. In his view, emotions are able to form the basis of literature because emotions function as mini-narratives. Borrowing from De Sousa's (1987: 181-4) proposal of paradigm scenarios, Hogan suggests that emotions involve both causes (typical elicitors) and effects (typical expressive or action consequences). Thus, Hogan argues, our understanding of an emotion "includes some account of the kinds of situations that give rise to the emotion and some account of the kinds of expression and action that result from an emotion" (82). In this respect, emotions are prototype based, representing standard situations that elicit the emotion; that is, they offer the seeds of stories (83): "our prototypical stories are, in their broad structure, expansions of the micronarratives that define our emotion terms" (89). Even lyric poems involve mini-narratives through emotion, tacitly evoking an outcome emotion and its implied narrative structure. Hogan's vision is comprehensive: based on the originating power of emotion and its narrative qualities, he thus seeks to account for the majority of world literature.

5. What are the most important open problems in this field and what are the prospects for progress?

The fields that engage with narrative issues remain somewhat fragmented, separated from one another, suggesting that a coherent approach to narrative remains elusive. The three main fields that I have in mind are narratology, cognitive poetics, and empirical studies. While each to some extent derives ideas from its neighbours, the principal problem from my perspective, and one that is likely to persist for some time to come, is that generally literary theoretical treatments are not empirical, and empirical treatments are not literary. There are exceptions: some scholars of cognitive poetics have shown a serious interest in empirical work (e.g., Alan Richardson 2004), but few have the competence in the field to develop experimental study (among the few exceptions: Cathy Emmott, et al. 2006; and, in a class of his own, Reuven Tsur 2008). But the field of cognitive poetics suffers from a degree of arbitrariness. As Jackson (2002) puts it, we are not in a position to modify or throw out cognitive theory, since we have "no controlled experiments, no quantitative data" (177). Such interdisciplinary work is in any case difficult to undertake, and experience of empirical studies has not been a part of the training typically offered graduate students in literature, so that empirical studies has remained a small field and has grown only slowly. At the same time, much of the empirical work on narrative has been carried out by scholars of cognition who, with a few exceptions (e.g., Graesser, as mentioned above), have taken little account of what may be distinctive to the literary domain. As Sternberg argued in a lengthy critique (2003), much of the work in this empirical tradition has overlooked important prior work in narratology, and is of limited value as a result (the work of Keith Oatley is a significant exception: e.g., 2002).

In the empirical field, among the problems that remain open and seem important, I will briefly mention three. First, as discussed earlier, studies of brain scanning here seem (as in a number of other fields) to hold promise of major advances in understanding. Currently, given studies showing a range of significant responses to language occurring during the first 400 to 500 milliseconds, further studies of the same kind, but focused specifically on narrative elements would be valuable. In addition to distinguishing the impact of foregrounded aspects on readers' sense of literariness in narrative (cf. Miall 2010), such studies would also forward our understanding of how central narrative constructs such as animacy and empathy first emerge (prior to conscious awareness or modification), and what their correlates are in the domains of the reader's self-concept and emotions. In referring to animacy (the second problem), I have in mind not only the enlivenment of characters, often through empathy, but also the endowment of significance on non-sentient aspects of narrative settings. A feature of literariness is that mention of, say, a chair, or a tree, or a distant chimney in the landscape is never made at random; it augments the reader's awareness and prescience as to what may be significant, and may serve to endow the object in question with dispositions or traits that will influence how the reader understands the human attitudes depicted in the text. As brain scanning studies suggest, these acts of valuation probably occur very rapidly, within the first 200 milliseconds of onset, showing that an important part of our response to narrative is initiated outside our awareness. A similar issue arises in the case of empathy, a much-discussed feature of narrative response. Here, too, readers seem eager to endow characters with feelings and attributes, even on the bare mention of a name: as Alan Palmer (2004) has noticed, "A character's name is a space or a vacuum into which readers feel compelled to pour meaning" (207). The larger issues of empathy have recently been considered in detail by Suzanne Keen (2007), whose discussion takes account of some relevant empirical studies. It is notable that her treatment too remains unsettled, leaving open a series of questions about the role, function, and even the validity of our concepts of empathy. She is sceptical, for example, of the altruistic influence that reading fiction is said to have, as in Hakemulder's (2000) studies of how representations of immigrants in Dutch culture modify the attitudes of native Dutch readers (89-90).

All of the issues I have mentioned can, in one way or another, be connected with our understanding of emotions and feelings—the affective impact of foregrounding, the emotional basis of the plots of world literature, the feelings instantiated by empathy. Thus, although it is by no means distinctive to the narrative domain, perhaps the greatest advances in narratology in the near future are likely to be made through careful theoretical and empirical studies in this domain. As Jenefer Robinson (2005) has put it, our emotional response to fiction reframes the world, or "regestalts" it; or, more specifically, "I see the whole world of the novel through the prism of that emotion" (128). It is in this domain that my own studies of narrative are most often located.

18
Jeff Mitscherling

Professor
Department of Philosophy, University of Guelph

Narrative Theory and Realist Phenomenology

We've always recognized that an effective story casts a spell. The modern word "spell" in fact comes from the Old English *spellian*, which meant "to tell, speak". Words themselves can fascinate, but stories mesmerize. Word by word and one word at a time, the narrator spins a web that snares the reader. And every good storyteller knows that the most commanding incantation grips the audience at the outset. In some cases a lengthy opening is appropriate, as in the case of *A Tale of Two Cities*:

> It was the best of times, it was the worst of times, it was the age of wisdom, it was the age of foolishness, it was the epoch of belief, it was the epoch of incredulity, it was the season of Light, it was the season of Darkness, it was the spring of hope, it was the winter of despair, we had everything before us, we had nothing before us, we were all going direct to Heaven, we were all going direct the other way–in short, the period was so far like the present period, that some of its noisiest authorities insisted on its being received, for good or for evil, in the superlative degree of comparison only.

Other stories—even novels longer than those of Dickens—have to begin with brevity, as does *Anna Karenina*'s "All happy families are alike; every unhappy family is unhappy in its own way" and *Moby-Dick*'s "Call me Ishmael". Whatever its length, the opening must be gripping, and what follows cannot disappoint. Both conditions are met only when the linguistic structure is appropriate to the content being presented. But exactly what is it that makes one structure appropriate to its content and another a total failure? What is it that makes one literary work, and particularly a literary work of art, more successful than another? And how do the linguistic structures of the successful literary work of art combine as parts and work together in such a way as to give rise to a unified, organic whole? These are the chief questions that drew me to the study of narrative theory, and it was the work of Roman Ingarden, which I first examined at length in *Roman Ingarden's Ontology and Aesthetics* (1997), that both introduced me to such questions and first suggested a philosophically sophisticated manner in which to pursue their answer.

In *The Literary Work of Art*, Ingarden describes how this work is a schematic formation that arises as an organic whole by virtue of the features belonging to its four distinct strata: (i) individual word sounds and higher-order word-sound formations; (ii) meaning units, such as word-meanings and sentence-meanings; (iii) schematized aspects; and (iv) represented objectivities, such as characters, events, and actions. Each of these strata is itself a complex structure exhibiting its own internal coherence, and Ingarden's analyses of the sorts of intentionality that are operative in each of the strata provide a detailed outline of the manner in which the reader is able to actualize the work as an aesthetic object during the course of the aesthetic experience. To state most briefly what I have found to be Ingarden's most profound insight, the reader is guided in his or her reading of the text by an intentionality that belongs to the work of art itself, and this intentionality operates already at the simplest of the strata and guides the reader's cognition of the literary work in the course of its reading. As a schematic formation, the literary work of art—and indeed, every sort of work of art—subsists as a set of guidelines or rules for cognition that direct the course of the aesthetic experience of the work. The work of art provides, as it were, an objective foundation and framework for the subjective aesthetic experience.

This conclusion is already exciting, for it not only establishes objectivity in aesthetics but also suggests a possible basis for literary criticism that remains largely unexplored. What I have found still more provocative, however, from an ontological and metaphysical point of view, is an implication that Ingarden himself does little more than mention: While it would seem that the author would bestow his or her intentionality on the work in the course of its creation—in much the same manner as does the reader in the course of the re-creation (or co-creation) of the work—the matter is not as straightforward as that, for entities like word-meanings and sentence-meanings have intentions of their own, and they largely dictate for themselves the manner in which they may be combined with other intentional entities. That is, an author may not do whatever he or she likes with the words being employed, and there exists increasingly less authorial freedom as the work in progress develops, for as the intentional structures build upon one another and thereby grow in complexity, they also grow increasingly demanding, setting guidelines not only for the reader's cognition of the work in the course of its reading but also for the author's cognition of that work in the course of its writing. The same intentionality is at work, in other words, in both the reading and the writing of the work, and this intentionality does not derive solely from the author or the reader. Rather, the work itself seems to develop, at least to some extent, through an internal logic of intentionality that dictates its course to author and reader alike. This internal logic in fact both dictates and is dictated by the development of character as well as of plot. As Philip K. Dick observed, contrasting the short story to the novel in his introduction to the collection *The Preserving Machine* (Dick 1995: 400):

> In terms of actions and events, the story is far less restrictive to the author than is a novel. As a writer builds up a novel-length piece it slowly begins to imprison him, to take away his freedom; his own characters are taking over and doing what they want to do—not what he would like them to do. This is on one hand the strength of the novel and on the other, its weakness.

In *The Author's Intention*, Tanya DiTommaso, Aref Nayed and I explored at some length the nature of this internal logic of a literary work, distinguishing between what we called the "dynamic intention" and the "energic intention". The dynamic intention of a text is immanent; it derives from and consists in the manner in which the words of a text exhibit meaning only in distinction from and in relation to the other words in the text. The energic intention is both immanent and transcendent; this kind of intention is that which drives the story itself, both evolving through and sustaining the ongoing narrative of the literary work. Our analyses of the operations of intentionality in the literary work rehabilitated the concept of authorial intention, which had notoriously fallen out of fashion in recent years, but at the same time it relocated the origin of intentionality. Whereas most apologists for the intentionalist position—for example, E.D. Hirsch in literary theory

(Hirsch 1967 and 1976), and Emilio Betti in legal hermeneutics (Betti 1954 and 1955)—have regarded the author's intention as belonging to and deriving from the subjective mental operations of the author, DiTommaso, Nayed and I argued, following the logic of Ingarden's provocative implication, that the author's intention is itself largely derivative, finding its origin in intentional structures, both dynamic and energic, that belong to a much wider narrative complex that the author merely taps into, as it were. This suddenly presented to us an entirely novel manner in which to regard the ancient and traditional concept of "inspiration", which we could now analyze not as some vague and mysterious, or indeed mystical, experience, but as an entirely natural phenomenon, but a natural phenomenon that is revealed as metaphysically profound. It suddenly became clear to us that our analyses had led us to an entirely new philosophical plateau—although we actually looked at it more as a gaping abyss at the time—from which to survey several major philosophical problems that have long proved impenetrable. Some of the most basic of these problems revolve around the question of the manner in which the human mind is related to the external world. If we were correct, our new way of looking at intentionality provided us with a way to approach that question that promised to avoid at least the most obvious of the problems encountered by such standard traditional accounts as those offered by idealism, materialism, and Cartesian dualism. But the actual elaboration of our position and the formulation of our arguments took some time.

It wasn't until six years later that I was finally able to complete this work—in *Aesthetic Genesis: The Origin of Consciousness in the Intentional Being of Nature* (2010)—and even this "completion" remains painfully programmatic. As it turns out, the analysis of the underlying structures and constitutive principles of narrative formations points to fundamental metaphysical features of every aspect of our experienced reality. Here, too, Ingarden appears to have led the way. While he remains best known for his work in aesthetics—and for that reason he is largely regarded chiefly as a philosopher of aesthetics—he in fact regarded himself as an ontologist and metaphysician. He devoted his entire life to the construction of a realist alternative to the metaphysical idealism he detected at the heart of Husserl's phenomenology, and his magnum opus, *TheControversy over the Existence of the World*, presents an extended elaboration (in three [untranslated] volumes, in fact, with the third remaining incomplete at his death in 1970: Ingarden 1981, 1987) of a realist existential and formal ontology and analysis of the causal structure of "the real world". In this work he consistently follows the lead of Aristotle—in fact, in 1938, just as he was returning after a forced break to the writing of *Controversy*, he actually immersed himself in the study of Aristotle's *Metaphysics*, offering a "free seminar" on the subject at Jan Kazimierz University in Lwów—and indeed, a close reading of all of Ingarden's work reveals that Aristotle was never far from his thought. And when we turn back to Aristotle we can easily see why, for it was Aristotle who first laid bare the essential ontological link between the mind and the world, and he also demonstrated the manner in which this link was exhibited quite clearly in the literary art of his day. Current research in cognitive science is discovering valuable insights in the Aristotelian account of perception and cognition in general (see, for example: Kafetsios and LaRock 2005; Green 1998; Shields 1991), and narrative theory similarly stands to gain much from a renewed study of the peripatetic philosophy.

According to the modern view, the mind and the world are two ontologically distinct entities, and in the act of cognition the two become related yet remain distinct. Of the countless attempts to explain the nature of this uncomfortable relation, the diametrically opposed accounts offered by the idealists and the materialists are perhaps the most widely known. Stated most simply, idealists maintain that the object of cognition, and indeed the entire world as we know it, first comes into being through the cognitive activity of the subject, while the materialists maintain that the physical operations of the objective, material world that impact upon our body and brain and that are involved in what we describe as the mental activity of cognition in fact give rise to what we call the mind. The problems involved in each of these accounts, and in all of those lying between these two extreme positions, have been the subject of heated debate for centuries, and the same arguments for and against each of them continue to be vigorously rehearsed today. The Aristotelians, however, viewed the relation between mind and world quite differently, and this is what has attracted the attention of many researchers in current cognitive science. According to the Aristotelian account, every individual entity consists in a particular combination of matter and form; basically, the form of a thing is that which determines the specific manner in which the "stuff" of the thing coheres so as to distinguish it as a particular, identifiable entity. Three points must especially be stressed regarding the form/matter combination, for each of them is basic to the Aristotelian account of cognition: (i) the form does not pre-exist apart from any combination with some matter—that is, the form is not to be confused with what is commonly understood as a "Platonic idea"; (ii) the "matter" of a thing need not be what we nowadays refer to as matter—that is, it need not be tangible, physical material, but may equally well be intangible, "intelligible" material (such as the "stuff" of a meaning construct, or proposition); and (iii) not only "objects" have matter and form, but also actions.

For the Aristotelian, everything that is, every activity as well as every object, consists in a quite particular combination of form and matter. (More precisely, the *being* of everything that is consists in such combination—but it sounds strange to use the word "being" like this.) Since cognition is an activity, it too has a form, and the specific form that a particular act of cognition assumes depends upon its particular object. In the act of cognition, according to Aristotle, the subject does not merely perceive or conceive an ontologically distinct object—rather, the cognizing subject actively assumes the same form as the object of cognition. In other words, the subject and the object are formally identical: for example, the form that determines the manner in which the material of the object is structured also structures the act through which I cognize that object. There is one form that participates in the being of two otherwise ontologically distinct entities and these two entities are identical with respect to that form. It is one and the same form that is "informing" both the activity of being of the object and the activity of cognizing of the subject. This ontological process of the "information" of the respective activities (of being and cognizing) of objects and subjects is an instance of what Aristotle referred to as "formal causality", and this same process is at work in the cognition of narrative structures. Each of the various strata of the literary work of art comprises countless smaller narrative structures—for example, the stratum of linguistic meaning units comprises sentence parts, sentences, sentence complexes, paragraphs, chapters, and so on—and each of these structures embodies its own form. This form is in fact that of the *intention* of the structure, and when we read a text we cognize the meaning by allowing ourselves to be guided by that intention. There is nothing particularly mysterious about this. For example, when we encounter a simple sentence that contains a subject and a predicate, we are presented with a grammatical guide that informs us of the manner in which to cognize this predication, and our thinking consists in the recognition of this predication. Our act of cognition is, in a sense, merely the actualization of a potentiality that the text presents to us, and this actualization consists in the fulfillment of the intention exhibited in the form of the text, which becomes also the form of the act of cognition. The form of the subjective act of cognition is one and the same as the form of the objective text. This achievement of formal identity of subject and object is not restricted to our cognition of a simple piece of text, or even to our more comprehensive aesthetic experience of an entire literary work of art. This is what happens every moment of our conscious life, in our ongoing engagement with our world. We are constantly taking on the forms of the world, and sharing in the intentional structures that bind it together as a whole. We are indeed a part of the world in the most fundamental sense, sharing with it the formal principles and structures that constitute us both, and modern philosophy and science have been mistaken in supposing that there exists an essential difference between the mind and the world.

An essential component of the investigation into the nature of the literary work of art is the analysis of the most basic logical relations of the linguistic structures underlying any narrative construction. As we have just seen, this analysis can reveal insights regarding the relation in which we stand to our world—how the mind or consciousness "relates to" its object or to the external world in general—and indeed regarding the nature of reality as a whole. This certainly points to the potentially overwhelming importance of narrative theory in philosophical research in ontology and metaphysics, which attempt to describe and explain "how the world is". But narrative theory has also been central to recent philosophical work in epistemology and hermeneutics, which attempt to describe and explain "how we understand the world". Paul Ricoeur's theory of narrative is here the most obvious example, and his theory has exercised a seminal influence upon researchers working in other academic disciplines—as David Pellauer has observed, his work "has been discussed by historians, literary critics, legal theorists and jurists, biblical exegetes and theologians" (Pellauer 2007: 2)—and the influence of his narrative theory in such seemingly unrelated disciplines as psychology and theology has subsequently proceeded to inform practice in everything from psychoanalysis and family therapy to pastoral counseling. The extent to which insights deriving from narratological investigation pursued by scholars in numerous disciplines have come to inform not only academic research but also the practice of non-academic professionals is simply astonishing, and this achievement suggests a possible development that would prove even more remarkable: Perhaps it will be further research in narrative theory that reveals those fundamental elements of the diverse range of human experience that will provide us with the means to link together systematically our academic disciplines, especially in the humanities and social sciences, and to integrate the efforts of scholars in fields that currently remain entirely cut off from one another. How such integration might subsequently inform human praxis and transform human experience into a united effort to find meaning in this world we all share would make for a spellbinding story indeed.

19
Ansgar Nünning

Chair of English and American Literary and Cultural Studies
Justus-Liebig-University Giessen

1. Why were you initially drawn to narratology or narrative theory?

For any narratologist, answering the question of why one was initially drawn to the theory of narrative—identifying the moment the story began, or the turning point, so to speak—is no straightforward matter. The business of the narratologist is, in part, to be aware of the ways in which narratives are constructed; and this involves recognizing that any narrative of the past will be in some way one story, or even fiction, among many other possible stories or fictions that one could also tell and thus, to some degree, a product of the present, generated with the benefit of hindsight. I might trace my initiation into narratology and narrative theory at many points: to my childhood delight in the stories told by my father and even the storytelling among the students and patrons of British pubs on afternoons or evenings in Cornwall, where I worked as a tourist guide and English teacher back in the 1970s. But down this anecdotal route, one cannot help but turn into Tristram Shandy—and so full an account of my Life and Opinions, Gentleman (and Ladies), would lie somewhat outside the remits of this interview...

Without entering into an eternal regress, then, and with the proviso that such origins and turning points are not given or found but made, I would nevertheless suggest that my professional engagement in narratology and narrative theory is, initially, an expression of a life-long fascination with stories and with human beings as "storytelling animals" (Graham Swift). This developed into an early fascination with literature, which developed into a desire to find an answer to the question "Why?", i.e. a desire to find explanations through stories and to understand how narratives work, which is itself already a wish to explore—to draw out the etymology of 'narratology'—the 'science of narrative'. It was as an undergraduate student of English Literature and History at the University of Cologne that this long-standing interest first encountered in narratology a rich and exciting field of inquiry that provided the means to express this fascination, and to systematically and rigorously explore the workings of narrative. I found in the insights and approaches of Russian Formalist theory, structuralist theoretical approaches in general, and most specifically the emergent field of narratology (*narratologie* being a term only coined, of course, in 1969 by Tzvetan Todorov), not only a locally focused body of insight into specific texts, but the foundations of a more widely applicable range of concepts, models and analytical tools for understanding narrative. My doctoral research on the foundations of a communications-model of narrative mediation and the functions of the narrator in George Eliot's novels (*Grundzüge eines kommunikationstheoretischen Modells der erzählerischen Vermittlung. Die Funktionen der Erzählinstanz in den Romanen George Eliots*), published as my first monograph in 1989, drew on and developed in this vein and marked my initiation into the field, which was fostered by some of my excellent and stimulating teachers at the university of Cologne, most notably Helmut Bonheim, Manfred Jahn, Gottfried Krieger and Natascha Würzbach, and the renowned historians—and great storytellers—Erich Angermann and Herman Wellenreuther.

2. What do you consider your most important contributions to the field?

The trouble with this question, and perhaps even the format of these volumes as a whole, is that they encourage you to adopt a somewhat egocentric perspective, but no (wo)man is an island, not even a scholar or narratologist working in (what fortunately is no longer) an ivory-tower. I have striven to contribute as a narratologist, and literary and cultural scholar and theorist generally, in three key areas: through research, teaching and institution-building. As a passionate advocate of what Wilhelm von Humboldt called the "unity of research and teaching", I regard these areas as being, in the best of all possible worlds, interlinked and equally important (though this is not always the case). One of the many attractions of narratology, as noted above, is that it involves developing concepts and models of understanding that are widely applicable in literary and cultural studies, providing the tools as well as the materials for the interdisciplinary study of the forms and functions of narratives, not only in literature but in culture at large, and this in itself has a pedagogical value, as well as an analytical one. It is my hope that one of my contributions to the field of narratology, on the most general level, lies in the integration of these three key areas, in the recognition and implementation of the potential of narratology to contribute to the unity of research, teaching and institutions in which both may thrive. That is also one of the reasons why I have always enjoyed writing and editing introductions and text books for university students, including e.g. *An Introduction to the Study of Narrative Fiction* which Birgit Neumann and I co-authored.

Among my sole-authored monographs, my first book—on narrative discourse and the functions of the narrator in George Eliot's novels (1989)—went through five editions until 1994 (before I decided that it should no longer be reprinted because I wanted to write an updated state-of-the-art introduction to narratology) and has been something of a theoretical foundation stone for my subsequent work, which has covered many different periods, genres and theoretical issues. My two volumes on the genre theory and development of British historical fiction since the 1950s (Nünning 1995) have proven an influential analysis of the genre, but also set out the theoretical spectrum that has informed much of my work in other genres and periods, as well as providing a narratological approach that has been fruitfully adopted by scholars working in other disciplines and areas, including Canadian, German, French, Spanish and Turkish literature.

In addition to these narratological monographs, my contributions to the field of narratology mainly revolve around a number of key narratological concepts, including the implied author, unreliable narration, multiperspectival narration, metanarrative and description, while also trying to gauge and extend the applicability of narrative theory to other genres (especially drama), media and nonfictional storytelling. My work on a cognitive reconceptualisation of unreliable narration, most notably in one of my edited volumes, *Unreliable Narration. Studien zur Theorie und Praxis unglaubwürdigen Erzählens in der englischsprachigen Erzählliteratur* (1998a), but also in a number of articles published in English in journals and collections of essays, has been a reference point in many other subsequent engagements with this question. The same holds true, albeit to a lesser extent, for some of my work on feminist narratology, on the relationship between drama and narratology (which I explored in a number of articles co-authored with Roy Sommer), and my modest proposals for defining, developing typologies of and gauging the historical development of relatively neglected narratological concepts, including e.g. the implied author, multiperspectival narration, metanarration and metarrative, description, and, most recently, crises, catastrophes and turning points as metaphors and narratives.

In developing my ideas on these and other issues, I have greatly enjoyed, and profited from, the dialogic research culture that fortunately prevails in narrative theory, and would like to take this opportunity to thank a number of colleagues whose work I admire very much and who have been very generous with (sometimes quite critical) feedback on my publications or papers given at conferences: Seymour Chatman, Dorrit Cohn, Monika Fludernik, Herbert Grabes, the late Gabriele Helms, David Herman, Luc Herman, Fotis Jannidis, Susan Lanser, Uri Margolin, Greta Olson, James Phelan, Manfred Pfister, John Pier, Bo Pettersson, Gerald Prince, Brian Richardson, Shlomith Rimmon-Kenan, Dan Shen, Franz K. Stanzel, Meir Sternberg, Werner Wolf and Tamar Yacobi as well as the members of the Hamburg research group "Narratology", particularly Wolf Schmid, Jörg Schönert, Hans-Harald Müller and Peter Hühn.

My work as an editor and contributor to edited volumes and journals has covered quite a broad spectrum of narratological concepts and issues, across periods and genres and includes two handbooks on new approaches in narrative theory and transgeneric, intermedial and interdisciplinary narrative theory respectively, both of which I co-edited with Vera Nünning (both published in 2002), and an encyclopaedia of literary and cultural theory (Nünning 1998b), which has become a standard work (the 4th enlarged and updated edition was published in 2008), and which features many entries on a broad range of narratological approaches, concepts and narratologists. The interface between literature, narratives and cultural memory has been a particular area of interest in which my colleague and friend Astrid Erll and I have contributed to bringing classical narratological tools to bear in broad literary and cultural areas of focus (see, for example, *Cultural Memory Studies: An International and Interdisciplinary Handbook, A Companion to Cultural Memory Studies*, 2010). Among the directions taken in my recent work are the move towards constructivist narratological theory (most recently in Nünning et al. 2010), towards applying the concepts, insights and methods of narrative theory to broader cultural concerns like a "Narratology of Crises" (2009) and also, as one of my article titles terms it, "Towards a Cultural and Historical Narratology" (2000).

I have dedicated much energy, too, to my work in building institutions—most prominently, the Excellence Initiative-funded International Graduate Centre for the Study of Culture (GCSC) at Justus-Liebig-University Giessen, which houses the International PhD Programme in Literary and Cultural Studies, the European PhDnet in Literary and Cultural Studies, and numerous other initiatives, including intensive co-operation with other universities and graduate centres around the world. The conception of the Centre around key concepts and research areas, including the interface between culture(s) and narrative(s), encouraging interdisciplinary exchange in working towards the development of new concepts for the study of culture, is in a sense the institutional realisation of the directions I have argued for in my scholarly research as a narratologist: interdisciplinary dialogue, cultural and historical contextualism, the pursuit and application of concepts across traditional boundaries, and culturally reflexive, internationally engaged research and teaching.

One of the happiest results of having dedicated so much time and mental energy to building research and teaching institutions is the pleasure of seeing former students and supervisees going on to produce pioneering work in the field. Since I am not only a teamplayer, but also, as a narratological friend of mine once observed, "take great pleasure in the success of others" (thanks, Jim, for this very generous compliment which made my day on the day, briefly overshadowed by a fully-fledged tornado, that you taught a master class at our Graduate Centre!), I consider the successful careers and insightful works of the former members of my research group "Cultural and Historical Narratology" to be probably my most important contributions to the field. The list of these impressive young scholars, most of whom have by now got chairs or tenured professorships at other universities, includes Roy Sommer, who has done excellent work on multicultural narratology and edited an important volume on *Narratology in the Age of Cross-Disciplinary Narrative Research* (2009), Carola Surkamp, who has written an important book on the perspective structure of narrative texts, Bruno Zerweck, who is best known for his essay on "Historicizing Unreliable Narration" (published in *Style* in 2001), Astrid Erll, whose seminal contributions have served to chart and stake out the field of cultural memory studies and the interfaces between that field and narrative theory, Marion Gymnich, who has made significant contributions to feminist narratology and linguistic approaches to narratives, and Birgit Neumann, who has fruitfully applied the insights and tools of narratology to fictions of memory and imagology. I should also like to mention some (even) younger postdoctoral researchers who have completed their PhDs with me and who have begun to make important contributions to narrative theory, including (in alphabetical order and with a keyword each to indicate their narratological contributions) Gaby Allrath (feminist narratology), Dorothee Birke (crises of memory, identity and narrative), Stella Butter (functions of narratives), Simon Cooke (travel writing), René Dietrich (the narratives implied in US-post-apocalyptic poetry), Janine Hauthal (narratology and metadrama), Sandra Heinen (narratology across the disciplines), Guido Isekenmeier (media events), Julijana Nadj (fictional meta-biographies), Kirsten Zierold (narratology of computer games), Martin Schüwer (narratology of comics) and Robert Vogt (unreliable narration).

3. What is the proper role of a narratology and narrative theory in relation to other academic disciplines?

The path taken by narratology over the course of its history as a discernible discipline or field, at least as I see it, has largely been one from a structuralist and formalist 'science' with a tendency towards description, neologisms, taxonomies and universalism, towards a broader, more culturally and historically contextual, interdisciplinary and international phenomenon. Equally, as classical narratology became "post-classical" (David Herman) and broadened its horizons, numerous scholars working in other fields—anthropology, ethnography, cognitive science, history, media studies, to give just a few examples—have shown an increasing interest in the ways in which narratives shape and re-shape our understanding of how worlds are made, i.e. illuminating the important role of narratives as a way of self- and worldmaking.

The proper role of narratology and narrative theory is, in my view, one of navigating and bringing together these various fields and trends: energetic and open engagement between the findings and tools of narrative theory and the research domains of other disciplines. Narratives are at work in literature, but also in so many dimensions of culture and society—from personal anecdotes and news reports to the innovative modes of storytelling developed by the new media—that narrative theory benefits from, and can contribute to, the understanding gleaned through other disciplines, and vice versa. Because narrative theory seeks out the meta-level workings of narrative forms, it can illuminate our understanding of a vast range of phenomena in culture in the widest sense; and given the growing interest in narrative in other disciplines, much can be learned from work carried out in those fields. In this day and age of cross-disciplinary interest in narratives what is crucial is fostering communication across the traditional boundaries of the disciplines: and in my opinion and experience, narratological concepts are extremely well placed to enable such dialogue. Mieke Bal's *Travelling Concepts in the Humanities: A Rough Guide* (2002) is a fine example of how narratological concepts and foundations can enable 'travel' through the disciplines and a seminal work demonstrating the potential of the discipline to stretch its own borders and enable movement across disciplinary boundaries.

4. What do you consider the most important topics and/or contributions in narratology?

The topics and contributions in narratology are so rich and varied, drawing on such an international and interdisciplinary range of scholarship, that one fears distortion by omission in attempting to highlight the most important among them. One might best begin, then, by recommending one of the best, most up-to-date and state-of-the-art reference works on narratology, the *Routledge Encyclopedia of Narrative Theory* (2005), which includes entries by many key figures in the discipline, and is edited by three of the most prominent and brilliant current contributors to the field in their own rights: David Herman, Manfred Jahn and Marie-Laure Ryan. There are of course some classics in the field from the heyday of structuralism that remain crucial as pioneering and foundational works, pre-eminently Gerard Genette's *Narrative Discourse: An Essay in Method* (1972) as well as Wayne C. Booth's earlier *The Rhetoric of Fiction* (1961), which, though it predates the birth of narratology proper, is an important point of reference for subsequent narratology, particularly concerning questions of unreliable narration. Paul Ric$\frac{1}{2}$ur's *Time and Narrative* (1984-1988), especially his lucid explication of the three-stage model of mimesis, has proven extremely enlightening as a basis for a wide range of literary analyses. And Shlomith Rimmon-Kenan's *Narrative Fiction. Contemporary Poetics* (2nd ed. 2002 [1983]), though billed as an introduction (and one of the first sustained attempts to outline the discipline as such), is also an important intervention as a work of critical theory in itself.

The more recent works that must be included in any bibliography of important works also demonstrate the versatility and scope of narratology in tackling broader topics than strictly structural concerns of narratology, which the book series "Narratologia" (published by de Gruyter, 20+ volumes to date) has done an excellent job to chart and clarify. The work of narrative psychologists such as Jerome Bruner (*Actual Minds, Possible Worlds*, 1986) and Paul John Eakin (*How Our Lives Become Stories: Making Selves*, 1999) have made important steps in understanding the nature of storytelling as a means of understanding how we make (our) selves, and point towards other recent work on cognitive narratology (the work of Manfred Jahn and David Herman again deserves mention) while, relatedly, Monika Fludernik's *Towards a 'Natural' Narratology* (1996) is the most robust contribution to the field of experientiality in narrative. I consider Jim Phelan and David Herman to be among the most influential and illuminating scholars working in narrative theory, and their books on the rhetoric of narratives and on cognitive narratology respectively—e.g. Phelan's *Living to Tell about It* (2005) and Herman's *Story Logic* (2002), but also their more recent monographs—are seminal works demonstrating the potential of the discipline to stretch its own borders and enable movement across disciplinary boundaries. An important trend (as I also have argued in favour of) has been towards more (inter-)culturally and historically contextualist kinds of narrative theory. The work of Roy Sommer deserves special mention here, and points towards one of the many key issues and open problems in the field.

5. What are the most important open problems in the field and what are the prospects for progress?

The problems of narratology and the theory of narrative are, almost by definition, open, inasmuch as the forms that narratives take are constantly changing—in terms of literary form, but also in terms of media, technology, culture and history. At the present moment, there are a number of specific issues that are well worth highlighting.

The issue of media (especially new media) is one area that has rapidly changed the contours of the object of study. Narratologies of other media, ranging from film and television to new forms of narratives on the internet and other new media, and the scope for applying and adapting narratological concepts derived from the theory of literary narrative is one major area of development in which considerable progress has already been made, but which will probably continue to keep (almost) as many professors busy as James Joyce. The role of other new media remains a relatively underexplored area: the impact of new media technologies in literary narrative (as evidenced in email-novels, for example, but also in contemporary novels that explore the modes of editing and storytelling of television and on the internet), and the changing role of narrative in different media formats (TV, internet, etc.), and indeed the question of how the ubiquity of such media affect narrative form generally, are areas of especial interest.

The issue of interdisciplinarity in narratological research, as noted above, is also an open question: how can narratology contribute to greater dialogue across the disciplines? Can its conceptual apparatus serve as the foundation of a language of communication that can illuminate the workings of narrative in different disciplinary areas of inquiry? The concepts developed in narratology can indeed perform this task, but it will require sustained engagement across the borders of disciplines as well as mutual exchange. I am firmly convinced that change and progress indeed depend on interdisciplinary and international dialogue and exchange.

What I consider to be particularly vital—pointing to another open problem in narratology itself—is the question of moving towards a genuinely cultural and historical narratology, i.e. a self-reflexive narratology that not only looks at the cultural variablity and historical development of narrative forms and genres, but also considers the historicity, and cultural specificities, of its own approaches, concepts and methods. Narratology in its classical form often aimed at a universalist science, while cultural studies have emphasised diversity and cultural and historical specificity. What seems crucial here, as in so much academic research, is intellectual reflexivity and adaptability: it is arguably possible, productive and illuminating to develop narratological concepts that have wide applicability (not least as a means of finding parallels and correspondences across cultural and historical borders), but it is necessary to maintain a reflexive consciousness of the conditions and pre-conditions that shape our modes of understanding and our cultures of research. This is, indeed, one of the fundamental insights that is gained through constructivist approaches to narratives (and metaphors) as 'ways of worldmaking' (Nelson Goodman).

The most promising prospects for progress here can be found, I would argue, in increasingly international and interdisciplinary research and genuine engagement across national, cultural and disciplinary borders—something of value in much research and teaching in the humanities today, and something that narratology is well placed to enhance. The future of narratology, and of everything else, of course, "is uncertain, but it will be interesting to watch", as the narrator at the end of David Lodge's novel *How Far Can You Go?* (1980) observes. And it will be even more fun to continue to make theoretical interventions that may serve to prevent narratology from degenerating into a 'narrowtology' (as a hilarious misspelling of one of our students once had it) and modest proposals to the blossoming field of interdisciplinary narrative theory that can serve to illuminate the important role that narratives have fulfilled, and will continue to fulfil, as ways of self- and worldmaking.

20
Alan Palmer

Independent scholar

1 Why were you initially drawn to narratology or narrative theory?

The story of my involvement in cognitive narratology is, I think, an unusual one and shows this subject area from what may be a surprising perspective. I mentioned some of it at the beginning of my book *Fictional Minds*. However, as it is, perhaps, quite instructive about the value of cognitive narratology, I'd like to tell it again now in a little more detail.

I studied at Birmingham University from 1969 to 1972 for a BA in English and philosophy. Unsurprisingly I suppose, given the time, there was no mention on the syllabus of narrative theory. However, in my final year, I was lucky enough to fall under the spell of Northrop Frye's wonderful book, *Anatomy of Criticism* (1957). I think that must have sowed a seed that took over twenty years to germinate. When I then did a teacher training course at the Institute of Education, University of London (1973-74), I was introduced to the work of the influential Russian social psychologist, Lev Vygotsky. After finishing this course, I decided not to be a teacher but to become a bureaucrat instead (as I still am). I had no involvement at all in academic life and did no research of any sort for over 20 years.

In the summer of 1995 I decided that I'd like to study the representation of consciousness in fiction. This was an aspect of narrative that had always interested me and I was curious to know what I could find out about it. I'm not sure now where this interest came from. I think the appeal lay in the fact that it was an opportunity to combine the three subjects that I studied many years before: English literature, philosophy and then psychology.

I was, at that time, still completely unaware of the existence of narratology as an academic subject. Obviously, I could have tried to find out whether or not there had been any theoretical study of consciousness representation. But I made a deliberate decision not to and decided simply to encounter and experience some fictional texts direct. I envisaged this activity as a kind of private, informal study that was not intended to lead anywhere and was purely for my own amusement. Reading theory didn't sound like as much fun as reading passages from novels. A chapter seemed about the right length for an in-depth analysis. The two texts I chose were the Box Hill chapter in *Emma* and, later, the Waterloo Ball chapter in *Vanity Fair*. I was attracted to them because they were about groups of people and I wanted to study the functioning of characters' minds in their social context. The influence of Vygotsky had clearly stayed with me.

My intention was to separate out statements about the physical surface of the storyworld (I only discovered this term later, of course) from statements about characters' consciousnesses. But I found immediately that this was not as easy to do as I had assumed. I frequently agonized over how to classify particular statements. For example—one that I've just recently encountered - "He went up to his room after dinner to be alone with his soul" (*Portrait of the Artist*). The first half of this sentence is a description of a physical action but the second half describes Stephen's mind.

This initial difficulty proved eventually to be very rewarding - it led directly to the discoveries described in *Fictional Minds*. I refer to the problem there as *Wittgenstein's question*. In the *Philosophical Investigations*, Wittgenstein quotes the sentence, "I noticed that he was out of humour," and asks: "Is this a report about his behavior or his state of mind?"

The other point that I want to stress about this early work is that I simply assumed, right from the beginning, that it would make sense to use real-mind disciplines such as the philosophy of mind and psychology to study fictional minds. I'll come back to this point later.

After doing an analysis of the Austen chapter along these lines, I changed my mind and decided that I would, after all, like to find out if there was any theory on this sort of thing. The project began escalating from a very early stage and I felt that I should go where it took me. I therefore wrote in the autumn of 1995 to the heads of two English departments within London University to ask for advice on theoretical texts. One replied, and he recommended books by Roland Barthes, Helmut Bonheim, Wayne Booth, David Lodge and Shlomith Rimmon-Kenan. From their bibliographies I discovered other treasures: Mieke Bal, Seymour Chatman, Dorrit Cohn (a particular favourite), Monika Fludernik, Gérard Genette, Marie-Laure Ryan (an important influence) and many others. I discovered, belatedly, that I was a narratologist!

After a few months more I had a second change of mind. I decided that what I was doing sounded like a thesis. In that case, it would make more sense to do it formally. In the spring of 1996 I applied to the Cultural Studies Department at the University of East London to do a PhD there. I started in October 1996 and submitted my thesis in January 1999. It was called 'The Presentation of the Mind in Narrative Fiction'. My two supervisors were extremely helpful and supportive and I'll always be very grateful to them for that. Neither were mainstream narratologists. My main supervisor (Bob Chase) was interested in narrative from a historiographical, Hayden White-esque perspective. I particularly value his introducing me to Bakhtin and reader response theory. My other supervisor (Couze Venn) was a specialist in poststructuralist and postcolonial studies. I have to say that I found the fact that neither had a mainstream narratology background an advantage - it gave me a lot of freedom to develop my own ideas without worrying too much about how they fitted into existing narratological paradigms. The downside was that I remained fairly isolated from the current trends in narratology and, in particular, from the cognitive turn. (I realise that I could have done a lot more to keep myself informed about recent developments. Unlike the initial decision not to find out about the theory, this wasn't deliberate.)

In 2000, I submitted an essay summarizing the thesis to *Narrative*. It was called 'The Construction of Fictional Minds' and a revised version of it was published in 2002. At the same time as this article was being accepted for publication, I was asked by David Herman, who had peer-reviewed the article, to write a chapter in his pioneering collection, *Narrative Theory and the Cognitive Sciences*. David also asked me to contribute a book to his Frontiers of Narrative series, and so *Fictional Minds* was published by the University of Nebraska Press in 2004.

It might look rather odd with the passing of time that *Fictional Minds* doesn't refer to the cognitive turn. The reason is because, strange as this may seem, I didn't know about the full extent of it at the time that I wrote the book. Although, as I say, I'd contributed to *Narrative Theory and the Cognitive Sciences*, I was not aware of the wider context to this volume and did not realize quite how ground-breaking it was. Of course, I knew about a lot of the other work being done in cognitive narratology. It's just that I didn't fully appreciate that cognitive approaches to literature had been very controversial. When I wrote my book I was still working in a very isolated way. For example, the first time I met other narratologists in person was at a conference in Hamburg in late 2003, 18 months after the book was finished.

I've been very lucky in my academic career. It was a lucky break that David Herman peer-reviewed my first article. I was also lucky to come along, unwittingly, at exactly the right time - just as cognitive approaches were becoming more acceptable to mainstream literary studies people.

I've told this story because it's the opposite of what I imagine is the standard progression towards cognitive narratology. What tends to happen usually, I'd guess, is that scholars arrive there after having typically progressed through the beginning of their career in literary studies and then gone on to choose a specialism, first in mainstream narratology, and then, if they're so inclined, in cognitive narratology. As I've explained, my experience was completely different. I chose narratology direct, as it were, before I knew that the subject even existed. More specifically, I chose *cognitive* narratology direct, not only before I knew that the subject existed, but also before I knew that it was, or had been, controversial. To me, the choice was not startlingly revolutionary, self-consciously new, or the Next Big Thing. It was not something that I felt I needed to justify to myself or to other people. It was just obvious.

2 What do you consider your most important contributions to the field?

I don't think it would be appropriate for me to try to answer this question in this form, so I'd like to answer a slightly different one: What do you hope will be your most important contributions to narratology? I'd like to suggest three.

1 *The social mind.* I've tried to argue in all my work that fictional minds have to be studied within the social context of their storyworld. Traditional literary theory tells only part of the story about how characters in novels think because of its undue emphasis on the inner, introspective, private, solitary, and individual mind. In addition, an externalist perspective is required, one that focuses on the outer, active, public, social, and embodied mind. This reveals, for example, that a good deal of fictional thought is intermental, or joint, group, shared, or collective. Social minds are not of marginal interest; they are central to our understanding of fictional storyworlds. I hope that it will be part of my contri-

bution to put the complex and fascinating relationship between social and individual minds at the heart of narrative theory.

Perhaps an example would help here. This is one that I've used quite a lot. One of the most important characters in *Middlemarch* is the town of Middlemarch itself. I call the intermental functioning of the inhabitants of the town "the Middlemarch mind". I go much further than simply suggesting that the town provides a social context within which individual characters operate, and argue that the town *literally* and not just metaphorically has a mind of its own. The Middlemarch mind is complex, interesting, clearly visible to a close reader of the text, and vitally important to an understanding of the novel because it explains a good deal of the motivation behind the actions of the other main characters. An analysis of the construction of the Middlemarch mind in the opening few pages of the novel (see chapter three of *Social Minds in the Novel*) shows that these pages are saturated with this group mind, and that the initial descriptions by the narrator of the three individual minds of Dorothea Brooke, her sister, Celia, and her uncle, Mr Brooke, are focalized through it. In fact, I would argue that it's not possible to understand the novel without following the workings of the intermental mind of the town. Many other novels, especially but not exclusively nineteenth century novels, also require an understanding of intermental thought. But this is not reflected in the theory.

2 *The whole mind.* I'd like the paradigm for the study of the representation of consciousness in fiction to be modified so that what is studied is the *whole* fictional mind. In other words, we need to *expand* the concept of the fictional mind. In addition to the social mind, some of the other aspects of the whole mind that I think would benefit from further exploration include action (in particular, how characters' actions are described in the discourse), dispositions and emotions. In parallel with the point I just made about intermental thought, readers have to rely on these aspects of the fictional mind while trying to follow characters' thought processes, but insufficient attention has been given so far to these aspects in the theory.

3 *The centrality of mind to narrative.* This is implicit in everything I've said so far. A lot of exciting work has been done on re-evaluating some traditional narratological concepts from a cognitive perspective (e.g. focalization). But I think that, once the centrality of mind to narrative is acknowledged, more can be done

to re-evaluate other topics such as character and story. Even the concept of narrative itself could be re-visited. I'm thinking of my suggestion (consistent with Monika Fludernik's notion of experientiality) that narrative is, in essence, the description of mental functioning.

3 What is the proper role of narratology and narrative theory in relation to other academic disciplines?

I agree with David Herman that narratology should be regarded as one of the cognitive sciences. However, I've been disappointed that, although several literary theorists have made good use of what might be called the "hard" cognitive sciences such as neuroscience, much less use has been made of the "soft" sciences such as social psychology, discursive psychology, sociolinguistics, and anthropology. David himself is a notable exception, but there's a lot more that can be done.

I also agree wholeheartedly with David that the exchange between narratologists and cognitive scientists (using the term in a broad sense) should be two-way. It shouldn't always be a case of narratologists borrowing from scientists. Speaking for myself, I'd be delighted if social psychologists found the evidence in my second book, *Social Minds in the Novel*, relevant to their work. For example, I look there in detail (chapter four) at the ways in which the social minds in *Little Dorrit* communicate with each other by such nonverbal means as facial expressions, nods, winks, shrugs and meaningful looks. I also analyse the workings of some large, medium and small intermental units. Examples of the last-named include the Dorrit family, Clennam and Mrs Clennam, Mrs Clennam and Flintwinch, and Little Dorrit and Pet. The analysis of the whole Dorrit family is informative, I think, about the dynamics of the relationships between subgroups of family members, for example, Little Dorrit and Mr Dorrit, and Little Dorrit and Fanny. It may be that social psychologists could find in this material some ideas for empirical research into the mechanics of relationships between family members, friends, work colleagues etc. in the real world.

As I'm British, I'm disappointed that narratology is still so marginal to the practice of literary criticism in the United Kingdom. Almost the only interest in narratology in this country comes from linguistics scholars who specialise in poetics or stylistics such as Cathy Emmott, Elena Semino and Peter Stockwell. It irritates me, to be honest, to look at the research interests listed in the websites of English studies departments in this country and to see how unthinkingly it's assumed that literary studies equate to literary history. Don't get me wrong, as the phrase goes. I think literary history is an extremely valuable subject. I just think there's more to literary studies than history.

Pursuing this point a little further - my impression as an academic outsider is that any dialogue that exists between narratologists and cultural historians is a pretty one-sided one. Perhaps I'm biased here but it seems to me that, on the whole, narratologists wholeheartedly embrace the concepts of history and culture and are open to the incorporation of them into their work. I've certainly never met one who doesn't and isn't. But, in my admittedly limited experience, literary historians are much less keen to accept the value of narrative theory and tend to be rather dismissive of it. This sort of parochialism can result in critics missing a lot about their particular period. For example, I think that there are some important discoveries about the nineteenth century novel in *Social Minds in the Novel*. But there'll be very few, if any, British literary studies specialists in that period who'll take any interest in the book or even be aware of it.

4 What do you consider the most important topics and/or contributions in narratology?

I don't really have anything to add here to my other answers. I think that the other narratologists in this volume will have much more interesting answers to this question than I would have.

5 What are the most important open problems in this field and what are the prospects for progress?

I think that what I want to say here may be somewhat controversial. I hope I don't offend anyone. Anyway, here goes ... I think that there is a danger of some narratological issues becoming overstudied. Brilliant work has been done on topics such as free indirect discourse, the unreliable narrator and narratorial omniscience. So brilliant, in fact, that the number of things worth saying about them is getting smaller and smaller. The possibility of severely diminishing returns is a real one. I would say that the concept of the implied author is different because there is a really interesting debate going on about its value. So I don't want to sound dogmatic about this, but I do think it's worth mentioning as a concern.

Putting the same point in a rather more positive way - My worry is that, when we approach texts through pre-existing conceptual frameworks, we can miss things. So I think we should be as imaginative as possible about finding new ways of doing narrative theory. I wonder sometimes if it would be a good idea for us to try occasionally to put all of our theory out of our minds for a while in order to respond *direct* to fictional texts. In that way, it's possible that we could identify some interesting recurring patterns that could then usefully be theorised. I accept that it's unrealistic to expect that deeply-embedded knowledge can be so easily set aside, but it may be that good would come simply from making the effort. I should stress that I'm not *guaranteeing* that there are undiscovered general properties of fictional texts which will remain undiscovered as long as we stick to the existing theoretical paths. I'm just saying that there may be.

I accept that there are some potential pitfalls. It would be very unfortunate if we all developed our own vocabulary and sets of concerns and became increasingly unintelligible to each other. This would certainly impede the development of the subject as a coherent body of knowledge. So there is a clear need to maintain a balance between creativity and originality on the one hand and consistency and coherence on the other. Monika Fludernik drew attention to this dilemma at a conference I attended in 2009 and I've been thinking about it a lot since. On the whole, I've come to the conclusion that my instinct, when in doubt, is to favour creativity over consistency. The fact is that narratology developed in historically contingent ways. It didn't have to be the way it is now. It could have been different. There is still much more to say.

21
Sylvie Patron

Associate Professor and Research Supervisor
University of Paris Diderot-Paris 7

1. Why were you initially drawn to narratology or narrative theory?

Without wishing to play on words, I would say that I became involved in narrative theory (more ezactly, in the history and epistemology of narrative theory) through the critique of narratology. It is important to know what I mean when I speak of *narrative theory* and *narratology*, or even *critique of narratology*. I will therefore begin by offering some precisions on these points.

1.1. By *narratology*, I understand a school of literary theory or, more precisely, of the theory of literary narrative, which was first formed in the mid 1960s and based at the École Pratique des Hautes Études (EPHE), then at the École des Hautes Études en Science Sociales (EHESS) in Paris. Gérard Genette swiftly became its leading figure. For historical reasons which deserve closer examination, his prominence began to extend outside France in the late 1970s, particularly in the Netherlands, the United States and Israel; it later reached other countries in Europe, often by an indirect route, particularly in German-speaking countries, which were subject to other influences. (This overall picture naturally needs to be drawn with greater nuance and emphasis on the fact that within narratology considered as a whole, Genette's dominance was never total, but rather tended to combine with national traditions, often with the result of revitalizing them.) As to the program put forward by narratology, it was expressed as follows in *Narrative Discourse: An Essay in Method*: "Analysis of narrative discourse will thus be for me, essentially, a study of the relationships between narrative and story, between narrative and narrating, and (to the extent that they are inscribed in the narrative discourse) between story and narrating" (Genette 1980 [1972], p. 29). It was reformulated in the preface to the French translation of Käte Hamburger's *Die Logik der Dichtung* (*The Logic of*

Literature), where the accents falls more strongly on the issue of fiction: "[...] the work of fictional narratology, always more or less focused on the comparison of discourse and story, assumes (by virtue of a provisional methodological decision) that the nonserious pretense of fiction — to tell a story that has actually happened — is taken seriously" (Genette 1993: 113). *Story*, *narrative* (or *narrative discourse*, or simply *discourse*), *narrating* (or *narrator*): narratology cannot do without the propositions these words encapsulate. They designate issues so essential that it cannot call them into question without undermining its own legitimacy.

(I) There is a story, which must be clearly distinguished from the narrative in which it is expressed.

(II) The narrative is always uttered by somebody addressing somebody else (even in the case of written narrative: "uttered", here, means "produced in verbal form, whether oral or written": this is what Genette terms the *narrating* (*narration* in French).

(III) In the case of narrative fiction, the story and the narrating (and thus the narrator and the narratee) are fictional. More exactly, a fictional act of narrating duplicates the author's real act, which narratology passes over, although in its absence there would simply be no narrative. The fictional narrator tells the narratee a series of events which he or she knows before recounting it. He or she is the one who makes use of the categories of *time* (*order*, *duration*, *frequency*), *mood* and *voice* in Genettian narratology. He or she is behind the selection and presentation (sometimes termed *focalization*) of narrative information in other schools of narratology.

This obviously does not mean that such propositions cannot be called into question (on the basis of conceptual redefinitions: "story/narrative" in the case of fictional narrative, "narrator", "fictional", etc., or refutation, in other words a demonstration of their falseness in some specific cases). However, it is clear that calling these concepts into question is admissible only in theories other than narratology.

Contemporary debates accord great importance to the difference between so-called *classical* and *postclassical* narratologies (this terminology was put forward not by historians, but rather by the protagonists of the second movement themselves). Postclassical narratology, they claim, is distinguished by a profusion of new methods and research hypotheses. They add that it draws on a range of sciences and that its corpus is much larger and more varied than that of classical narratology. Nevertheless, it seems to me that retaining the term *narratology* is at least as important as the distinction between classical and postclassical, as long as it is understood what using this term means: it designates this very set of propositions even if they survive in different, but still translatable, forms.

1.2. I have already situated *narrative theory* on a different level from narratology. I understand narrative theory in its largest extension: all forms of knowledge based on narrative or the faculty of narration, apprehended through the whole range of narrative discourses or texts. Narrative theory includes both classical and postclassical narratology, but also theories other than narratology, theories older than narratology, theories belonging to different cultural areas from narratology, etc.. Some authors use the term *narratology* (or even *postclassical narratology*) to designate the domain I am calling *narrative theory*, however such terminology has its drawbacks.

1.3. By *critique of narratology*, I understand a study of the conceptual and empirical basis of narratology. This study is grounded notably in the existence and the theoretical and empirical value of theories other than narratology.

2. What do you consider your most important contribution(s) to the field?

My major contribution to the history and epistemology of narrative theory is my 2009 volume entitled *Le Narrateur* (The Narrator), initially subtitled *Un problème de théorie narrative* (A Problem in Narrative Theory) and renamed *Introduction à la théorie narrative* (Introduction to Narrative Theory) at the publisher's request. It differs from narratological studies, whether classical or postclassical, in its *object*, the narrator (narratology cannot study the narrator to the extent that it takes it as axiomatic), its *method*, a historical and critical approach to different theories focused on the opposition between *communicational* theories of narrative and *non-communicational* theories, which can also be termed *poetic* theories of narrative fiction, and finally, its *conclusions*, which call into question the dominance of the communicational paradigm in the theory and analysis of narrative fiction.

2.1. The question is as follows: is there a narrator for all narrative fiction, or only in certain cases (which would imply that narratives can be "narratorless")? This question separates communicational theories of narrative, according to which communication between a narrator and a narratee constitutes the definition of narrative, including narrative fiction, and non-communicational or poetic theories of narrative fiction, which consider that narrative fiction, or a certain type of narrative fiction, and communication are mutually exclusive categories. According to these theories, narrative fiction is not, or is not always, the product of an act of communication. These theories also aim to rehabilitate the function of the author as the creator of the narrative fiction.

Now let me cite the three basic propositions of narratology once more: (I) there is a story, which must be clearly distinguished from the narrative in which it is expressed; (II) the narrative is always uttered by somebody addressing somebody else; (III) in the case of narrative fiction, the story and the narrating (and thus the narrator and the narratee) are fictional. In other words, for narratology, all narrative has a narrator, whether real or fictional, who communicates narrative content to a narratee, whether real or fictional. More exactly:

— in the case of non-fictional narrative, a real narrator (the author) communicates narrative content, which is given as authentic, to a real narratee (the reader);
— in the case of narrative fiction, the author communicates narrative content which both of them know has no claim to authenticity, via the mediation of communication by a fictional narrator to a fictional narratee, of narrative content which is given as authentic.

Narratology is only interested in the second situation of communication, which can be summarized by the questions "who is speaking?" and "to whom?" (implying: fictionally). It frequently does without the operator "It is fictional that..." and considers narrative fiction as an *analogon* or an imitation of non-fictional narrative.

For non-communicational or poetic theories of narrative fiction, on the contrary:
— it is not at all obvious that the relation between the author and the reader is one of communication, in an essential and interesting sense of the term *communication* (based on a linguistic and potentially pragmatic interpretation of what communication is, as opposed to what it can be considered not to be);
—it is not at all obvious either that there is always a fictional situation of communication implying a fictional narrator and narratee. The presence of a fictional situation of communication must be established on the grounds of a logico-linguistic analysis rather

than presupposition. Its absence enables the appearance of other forms that are always more or less closely linked to the representation of the "third-person subjectivity" (or to that of "subjectless subjectivity") and which have become indissociable from third-person narrative fiction.

In fact, for non-communicational or poetic theories of narrative fiction, the most interesting question in the case of narrative fiction is not "who is speaking?" (implying: fictionally), but the question "how is it written?" (implying: given the possibilities offered by the structure of language).

2.2. Communicational theories of narrative are theories implying the absence of linguistic differences between non-fictional narrative, fictional narrative and communicational discourse. The problem is that they are also non-linguistic theories of narrative fiction (with the exception of part of Lubomír Doležel's theory in *Narrative Modes in Czech Literature*, 1973). I disagree with certain representations of classical narratology, generally those prompted by a concern to define postclassical narratology, which see the former as a linguistic theory of narrative inspired by structural linguistics. Such representations do not withstand rigorous scrutiny. On the other hand, non-communicational or poetic theories of narrative fiction are linguistic theories of narrative fiction (except Hamburger's, which is more akin to logic and the philosophy of language; some of her propositions are nevertheless translatable into linguistic discourse). For the representatives of these theories, the narrating of fiction is distinct in some respects from non-fictional narrating, and similar to the latter in others; it can only be theorized within the framework of a linguistics of written language and a historical stylistics of discourses and genres.

2.3. Communicational theories of narrative fiction are theories of omni-fictionality in fictional narrative. They are not interested in the distinction, which stems from the study of the reception of works of fiction, between those elements that relate to the content of the fictional representation (the characters, events, the narrator if there is one) and those relating to the means employed in the construction of the representation (the language, style and composition of the text on different levels). On the other hand, non-communicational or poetic theories of narrative fiction make this distinction more or less explicitly. Ann Banfield writes, for example, on the subject of the author's style: "[...] style approached in this way is not on a par with those aspects of style which create the intentional construct which is fictional subjectivity. A writer may leave his signature in his writing — it may even contribute a major proportion of what is valued in it — but this is not what his writing creates [...]" (1982: 253). Mary Galbraith uses more explicit formulations: "In a fictional narrative without a narrator, the language of narration is not itself part of the fiction, except where it represents the verbal expressions of characters [...]. Rather, the language of narration is the mode of being of the fiction. Fictional people, events, experiences and verbal expressions are all represented and come to life through the language of the text, and the style of the language makes each fiction a different kind of experience, a different texture, a different self-world relation" (1995: 49). In my own article entitled "The Death of the Narrator and the Interpretation of the Novel: The Example of *Pedro Páramo* by Juan Rulfo" (Patron 2010b), I have aimed to show the benefits to be gained from this distinction for the analysis and the interpretation of a particular work of narrative fiction.

2.4. Beyond the preceding formulation of oppositions, I consider as my own contribution:

(I) Identifying the point at which the concept of the narrator took on a stabilized form (coinciding with the first descriptions of the first-person novel as opposed to the third-person novel) and observing the persistence of the traditional conception of the narrator in communicational theories of narrative (where it is never integrated without the introduction of an imbalance or disparity between criteria) and in non-communicational or poetic theories of narrative fiction (where it is integrated but reinterpreted).

(II) Compiling a corpus and studying the succession of theories in the case of communicational theories of narrative fiction (in the case of non-communicational or poetic theories of narrative, I was able to adopt an existing corpus and examine relationships of succession which had already been established).

(III) Offering a renewed account of non-communicational or poetic theories of fiction (which had been the object of a number of erroneous readings and representations). As in the case of communicational theories, I endeavored to evaluate the common characteristics and differences between these theories on the level of the issues raised, the concepts and the terminology used and the literary examples cited.

(IV) Establishing the genealogy of certain concepts or ideas, and exposing several errors linked to conceptual transfers between narratology and enunciative linguistics, or between narratology and speech act theory, for example.

2.5. My book calls into question the dominance of the communicational paradigm in the theory and analysis of narrative fiction. Despite some obscurity or approximate reasoning and the different extension given at times to *narratorless narrative*, I consider than non-communicational or poetic theories of narrative are sounder on the theoretical level, more precise and adequate on the descriptive level and more fertile on the interpretative level than communicational theories of fiction.

3. What is the proper role of a narratology and narrative theory in relation to other academic disciplines?

As far as I am concerned, the pertinent question is the following: what is the role of the history and epistemology of narrative theory in relation to narrative theory and potentially to other academic disciplines? The answer to this question would require more space than I have available here, however I will try to give a few indications along with some examples.

3.1. Historicizing narrative theory consists in making information available to researchers which may broaden their *retrospective horizon* (*horizon de rétrospection* in French): the memory of results, problems and concepts developed before their time (I am taking the term and its definition from French historians of linguistics). To cite a simple example, Genette's discussion of *person* based on the expressions "first-person narrative" and "third-person narrative" contains very limited retrospection. When he writes that "these common locutions seem to [him] inadequate, in that they stress variation in the element of the narrative situation that is in fact invariant — to wit, the presence (explicit or implicit) of the 'person' of the narrator" (1980: 243-244), Genette shows that he is not familiar with the traditional definition of these expressions, which focuses on the "person" of the protagonist, rather than that of the narrator (even if the first-person novel is characterized by the protagonist *also* being the narrator of the novel). Clearly, had he been aware of this definition, Genette would not have formulated the issue in the same way and the discussion would no doubt have continued on different grounds. The importance of historicizing contemporary narrative theory is readily seen: dissipating the illusion of natural concepts (the theories and concepts they employ, the terms used, etc. are not natural entities, but historical realities; in other words, nothing is obvious, nothing is given, everything is constructed); fighting "presentism", showing the continuity of sets of problems which often prefer to be seen as radically distinct; showing oversights, too, the gaps in the memory of the discipline; potentially re-opening debates which were thought to be closed; conversely, helping history become truly cumulative, rather than cyclical, by avoiding questions being asked repeatedly in the same, or synonymous, terms.

3.2. The history of narrative theory therefore provides the conditions for informed study of the epistemology of narrative theory. Historical inquiry reveals, for example, that the modern, narratological concept of the narrator is the fruit of syncretism between:

— the traditional concept of the narrator (referring to the character who has the status of narrator, in the ordinary sense of the term, in the first-person novel);
— the personification of a generic opposition, the opposition between narrative and dramatic genres (the narrator referring here to the mediating agent of the narrative, in particular the dialogs contained in the narrative, of whatever type);
— the personification of a methodological principle, the principle of immanence, according to which the coherency of an analysis implies that an object only be grasped through the interplay of its internal relations (the narrator referring, here, to the speaker within the narrative, of whatever type);
— the personification of a methodological decision, the decision to treat narrative fiction as an *analogon* or imitation of non-fictional narrative (the narrator referring, here, to the fictional producer of the narrative fiction, of whatever type);
— lastly, the personification of John Searle's theory of illocutionary pretense (the narrator referring here to the speaker who conforms to the characteristic, constitutive rules of the assertions contained in the narrative fiction, of whatever type, which is a mistake from Searle's point of view).

In some narratologies (I am thinking in particular of those tackling literary narrative and cinema, and even theater all at once), the concept of the narrator is so thoroughly stripped of all empirical determinations that one wonders how it can still be applied in its original domain, to wit, the first-person novel.

Postclassical narratology has not eliminated such contradictions; far from it. It could even be said that it has made them a core element of its theoretical programs.

3.3. Thus we come to the idea of *evaluative* epistemology. Evaluating theories is a necessity within any discipline. The relativism of historical description must therefore be moderated by taking into account the theoretical and empirical value of theories, in the case of narrative theory as with other academic disciplines.

4. What do you consider the most important topics and/or contributions in narratology?

The formulation of this question worries me for two reasons: first, it appears to be looking for a list of winning contributions, which I do not feel entitled to put forward; second, it abandons the distinction between narratology and narrative theory, which I believe to be important, in the sense that I have made clear.

4.1. One way for me to reply to this question without replying as such is to outline the principles on which I based the compilation of my corpus: distance with regard to pure erudition; choice of representativity over exhaustiveness. I favored Gérard Genette's and Seymour Chatman's theories over Shlomith Rimmon-Kenan's for example, which does not offer an original understanding of the narrator or narration (the same goes for Mieke Bal, who has an original understanding of narrative focalizations, while her understanding of the narrator is strictly equivalent to Genette's). I gave Franz Stanzel's theory a prime position because of its originality, as well as its reception and the influence it has borne (which is shown in the book with the examples of Gottfried Gabriel and Monika Fludernik). In the case of Lubomír Doležel's narrative theory, the criterion of influence was not the most important, since this theory is not well known outside the circle of specialists in Czech literature. It was rather the criteria of originality, interest and difference from Genette's narratology in its relation to linguistics, and also the fact that it is necessary to be familiar with this theory in order to understand the theory of authentication, a branch of Doležel's theory of fiction. In the case of non-communicational or poetic theories of narrative fiction, which are less numerous and more concerned to publicize the cumulative grounds of their knowledge, as I mentioned already, I only had to adopt a corpus and examine relationships of succession which had already been compiled, from Käte Hamburger to S.-Y. Kuroda and Ann Banfield, and from the latter to the representatives of deictic shift theory (Buffalo school). I did not devote a chapter to Dorrit Cohn, whose eclecticism (Hamburger's understanding of fiction, Genette's view of the narrator, her rejection of Banfield's theory without further argument) appear to me as a theoretical compromise, or rather, fundamentally, a non-theory. (I am only referring, of course, to the part of her theory which concerns the narrator without calling into question Cohn's considerable contribution to the theory of narrative fiction in general.)

4.2. As for the topics, which I have not yet mentioned, it seems to me that narratology has placed too much value on the question of the narrator ("who is speaking?") and in a different way, of its corollary, the narratee ("to whom?"), and focused attention on a few macrostructural figures seen as relating to the communication between the two, to the detriment of other major questions and phenomena. I have already noted the question of the language of fiction and that of the biplanar reception of narrative fiction. I will mention, here, the issue of plot production *(narrative tension* in Raphaël Baroni's terminology), which has long been neglected for reasons to do with the history of narratology and its trends. As Baroni puts it, "[...] one can [...] criticize the relegation of "narrative sequence" to the register of a narrative theme, function or motif, in other words its assimilation with the logical form of the story, to the detriment of the study of the complex relations formed between what is told, the manner in which it is told, and the aesthetic aim of the arrangement of the events to form a plot"; "[t]o remain within a structuralist framework, the plot would [...] fall into the domain as much of Genette's modal narratology as of thematic narratology, even if, at the time, questions pertaining to narrative sequentiality were monopolized by the latter trend to the detriment of the former" (2011:186, 188) (It could also be said that these questions were overlooked by the former trend, since they were considered to be the prerogative of the latter — chronologically the former.)

5. What are the most important open problems in this field and what are the prospects for progress?

I have no foresight as to the fate of narratology (even if I have suggested that part of its program of study, developed forty odd years ago, can no longer be considered valid). I will therefore limit myself to briefly concluding this article by insisting on two points which I believe to be important. First point: the relation between history and epistemology. In the humanities, historical inquiry must palliate the near impossibility of experimentation (I am more skeptical than many contemporary narratologists about the contribution of the cognitive sciences in this domain). There are a certain number of problems in narrative theory which would clearly benefit from solid historical input. Second point: interdisciplinarity and its limits. The theory of narrative fiction certainly has a lot to learn from other disciplines which are interested, however closely, in narrative in general and in narrative discourses or texts in particular. However, it should not forget the theoretical method of discriminating tasks and specifying objects which has been employed by literary theory since it was formed as a discipline.

Translated by Susan Nicholls

22

Thomas Pavel

Gordon J. Laing Distinguished Service Professor
Romance Languages and Literatures, Committee on Social Thought, University of Chicago

---

1. Why were you initially drawn to narratology or narrative theory?

I shall use the term 'narratology' for the discipline that includes

– the study of plot structure, pioneered by Vladimir Propp and continued, among others, by Roland Barthes, Claude Bremond, and Tzvetan Todorov; and
– the rhetoric of telling stories, founded by Wayne Booth and further developed by Gérard Genette and other scholars.

Both branches seemed to me to be, not unlike stylistics, healthy auxiliaries of literary analysis. Plot analysis, in particular, appeared promising because of its direct links to the human content of literature. Its results, I believed, could not only help us better understand particular works, but could also be used to check the validity of literary interpretations and clarify the historical evolution of literary genres and forms.

For example, it is quite helpful, before engaging in speculative interpretations of Shakespeare's *Hamlet*, to figure out the structure of its plot and relate it to the sub-genre of Elizabethan revenge tragedies. In Shakespeare's play, the young prince's tendency to postpone acting is presented as a flaw. At the same time, it corresponds to a structural feature of most revenge tragedies, which reveal a horrid crime quite early in the play, but let revenge take place only during a final, general massacre. Once we realize this, it becomes clear that Shakespeare did not select procrastination as a peculiar feature that would make Hamlet more interesting, but that he used this feature to add plausibility to the routine postponement of revenge in tragedies of this kind. Examining plot structure is equally relevant for the history of genres and forms. The double plot, for instance, while essential for Elizabethan drama, was considered a fault in French neo-classicist tragedy.

2. What do you consider your most important contribution(s) to the field?

In my work on Corneille (Pavel 1976) I proposed a formal model of the links holding together the moves of a plot. Although this model, inspired by a version of Noam Chomsky's generative grammar, seemed to me to go farther than the earlier proposals of Vladimir Propp and Roland Barthes concerning plot-organization, I gradually realized that the model was still dependent on the misleading analogy between stories and sentences that was popular in the 1970s. A story is a long sentence, narratologists used to believe. It is not. Sentences are *word*-structures, while plots put together human *actions*.

In a subsequent book (Pavel 1985), I simplified the syntactic model of the plot, but I am far from certain that the result is satisfying. In this book, however, I made a first attempt to link plot to the social and moral norms that govern action. A quite simple, obvious, fact attracted my attention: we immediately understand what makes characters act—the maxims they follow—although these maxims are quite different from our own. The maxim "An earthly crown is the highest good" governs all Shakespeare's historical plays, but certainly not our own world. Each action (each move) belonging to a plot rests on such maxims, which tell the characters what goods to pursue and how to react to the moves of other characters. I gradually understood that plot-based literary works imagine fictional worlds populated by characters governed by certain maxims and whose actions and fate generate interest much more directly and intensely than the textual, stylistic aspects of the work. Following a line of research initiated by Umberto Eco and Lubomír Doležel, my book *Fictional Worlds* (1986) describes the way in which these worlds are organized.

Working on fictional worlds, I also realized the extent to which the linguistic models used by structuralists in the 1960s and 1970s were inadequate for an in-depth study of literature. *The Spell of Language* (French edition 1988, English version 1989, new revised edition 2001) examines the misuse of linguistic notions in structural anthropology, philosophy, and literary studies.

Since the early 1990s, I turned to the history of literature and culture and published a study of 17th-century neo-classicist French literature (Pavel 1996) and a history of the novel (Pavel 2003, an English revised version forthcoming). My earlier studies of plot, maxims governing action, and fictional worlds were very helpful for both projects.

3. What is the proper role of a narratology and narrative theory in relation to other academic disciplines?

Narratology can provide useful support and assistance to literary history and interpretation. But I am uncomfortable with the occasional attempt to present narrative theory as an all-encompassing model for the humanities and even more so with those philosophers who use the term 'narrative' in a vague, incantatory fashion.

4. What do you consider the most important topics and/or contributions in narratology?

The three main fields seem to me still to be plot and action, fictional worlds, and the rhetoric of story-telling. As for contributions, the work of the scholars who are included in the present volume has been and still is crucially important.

5. What are the most important open problems in this field and what are the prospects for progress?

The main challenge facing narratology is the imperative to bring its research closer to human interests. Abstract, algebraic plot-formulas don't help us grasp better the stakes and solutions of this or that particular play or novel. Fictional worlds cannot be reduced to mere logical constructions: they host characters and issues that are deeply relevant for readers and spectators. No one reads Flaubert's *Madame Bovary* in order to enjoy free-indirect discourse; this stylistic feature is there to help us grasp the heroine's personality and her fate.

The present challenge of narratology is to bring the results of formal speculations closer to literature's moral and artistic substance.

23
James Phelan

Distinguished University Professor
Department of English, Ohio State University

Five Questions, Five Answers; Or, A Few Stories, Proposals, and Off-the-Wall Ideas

1. Why were you initially drawn to narratology or narrative theory?

I was drawn to narrative theory through my study, during graduate school, of the work of the Chicago School neo-Aristotelians and especially through the teaching of Sheldon Sacks. At the end of my graduate coursework, I had the good fortune to study with Wayne C. Booth, and, as anyone who has read both his work and mine will notice, he has also been a major influence on my thinking about narrative. But if I had not encountered Sacks when I did, I am sure I would never have been asked to answer these five questions. For that reason, I will answer this first question by means of a short portrait narrative with two subjects, Sacks and my graduate school self.[1]

In the Spring of 1973, two-thirds of the way through what was proving to be a difficult year in the MA program at Chicago, I decided to enroll in "The Eighteenth-Century Novel." I signed up not because I had a burning desire to re-read *Pamela* and *Tom Jones* but because so many of the Ph.D. students advised me to take a course from Sheldon Sacks. He opened the course by asking, "Do we read the same books?" In 1973, before the widespread influence of reader-response criticism, Sacks could assume that we'd all answer in the affirmative. He therefore moved quickly to a demonstration of the gap between that "yes" and our ways of talking about books. He asked us what *Pride and Prejudice* was about and then suggested that, on the basis of our thematic

---

[1] This portrait narrative is adapted from a longer essay "Listening to Shelly." in a small-circulation newsletter called Hypotheses

answers ("the interrelations of pride and prejudice"; "marriage in an acquisitive society"; "the unreliability of first impressions"), we should either revisit our assumption that we do read the same books or re-examine our ways of talking about our experience. By the end of the class, through further questioning and some well-chosen interventions of his own, Sacks had begun moving us toward his way of thinking about novelistic form by suggesting that one powerful way of connecting our critical commentary to our experience would be to focus on our emotional investment in Elizabeth's progress toward her eventual marriage to Darcy.

All this was music to my ears, though I was not yet able to recognize the larger symphony to which these pleasing notes belonged. As the course went on, I felt that I was learning not just Eighteenth-Century Fiction but why I had been struggling so much during my first two quarters of the M.A. program: I had been living in that gap between experience and critical discourse, reading with pleasure (and other responses) on my own and then ignoring those responses as I participated in class discussions and wrote papers about themes and historical contexts and other things I barely understood. Sacks's approach not only emphasized the link between the experience of reading and the work of analysis but his questions also made interpretation a much more rigorous and challenging enterprise than anything I had previously encountered. "Based on what we see of Mr. and Mrs. Bennet in the first two chapters of *Pride and Prejudice*—his heartless teasing of her, her distorted values—why do most readers intuit a comic rather than a tragic or pathetic form?" "How does Fielding construct the form of *Tom Jones* to assure his audience both that Tom will marry Sophia Western and that if Tom were a real person rather than a fictional character he would meet a very different end, one consistent with the prophecy that he was born to be hanged?" "How is the principle of progression underlying *Tristram Shandy* different from the principles underlying Fielding's and Austen's novels?" With every new question, I found myself intrigued but initially stymied, and thus increasingly impressed with the way Sacks reasoned to the answers, sometimes with our collaboration but often on his own. I doubted that I'd ever be able to reason about experience and interpretation—or narrative technique, form, and effects—the way he did, but I loved trying to, almost as much as I loved listening to Sacks do it.

In the summer of 1973, my wife, Betty Menaghan, and I fled Chicago, returning to the friendlier confines of Boston, the city where we'd been happy undergraduates. Betty had just completed the first year of a three-year graduate fellowship in the Committee on Human Development, so we knew we would be returning to Hyde Park in the fall. We didn't know, however, whether I'd be returning to the University. My record as an M.A. student was good enough to get me accepted to the Ph.D. program, but not good enough to get me any financial aid. The job market had recently turned nasty. I had many doubts about my ability to succeed in the program. Ultimately, however, as I thought about my options from behind the wheel of a Town Taxi in the Boston heat, I decided that, even if I didn't make it all the way to the Ph.D., what I most wanted to do in the immediate future was to listen to more of Sacks's music.

If Sacks's Eighteenth-Century Fiction course served as my launch into narrative theory—and, more specifically, into Chicago school theory of the novel—his year-long seminar in 1973-74 committed me to the rest of my voyage. Called simply The Novel, this seminar met every Monday afternoon—officially from 1:30 to 4:30 but more often till 5 or 5:30. Autumn and Winter quarters were devoted to Sacks' version of Chicago school theory as it applied to—and was tested by—the novels our group of first-year Ph.D. students had chosen to work on. The list included, among many others, *Tom Jones* (again), Austen's *Persuasion*, Eliot's *Middlemarch* (my choice), James's *The Portrait of a Lady*, Hardy's *Tess of the D'Urbervilles*, Woolf's *To the Lighthouse*, and Hemingway's *A Farewell to Arms*. In Spring quarter about six of us stayed on and another half-dozen or so of Sacks's dissertation students joined the seminar as its focus shifted from the application and testing of the theory to the specific dissertation projects of the advanced students. Sacks believed that all of us would benefit by seeing projects at different stages of development and that the more advanced students would find the structure and companionship of the seminar a welcome relief from the isolation of dissertating.

In the over one hundred hours I spent in these thirty-three sessions, I never grew tired of Sacks's voice. The classes ran over because Sacks concentrated so intently on us and on the ideas he was pursuing that he would lose all track of the time. And so would I. I've never encountered anyone more animated by ideas, more passionate about the challenges and pleasures of thinking rigorously about narrative and how it works.

By the end of that year, I was able to recognize not only the Symphony from which the Eighteenth-Century Fiction course had been extracted but also several others as well. Like all good music, these symphonies entered my whole being; more than ideas to think about, more even than articles of critical faith, they became the air that I breathed, the blood circulating through my veins.

Symphony #1 was the loudest and most frequently played. It might be called The Power of Form, and some version of it is familiar to all who have carefully studied Chicago School criticism. Under Sacks's conducting, its recurring themes were (a) that the material action of a narrative was radically different from the plot proper, since the effect of any event could not be predicted from an examination of the event itself but only from an analysis of its particular treatment and its particular relation to the larger context of the narrative; (b) that there was no one-to-one correspondence between any narrative technique and a given effect on an audience, because techniques, like events, could be used in different contexts for different ends (Sacks's version of what Meir Sternberg later called the Proteus Principle); (c) that by considering every major novel as an experiment in form, we could begin to imagine a formal history of the novel (the approach was not ahistorical but it resisted the idea that extraliterary history determined the history of literary form); and (d) the most distinctively Sacksian theme, that intuiting a narrative's principle of coherence was an inevitable consequence of reading narrative.

Symphony #2 might be called Ode to Critical Reason; its recurring themes were (a) that virtually every statement about a particular novel had some larger theoretical implication; consequently, our investigations of particular novels were important both for what they might tell us about those novels and for what they might tell us about narrative technique, character, plot, and the form and the history of the novel more generally; and (b) all interpretations were hypotheses and all hypotheses need to be tested—against the details of the text, alternative hypotheses, and their logical implications.

Symphony #3 might be called the Quest for a Question, and it had a single recurring theme: to do criticism of any quality one needed to distinguish between productive and unproductive questions; unproductive ones were dead ends—once answered, the world's store of facts would be increased but not much else; productive questions, on the other hand, required answers that went beyond fact and, indeed, beyond their own overt subjects, to theory, to prediction—and to more questions. Symphony #4 might be called Passionate Humanity; its theme, more pervasive than all the others, was love what you do, care about it intensely, do it as well as you can, and everything else be damned.

I found Sacks's composing and conducting of these symphonies so exciting because his own effort exemplified the Fourth Symphony and because he envisioned the First Symphony as a variation on the themes of the Second and Third. In other words, for him, the Power of Form was not a fixed body of conclusions but a set of hypotheses to be tested and a set of questions to be answered.

Over the years I've come to disagree with Sacks about some of his hypotheses and answers, and I've come to be enchanted by other kinds of symphonies. But I've also continued to be sustained by listening to the music Sacks set playing in my head those many years ago—and for that I'm extremely grateful.

2. What do you consider your most important contributions to the field?

I've tried to contribute in different ways—through writing, editing, teaching and rendering service to institutions that promote the study of narrative. I leave it to others to pass judgment on which contributions are most important, but here are a few that I regard as highlights:

In my writing, I've tried to develop a comprehensive rhetorical poetics of narrative. But I should emphasize that such a statement imposes a retrospective coherence on my work that it didn't have until I was writing my third book. At first, I just wanted to write a decent dissertation about style in the novel. After that dissertation became a book (*Worlds from Words*), I wanted to answer some questions about character. Once I got to the point where I was relatively satisfied with those answers (*Reading People, Reading Plots*), I also began to feel that I was working out a way of thinking about narrative that was a useful, albeit incomplete, development of what I'd learned from Sacks, Booth, the essays of Ralph Rader, and the work of others in the neo-Aristotelian tradition, especially the work on audiences by Peter J. Rabinowitz. In writing the Introduction to *Narrative as Rhetoric*, I tried to articulate the basic principles of this approach. Since that point, I have been consciously pursuing this larger project.

The grounding idea is that narrative is not simply an account of related events but rather a rhetorical action: somebody telling someone else on some occasion and for some purposes that something happened. My goal, in a sense, is to explore what this conception of narrative means for our understanding of authors, narrators, audiences, and the elements of narratives through which they communicate (events, characters, plots, and narrative techniques). And as I conduct that investigation I seek to remain open to what narrative artists themselves can teach us about this conception of narrative. In that respect, I regard my work on the interpretation of individual narratives to be not simply illustrations of the theory but integral parts of its development. My main books, as their subtitles suggest, devote themselves to different aspects of this rhetorical poetics: *Worlds from Words: A Theory of Language in Fiction*; *Reading People, Reading Plots: Character, Progression, and the Interpretation of Narrative*; *Narrative as Rhetoric: Techniques, Audiences, Ethics, Ideology*; *Living to Tell about It: A Rhetoric and Ethics of Character Narration*; and *Experiencing Fiction: Judgments, Progressions, and the Rhetorical Theory of Narrative*. My current project, whose working title is *Conversation as Narration: A Rhetoric and Ethics of Dialogue*, investigates how authors use character-character dialogue to accomplish tasks that would otherwise be assigned to narrators.

Within this body of work, what I see most often cited are the rhetorical definition of narrative (quoted above) and my proposals about character, progression, unreliable narration, and narrative ethics. I think that the definition gets cited because it briefly encapsulates one view of narrative and that the proposals get cited because they are portable, that is, extractable from the larger edifice of the theory-in-progress.

In brief, I propose that

A. *Character* is an element with three components: mimetic (a fictional character is, to a greater or lesser degree, a possible person; a character in nonfiction is a representation of an actual person); thematic (a character has a representative or ideational function); and synthetic (a character is an artificial construct).

B. *Narrative progression* is a synthesis of textual dynamics and readerly dynamics. Textual dynamics arise from the introduction, complication, and resolution of instabilities (at the level of story, particularly in character-character relations) and tensions (at the level of discourse, as, for example, when a narrator clearly withholds information). Readerly dynamics arise from the audience's cognitive, affective, and ethical responses to the trajectory of the textual dynamics.

C. *Narrators* perform three main functions—*reporting, interpreting, and evaluating*—that they can carry out reliably or unreliably (that is, in ways that the author would or would not endorse). This reasoning leads to my taxonomy of *six types of unreliability*: misreading, misinterpreting, and misevaluating; underreading, underinterpreting, and underevaluating. I couple this taxonomy of the kinds of unreliability with an interest in its effects, which I locate along a spectrum from estranging (think of Jason Compson in *The Sound and the Fury*) to bonding (think of Huckleberry Finn and his decision to go to hell).

D. *The ethics of narrative* arise from the dynamic interaction of the ethics of the told and the ethics of the telling. The ethics of the told consists of the ethical dimensions of character-character relations while the ethics of the telling consists of the ethical dimensions of author-narrator-character-audience relationships. The ethical component of narrative progressions results from the interactions of the ethics of the telling and the ethics of the told.

As an editor, I have worn three different hats:

E. The single-collection-of-essays hat, worn for seven volumes, often in a matched set with one or more co-editors: *Reading Narrative* (1989); *Understanding Narrative* (co-edited with Peter J. Rabinowitz, 1994); the Blackwell *Companion to Narrative Theory* (also co-edited with Peter, 2005); *Joseph Conrad: Voice, Sequence, History, Genre* (co-edited with Jakob Lothe and Jeremy Hawthorn, 2008); *Teaching Narrative Theory* (co-edited with David Herman and Brian McHale, 2010); *After Testimony: The Ethics and Aesthetics of Holocaust Narrative* (co-edited with Jakob Lothe and Susan Suleiman, forthcoming), and *Fact, Fiction, and Form: Selected Essays of Ralph W. Rader* (co-edited with David H. Richter, forthcoming). These collections have each had their own distinct genesis, but each has made me grateful for the opportunity to collaborate with others in our efforts to influence conversations about important aspects of the field.

F. The book-series co-editor hat, passed back and forth between me and Peter Rabinowitz as we have worked, since the early 1990s, on the Ohio State University Press's series on the Theory and Interpretation of Narrative. Here our work has varied from nurturing younger scholars writing their first books to challenging more senior scholars to deepen their arguments to, on some occasions, simply facilitating the publication of the work. (Peter and I are grateful that in 2010 Robyn Warhol joined us as a third co-editor of the Series.)

G. The journal editor hat. Since 1993, I have been editor of *Narrative,* the journal of the International Society for the Study of Narrative. This work, too, has an important collaborative dimension as reviewers and especially authors help define and shape the way the journal contributes and responds to developments in the field.

In rendering service to the field, I have found much good company in the International Society for the Study of Narrative. With George and Barbara Perkins, I co-organized the 1986 Narrative Conference, which became the Society's first annual conference. I was coordinator for the third conference in 1988, and assisted Rick Livingston who organized the 1996 Conference. I will be one of the co-organizers with Alan Nadel, Robyn Warhol, and Eddie Maloney of the 2012 Conference in Las Vegas. I served as President of the Society in the late 1980s, and for the last several years, have been Secretary-Treasurer.

At Ohio State University, I have worked with my colleagues Frederick Aldama, David Herman, Brian McHale, and Robyn Warhol to establish Project Narrative, whose mission is to promote teaching and scholarship in the field. We have been able to do that through various means, including the development of courses in narrative theory, the sponsoring of symposia, and the hosting of visiting scholars.

3. What is the proper role of narratology and narrative theory in relation to other disciplines?

First, I think it's important that narrative theory not be subordinated to any discipline—literary studies, rhetoric, legal studies—but instead continue to develop as a distinct discipline focused on the nature of narrative as a distinctive mode of representing and exploring the varieties of human (and even some nonhuman) experience. Second, I think that narrative theory needs to establish a kind of two-way traffic with other disciplines. Traffic should flow from narrative theory and its findings and hypotheses to other disciplines, even as those disciplines put narrative theory's findings and hypotheses to the distinctive tests afforded by their objects of study and ways of approaching them. As Rita Charon and others have shown, bringing narrative theory to the stories that patients tell doctors can improve medical practice because it helps doctors understand their patients better, which in turn influences their treatment. Traffic should also flow from other disciplines back to narrative theory as their distinctive narratives and discipline-specific ways of thinking about them reveal places where narrative theory has been short-sighted or in other ways in need of revision. Shlomith Rimmon-Kenan and others have shown that illness narratives often challenge our ideas about such things as consistency of character and the coherence of narrative itself.

4. What do you consider the most important topics and contributions in narratology?

I'm reluctant to make a top-ten list, especially of topics (though I don't believe that all topics are created equal, I sometimes wish they were), but I will point to categories of contribution that I regard highly and cite just a few examples of each. I also want to emphasize that I think the field advances not just through the interventions of individual great books and essays but also through the cumulative effect of less-heralded contributions that revise received wisdom, extend previous work, and otherwise develop productive dialogues with other scholarship. (This belief underlies my work as editor of a journal and co-editor of a book series.)

1. Foundational work that has helped define the field and that remains part of our ongoing conversations. A few examples: Aristotle's *Poetics*, Shklovsky's *Theory of Prose*, Barthes' "Introduction to the Structural Analysis of Narratives," Bakhtin's "Discourse in the Novel," Booth's *Rhetoric of Fiction*; Genette's *Narrative Discourse*.

2. Work that opens up new areas of inquiry. Examples: Susan Lanser's and Robyn Warhol's work on feminist narratology; Martha Nussbaum's *Love's Knowledge* and Booth's *Company We Keep* with their turn toward ethics.

3. Work that taps into what we intuitively know but have not explicitly articulated: Prince's identification of the narratee; Genette's distinction between vision and voice; Rabinowitz's distinctions among the authorial, narrative, and actual audiences.

5. What are the most important open problems in the field and what are the prospects for success?

I'm bullish on the future of the field. Narrative theory has attracted and should continue to attract scholars with first-rate minds (but see point A below) in part because narrative itself is such a significant, varied, and challenging phenomenon. The Narrative Turn means that the field should continue to attract such thinkers. This confidence means that I believe my list of open problems is less important in its specifics than it is as an example to be put alongside others as a larger sign of the vitality of the field. My list starts with an institutional issue and then moves from general problems to more specific ones.

A. I'd like to see narrative theory more firmly established within the institution of the academy, especially in the United States. Its interdisciplinary nature should allow it to have many academic homes (in departments of literature, business, law, medicine, and so on) and even perhaps its own freestanding academic units. But the larger point is that narrative and narrative theory need to attain the status of, say, Victorian literature in the standard English Department: something that is part of the core of the unit (whatever the unit) rather than something that is seen as a nice extra. Furthermore, as narrative theory becomes more firmly established in the academy, it needs both to continue its emphasis on a diversity of approaches and of objects of study and to expand the demographic diversity of narrative theorists.

B. I'd like to see more work on the agreements and disagreements among different approaches to narrative. On the one hand, the proliferation of approaches—cognitive, feminist, unnatural, rhetorical, psychonarratological, postcolonial, and more—is a sign of the field's health, but, on the other hand, I worry that there's too much parallel play and not sufficient understanding of how the approaches relate to each other. Identifying what the approaches share and what the fundamental disagreement among them are will help clarify the state of inquiry and debate in the field as a whole.

In this connection, I am very grateful for Brian Richardson's initiating a project that is now coming to completion under the title of *Narrative Theory: Core Concepts and Critical Debates*. Brian invited David Herman representing the cognitive or, as David prefers, "mind-oriented" approach, Robyn Warhol representing feminist narratology, and Peter and me, representing rhetorical theory, to join him (as representative of unnatural or antimimetic narratology) in the conversation mentioned in the book's subtitle. That conversation has two parts: in the first we each demonstrate how our approach deals with the basic elements of narrative (authors, narrators, plot, time, etc.), and in the second we comment on each other's demonstrations. One measure of the project's eventual effectiveness will be whether it generates similar conversations among other narrative theorists.

C. I'd like to see more systematic work on the relations between the formal and the extraformal dimensions of narrative. Feminist narratology, with its emphasis on the interrelations among form, politics, and history (in a way that challenges traditional notions of form), provides one powerful example of such systematic study. It seems to me that feminist narratology could serve as a model—to build on, to revise, or to challenge—for other kinds of inquiry into the interrelations of the formal and the extraformal such as how and why narrative forms change, and what combination of experiences, contexts, and talents influences the formal innovations of individual narrative artists.

D. Within rhetorical theory, I'd like to see more attention not only to the previous three problems but also to relations between actual audiences and textually-inscribed audiences and, as my current project suggests, to the functions of character-character dialogue as narration. Both of these projects have the potential to blow up what I'm coming to regard as the increasingly misleading narrative communication diagram—misleading because it uses linear means to represent non-linear relationships (actual audiences can simultaneously retain their identities and join the narrative and authorial audiences) and because it contributes to the tendency to rigidify the story-discourse distinction (characters aren't part of the diagram because they're relegated to the story side of the dichotomy).

24
John Pier

Professor
Department of English, Université François-Rabelais

---

1. Why were you initially drawn to narratology or narrative theory?

My decision to take up narratology as a field of research was the result of an encounter—one partly of chance, but also by predisposition. Having studied English, philosophy and French as an undergraduate, I was not oriented toward any particular specialization; nor during the early years of graduate studies in French and comparative literature was it certain what line of research would ultimately define me as a scholar. It was during a year in the early 1970s at NYU in France that, enrolled in seminars taught by Roland Barthes and Gérard Genette, I discovered the exciting work going in on France at the time. It then so happened that, when I was searching for a dissertation topic, "Discours du récit: essai de méthode" (Genette 1972) had recently come out, and on discussing the matter with the author, I found myself not only a topic but with an advisor. What appealed to me in the structuralist approach to literary studies at the time was the project of developing a comprehensive system for the description and analysis of literary works, a possibility I found lacking in the New Criticism still prevailing in English-speaking countries, given to interpretations insufficiently grounded in textual and discursive criteria or that tended to resort to criteria and methodologies developed in an *ad hoc* or piecemeal fashion for individual works, but with little attention to a general theory of literary discourse.

My entire academic career has been in France teaching in the English Department, first at the University of Besançon and then at the University of Tours. A delegation from 2000 to 2002 at the Centre de Recherches sur les Arts et le Langage (CRAL) in Paris, a research unit founded in 1983 by Genette, Tzvetan Todorov, Claude Bremond, Christian Metz, Raymon Bellour and Louis Marin at the Centre National de Recherche Scientifique (CNRS) and having close ties with the École des Hautes Études en Sciences Sociales (EHESS), afforded me the opportunity, in November 2002, to co-organize (with the Comparative Literature Department at the University of Paris III and the Research Group in Narratology at the University of Hamburg) an international conference, "La métalepse, aujourd'hui" (see Pier and Schaeffer 2005 for the proceedings). This conference took place at a time when, some ten years after the "narrative turn" had taken root in English-speaking and in German-speaking countries, French researchers, for various reasons, had taken up pursuits that were often remote from narratology. In conjunction with various other factors, the conference served as a stimulus to reconsider narratology in light of the new paradigms and dimensions of inquiry cultivated by postclassical narratology. Thus in February 2003, a seminar entitled "La narratologie, aujourd'hui" (since renamed "Narratologies contemporaines") was inaugurated, the first such seminar at the CNRS-EHESS in more than ten years. Numerous French and foreign scholars have taken part in the seminar, contributing to a renewed interest in narratological themes and in their epistemological and transdisciplinary ramifications beyond literary narrative and beyond the strictly textual dimension of narrative focused on during the earlier phases of narratology (the seminar website can be visited at http://narratologie.ehess.fr).

2. What do you consider your most important contribution(s) to the field?

Whatever role I have been able to play in the remarkably diverse and innovative developments of recent narratological research cannot be dissociated from the scientific context described above. In addition, the inescapably international and increasingly interdisciplinary dimension of theoretically oriented narrative research has opened up perspectives and provided opportunities which are heartening for the future of narratology. Concretely speaking, this has resulted, firstly, in a fruitful collaboration with the Interdisciplinary Center for Narratology (ICN) at the University of Hamburg (website: http://www.icn.uni-hamburg.de) and in involvement in the recently created European Narratology Network (ENN), itself a manifestation of the rich exchanges now taking place among narratologically-minded researchers (website: http://www.narratology.net). From this vantage point, moreover, it has been possible to formulate themes of current narratological interest and to invite leading narratologists to contribute to a number of anthologies. *The Dynamics of Narrative Form* (Pier 2004b) includes studies that confront narrative forms and categories with their functioning in specific works, that expand and reconfigure these forms and categories beyond their preconceived theoretical contexts or that re-conceptualize and specify established categories in light of recent paradigms. *Métalepses* (Pier and Schaeffer 2005) takes a sustained look at what was long one of Genette's least debated theoretical innovations, seeking to determine the broad implications of metalepsis for narrative representation. *Théorie du récit* (Pier 2007), a collection of articles by the members of the ICN, presents German narrative theory to the French-reading public and also reflects the impact of French narratology in the German-speaking countries; the only book of its kind in French, it reveals a need for further research in comparative narratology. *Theorizing Narrativity* (Pier and García Landa 2008) includes studies that underscore one of the most pressing issues of narratology at a time when the scope and varieties of narrative taken into consideration and the criteria for describing, analyzing and interpreting narratives have expanded dramatically; among the questions raised are: Why is a narrative a narrative? What makes a narrative more or less narrative? What elements in a semiotic representation can be qualified as properly narrative? How is a narrative affected by its realization in various media? *Handbook of Narratology* (Hühn, Pier, Schmid and Schönert 2009) gathers together a body of 32 full-length articles, each devoted to a key concept or category of narratology and providing a concise definition, a systematic explication, a historical account and summary of differing positions and topics for further research. Now also available online as *the living handbook of narratology* (http://hup.sub.uni-hamburg.de/lhn/), this resource is open to the public for commentaries and will be periodically revised and re-edited for publication in book format. Finally, *Narratologies contemporaines* (Pier and Berthelot 2010), a collection of essays developed out of the seminar at the CNRS-EHESS, treats a variety of subjects, among them postclassical narratology, cognitive aspects of narrative, enunciative analysis of narrative, a genealogical study of *histoire* and *récit* in French narrative theory, narrativity in music, and it is intended to provide the French-reading public with insight into recent developments in narratological research.

My own research, carried on within this environment, can be described as an attempt to partially reformulate narratology along lines that incorporate certain concepts and principles drawn from

Peircean semiotics.[1] Still relatively undeveloped, although a fair number of narratological, semiotic and interdisciplinary studies lend support to this undertaking, such a semiotically informed narratology is characterized by a number of foundational considerations. To begin with, by adopting the triadic conception of the sign as opposed to the dyadic Saussurean model and its attendant battery of binarisms that have persisted in narratological discussions even beyond the demise of structuralism, such a narratology favors a signifying system based on inferential reasoning rather than on codes: under this system, both the referent and the interpretant, bracketed out of (post)structuralist theories, form an integral part of narrative signification. The ramifications of this orientation for existing narrative theories and its implications for future research are too numerous and far-reaching to take up in detail here. Among the principal consequences of the triadic conception of the sign is the fact that it opens the way toward a narratology rooted in text semiotics, the three dimensions of which—syntactics, semantics and pragmatics—offer a balanced approach to the process of semiosis. From this perspective, it can be seen that, for instance, the widely and uncritically adopted story/discourse pair, by restricting itself to a specific type of text, may well have something to gain from a general semiotic theory of text. Viewed dynamically as discourse (rather than as a text in which a message or an image is encoded), narrative is generated out of a dual movement: prospectively, as one progresses through a story by conjecture, anticipation, etc., and retrospectively, as one seeks to fill in gaps and causes after the fact, culminating with a configurational perception of complex relationships characteristic of narrative comprehension. Inextricably bound up with the process of communication, these operations are projected onto the backdrop of a semiotic "encyclopedia" composed of cognitive and intertextual frames, including prototypes (narrative, descriptive, argumentative, etc.), which are actualized to greater or lesser degrees in the reception process. This being the case, narrative is intrinsically intertextual (*pace* textual imminence). It is maintained in these publications, moreover, that intertextuality is one of the conditions of narrativity—the semiosis peculiar to narrative. Narrativity, however, is not a category or device of narrative such as focalization or free indirect speech but, rather, results from a pro-

---

[1] The following summary is based loosely on Pier (2003, 2004a, 2008, 2011a, 2011b).

cess that, like narrative configuration, emerges in the articulation between a theoretical framework and analysis of individual works, confirming once again the need for narratology to account for the intertextual. Another point of interest of a semiotic framework for narratology is that it relies on a signifying system which is not media-bound: Peirce's triadic conception of the sign is as valid for non-linguistic media as it is for linguistic media, and for this reason a narratology rooted in semiotics is both transmedial- and intermedial-friendly. It is also important to bear in mind that narratology conceived in these terms places narrative within a more general theory of discourse and thus avoids the risks of "narrative imperialism," i.e., the tendency (which has become widespread) to superimpose narrative paradigms onto signifying phenomena that may in fact be only marginally narrative or that exist in conjunction with other, non-narrative modes of signification. And finally, a semiotically informed narratology seems to offer an alternative to the hyphenated or double-entry postclassical narratologies in that it sees narrative in its innumerable manifestations as one—albeit pervasive and potent—form of social semiosis among others, thus coming within the purview of a broader semiotics of cultural representation.

3. What is the proper role of a narratology and narrative theory in relation to other academic disciplines?

Narratology is but one type of narrative theory and narrative theory one aspect of the amorphous field of narrative studies. Its status must thus be assessed in terms of its scientific program and its institutional role.

With regard to the former, it has long been debated whether narratology is a theory, a method, a group of methods or a discipline. However the case for one or the other might be argued or whether, as Jan Christoph Meister (2009) contends, narratology has evolved into a discipline that subsumes theory and method, it is worth bearing in mind that a substantial portion of the narratological issues debated even today originated long before or have been elaborated independently of the term coined by Todorov in 1969 to designate a "science of narrative." With its fluid, irregular history and its divergent and sometimes contested developments and claims, narratology seems nonetheless to set itself off from other theoretically-oriented approaches to narrative. This is due in no small measure to the fact that it seeks to frame its concepts, theories and methods by drawing on and positioning itself in relation to the social and human sciences (and much less so the natural or exact sciences that Todorov is often thought to be referring to). Such an enterprise is not without risks, of course, for it is not always the case that the narratologist is on the same wavelength as the linguist or the cognitive scientist—or vice versa. At the same time, narratology, like any scientific program, must define its own criteria of coherence and object of study. On this basis, Gerald Prince, contending that "[n]arratology is concerned (significantly if not exclusively) with the *differentia scientifica* of narrative, what in narrative is distinctive of narrative" (2003: 3), and acknowledging that this postulate, which focuses on the "core interests" of narratology, is open to elaboration both restrictively and expansively, has provided a broad and encouraging assessment of the field. Narratology, he argues, cannot and should not seek to cover each and every facet of narrative ("There is a lot more than narrative in narrative [...]"; ibid.); indeed, the role it plays is unique and crucial in that it specifies criteria, (re)draws boundaries, (re)defines domains and accounts for diversities and specificities.

Institutionally, narratology has made significant inroads as a discipline, as Meister (2009) has shown. Yet it seems unlikely that narratology will ever achieve the status of an academic discipline such as physics, law, history or Germanic languages and literatures. This, however, may be its very strength. Interdisciplinary by its origins, whether through the disciplines it allies itself with or by virtue of the conceptual and methodological criteria it endeavors to assimilate from other disciplines, the object of its study, as the "narrative turn" can only confirm, has become highly diversified. Narratology's disciplinary coherence can be validated and expanded only through the analysis and confrontation of a broad variety of corpuses drawn from all domains of social life, both synchronically and diachronically, and it can therefore best thrive in an environment of interdisciplinary exchange. Because the findings of narratological research are now working their way into other fields of study, it has been suggested that narratology has gained the status of master discipline (Fludernik 2005). However, this may be pushing the claims of narrative theory building too far. As was seen with structuralist narratology's attempt to adopt linguistics as a "pilot science" or as it may one day be seen with the role of the cognitive sciences in postclassical narratology, scientific disciplines are defined by criteria, goals and objects of study that do not easily translate into other disciplines. This being the case and given that, as stated by Roland Barthes (1966) nearly fifty years ago, narratives are numberless, international, transhistorical and transcultural, the unique role of narratology as a discipline is its potential to serve simultaneously as a meta-discipline.

And finally, at a time when universities and research institutes in many countries are undergoing the rigors of market-driven reforms and as curricula, particularly in the humanities, continue to feel the effects of an "interdisciplinarity" designed and implemented by government administrators and budget planners, narratology may emerge as a catalyst of innovative yet-to-come contours of teaching and research.

4. What do you consider the most important topics and/or contributions in narratology?

The contributions of narratology are numerous and varied, but perhaps its essential legacy is to have focused attention on narrative *qua* narrative. Although consensus as to what constitutes narrative *qua* narrative is and will remain relative at best, the fact that the question is raised is in itself an indispensable precondition to scientific debate, liberating inquiry from *ad hoc* methodologies and claims whose validity may not extend beyond limited insights into individual narratives, (sub)genres or corpuses or that remain restricted to specific domains (prose fiction, history, folktales, etc.). In this way, the implications of Propp's 31 functions for a general theory of narrative are not limited to a specific corpus of Russian folktales, while research on storytelling in everyday oral discourse has shed light on previously neglected aspects of prose fiction, etc. Paradoxically, then, at first sight at least, the question of narrative *qua* narrative, by encouraging scholars to work out a verifiable body of concepts and methods and to specify the theoretical framework within which they operate, opens the way to interdisciplinary narrative research and to the role narratology can play in a semiotics of cultural representation.

5. What are the most important open problems in this field and what are the prospects for progress?

Narratology's strengths also expose it to a number of risks. One is that, in pursuit of the coherence that befits any scientifically-oriented research, the narratologist may lose sight of the untheorizable elements of actual narratives, force recalcitrant features into a pre-determined mold or overlook or ignore an apparently insignificant detail that fails to meet the criteria of the adopted model. The perils of an autonomous narratology that cultivates theory for theory's sake or that strives to "model" narrative or narratives are best evidenced by the thorny problems encountered in the close analysis of literary narratives. And indeed, it is in the literary field that narratology places particular demands on discrimination and flexibility of method. At the opposite (though not unrelated) extreme is the risk of the "centrifugal force" of narratology, described by Jackson G. Barry (1990) as the questionable appropriation of narratology by the social sciences and philosophy, subverting their own epistemological and methodological claims, and that was to later spawn a proliferation of narratologies putting an emphasis on thematic and interpretive issues, but whose narratological rigor and pertinence are in many cases questionable (cf. Nünning 2003). These risks result, in part, from postclassical narratology's break with poetics and aesthetics (cf. Pier 2010).

The major lines of current research, which got its initial boost beginning with contextualist narratology in the early 1990s, are cognitive narratology (emphasis on how the mind recognizes and processes narratives in any medium) and transgeneric and trans-/intermedial narratology (analysis of narrative dimensions of poetry and drama; expansion of the field of study to include nonverbal or multimodal forms of narrative); however, research has recently also taken an interest in comparative narratology, engaging in a critical examination not only of its past but also of its local and national inflections, and perhaps modulating the *grand récit* of mainstream narratology (cf. Olson, 2011; Lavocat and Duprat 2010).

25
Gerald Prince

Professor of Romance Languages
University of Pennsylvania

Some Answers

Like many others, I started to do something akin to narratology before the term was coined by Tzvetan Todorov and before Roland Barthes's famous "Introduction to the Structural Analysis of Narrative." After a couple of years in graduate school, I had gotten bored with "hard" scholarly research like determining the publication date of this or that pamphlet by checking watermarks. I had grown equally tired of interpretation (more or less fun cocktail party talk). I preferred description, forms rather than meanings, general principles more than ad hoc results. My favorite book was *The Pooh Perplex*. But I wasn't quite liberated: I liked parties. Besides, I liked to joke and I enjoyed the French naturalists. I came up with a great thesis topic: "The Comic in Emile Zola." But I thought it wouldn't be very funny. I also enjoyed Sartre: *Nausea*, in particular, and his early critical essays. In one of them, he'd written: "A fictional technique always relates back to the novelist's metaphysics. The critic's task is to define the latter before evaluating the former." Since I understood his metaphysics ("Being is; non-Being is not"), I figured I'd study his technique.

I read a lot about narrative fiction and I liked a lot of what I read, especially *The Rhetoric of Fiction* (Booth 1961). I wasn't crazy about perhaps its most important contributions to narratology: the implied author and the unreliable narrator. Though the former helped to bracket biography and the latter helped to describe strategy, they both were too loosely drawn for my taste. But I admired Wayne Booth's style, his rehabilitation of the "author's voice," his chapter on "Types of Narration" (in spite of its conflations), and I relished these lines about "Brimgem young, bringem young, bringem young" and *Finnegans Wake*: "Will someone, by the way, someone who *has* read this unreadable work, tell me whether that first 'm' in the first 'brimgem' is a typographical error? You don't know? Or care? We are in trouble you and I."

After finishing my thesis and proving conclusively that Sartre's fictional technique related back to his metaphysics (I wouldn't have had it any other way), I continued to work on narrative and to read all about it. I loved the special number of *Communications* (no. 8) devoted to the structural analysis of narrative. No. 11, too, and no. 4, and more, much more. In particular, I relished Barthes's "Introduction," with its memorable beginning, its wonderful end, and its general model of narrative analysis. I would similarly feast on Barthes's *S/Z*. Though, in it, Barthes neglected the narrational code and though he dismissed the very attempt to describe narrative *langue* as an exhausting and silly enterprise, he developed various aspects of the "Introduction" (e.g. functional analysis) and provided numerous tips on description, characterization, thematization, and narrativity. There were many further delights: Tzvetan Todorov's serene ambition ("a science of narrative"), his "narrative quests" and "narrative men," and his view that, just as linguists try to characterize the grammar of language, narratologists should try to describe the grammar of narrative; Claude Bremond's firm and patient investigation of the logic of (narrative) action and his intricate typology of roles; Algirdas J. Greimas, because of his actantial model, his contracts, his tests, his transformations, and in spite of his tendency to find narrative everywhere except in narrative; Genette, of course, whose learned, supple, and sparkling studies of narration and focalization, narrative time, narrative motivation, narrative boundaries, provide countless narratological pleasures.

This was just the beginning. I reread Claude Lévi-Strauss (Mr. Structuralism). I carefully went through Vladimir Propp (the number of functions he isolated—thirty-one—smacked of reality effect). I discovered the Russian Formalists (fabulous). I learned about Müller and Lämmert, Friedemann and Hamburger, Kayser and Stanzel. There would be many other goodies, from Seymour Chatman's syntheses, Philippe Hamon on character or on description, and Marie-Laure Ryan on narrative semantics and on narrativity to Susan Lanser's feminist narratology and David Herman's postclassical ones. Some day I'll have to list them all.

The Rhetoric of Fiction had introduced me not only to the implied author but also to Walker Gibson's "mock reader," a textually implied figure similar to Booth's own "postulated reader" (the "reader's second self"). Barthes, too, in his "Introduction," and Todorov—like Genette a little later and Kayser (or Sartre!) a little earlier—had drawn attention to the signs of a reader's presence in narrative and to the narratively signified communication between narrator and audience. Inspired by them, by narrative analysts of all stripes, and by semiotics (which was still pretty big in literary circles) as well as by the realization that the figure symmetrical to the narrator had hardly been studied, I tried to correct this imbalance. I elaborated the narratee, whose specificity lies in the fact that it is constituted and signified by textual signs of the "you" narrated to, just as the narrator is constituted and signified by textual signs of the "I" narrating (See (Prince 1971, 1973, 1982).

The same interest in describing the nature and functioning of (various sets of) textual elements through which narratives take shape and make sense motivates much of the narratological work I have done: on the metanarrative dimension of narrative, for instance, on attributive discourse, or on the disnarrated. (On metanarrative signs, see (Prince 1977, 1980a, 1981a, and 1982: 115-28. On attributive discourse, see (Prince 1978, 1980b). As for my work on the disnarrated, it includes (Prince 1988, 1989).)

Metanarrative signs—which constitute one of the ways a narrative reads itself—are explicitly predicated on other signs viewed as elements in the codes framing the narrative in which they all appear. Attributive discourse, which serves as an element of theming and characterization, an inflector of point of view, a mark of textual self-awareness, an ingredient of textual legibility, comprises the signs accompanying the characters' speech acts and identifying the speakers, specifying the acts, and indicating various aspects of the latter's makeup or context. As for the disnarrated, whose functions are equally diverse, it consists of the signs that explicitly represent what did not happen (but could have) as opposed to what did happen.

If signs, along with European-flavored semiotics (or semiology) proved enticing, so did their configurations and so did American-grown linguistics (generative-transformational grammar). By combining a Proppian approach with concepts from traditional grammar, Todorov had tried to describe the syntax of actions in Boccaccio's *Decameron* and to lay systematic bases for narratology; but Chomsky too beckoned; and, as early as 1964, George Lakoff had rewritten Propp in generative-transformational terms. I found arguments about competence, intuition, or differences between Chimpsky and me stimulating. So I attempted to account grammatically for the infinitely large and diverse set of (all and only!) possible narratives rather than for only (specific subsets of) extant ones.(See, for example, Prince 1973a, 1980c, and 1982: 79-102. See also Prince 1993 and 2011). More than once. Though my grammars were not without weaknesses, which I'd rather not go into here, they did achieve a number of objectives: assigning a structural description to narratives, for example, describing the way complex ones can be taken to consist of simpler ones, or pointing to their hierarchical organization. They also encouraged me to investigate the properties making these narratives more or less immediately identifiable as such. In other words, they encouraged me to explore degrees of narrativity.(On narrativity, see Prince 1981b; 1982: 145-61; 1999 and 2008).

Grammars specifying the basic components of narratives (and, more particularly, of narrated worlds) as well as at least some of their interrelations were devised not only by literary theorists or budding narratologists but also by linguists, semioticians, and text grammarians, by folklorists, by computer scientists, by psychologists. They were used for studying such varied topics as regularities in folktales, compositional patterns in music, or memory and comprehension. Similarly, narratological inquiries not taking the shape of a (generative-transformational) grammar also—indeed, much more so—influenced domains far transcending the bounds of "literary or textual studies proper." In fact, they played a major role in bringing about the so-called narrative turn. By the middle of the 1970s, the very term "narrative" (or "story") begins to occupy a large number of (discursive) terrains and to replace the more triumphal "explanation," the more scientific "hypothesis" or "evidence," the more judgmental "ideology," the more authoritative "message." The category "narrative" repeatedly serves to characterize a multitude of activities and texts, from political maneuvers or business transactions to mathematical proofs, legal briefs, and L. L. Bean catalogues. Narrative becomes one of the most common hermeneutic grids of the times.

The narrative turn may have receded and narratology is not what it used to be. If it originally aimed to examine what all and only narratives have in common as well as what allows them to differ from one another and tried to characterize narrative competence, narratology is now often viewed as more or less equivalent to narrative studies. Nothing about narrative texts seems alien to it. Even more than in its "classical" phase, in its "post-classical" one it interacts with and is invigorated by other disciplines. It draws on literary, textual, and cultural studies, on historical and sociological (but fortunately not economic) knowledge, on cognitive science, and, of course, on biology. In addition to rhetorical, feminist, postmodern, or postcolonial narratology and to socionarratology, psychonarratology, cognitive narratology or historical narratology, there is now unnatural alongside natural narratology and there is an evolutionary narratology group on Facebook.

One might prefer, as I still do, to keep poetics and interpretation, narratological "theory" and narratological "criticism" separate, or to distinguish as much as possible between text and context, or to promote a relatively homogeneous set of disciplinary methods and terms. But one should remember, as I still do, that, throughout its history, narratology was methodologically diverse and borrowed terms from or shared them with biology (morphology), linguistics (signifier and signified, deep structure and surface structure), optics (focus and focalization), topology (homotopic or heterotopic), the visual arts (framing), game theory (moves), and sexology (climax). One should also acknowledge that context always informs text. Besides, one must admit that, by addressing many kinds of question, orienting its inquiries in diverse ways, adopting many different points of view to consider narratives, postclassical approaches discover and invent a variety of narrative elements, procedures, techniques, and forms (in areas ranging from voice, character, and temporality to narrative tension and metalepsis). It is even said that some of these approaches may save the humanities (at least in the U.S.A.).

Whether they do or not, they attest the vigor of narratology, the scope of its ambitions, the reach of its results. Cognitive narratology, for instance, not only exploits the cognitive sciences to illuminate various aspects of narrative and narrative understanding; it endeavors to show that narrative is a basic human instrument for making sense of things. In this, it calls to mind some of its forerunners, according to which the ultimate narratological goal is to characterize narrative competence—the ability to produce narratives and to process texts as narratives—that is, to deepen our comprehension of ourselves. Of course, this goal, like its relatives, requires the pursuit or completion of a number of tasks so as to answer such basic questions as: what would constitute the set of all and only possible narratives? what is understanding (or, more modestly perhaps, not understanding) a narrative? or what in a text (and its context) promotes its identification and processing as narrative?

One important task is to undertake experimental, cross-cultural, cross-media studies of the function and significance of (controversial or unproblematic) narratological claims and narrative traits in order to ground narratology empirically. Though I have not undertaken any myself (I wouldn't really know how), I have frequently lamented the relative paucity of such studies: we have too often been given to take locally attractive or persuasive arguments about narrative for globally true statements instead of examining what actually is the case. Another important task is to develop an explicit, complete, and empirically grounded model of narrative. The modeling drive in narratology has probably decreased (I know mine had, for a while). Yet the elaboration of such a model will strengthen the coherence of the discipline and facilitate the systematic exploration of its object. Finally—*ceci n'est pas une blague*—there is a (less important but no less fun) task I have set for myself: to compile a book of jokes about narrative and narratology.

26
Peter J. Rabinowitz

Professor of Compatative Literature
Hamilton College

---

1. Why were you initially drawn to narratology or narrative theory?

As a kid, I liked to know how systems fit together, how they worked; as a result, my favorite subjects were math and physics. Although I read voraciously on my own, I was put off by the routine of English classes—and I was more likely to lose sleep trying to figure out why my latest attempt to prove the four-color problem had fallen flat than I was to stay up late making sure that I had caught *all* the metaphors in Alfred Noyes's "The Highwayman." My conversion to narrative began in my senior year of high school, when my teacher Edward Ducharme showed me that literary study could be a lot more exciting—intellectually, ethically, and politically—than a mere tabulation of figures of speech. I was given another push when I got to college at the University of Chicago and realized that really *good* math students were so far ahead of me that I could barely understand what they were talking about. My literary interests became stronger and more focused the next year when Wayne Booth—fresh from the publication of *Rhetoric of Fiction*—showed up as a guest lecturer for a course I was taking in contemporary French novels. In just over an hour, Booth showed me that my interest in exploring the underlying structures of things could actually be productive in literary studies, too, without deadening the emotional impact of literature as so many high-school analyses had done. Booth remained a mentor, colleague, and friend for over forty years. I suppose, though, that it wasn't until after I met James Phelan that I began to think of myself primarily as a *narrative theorist*, as opposed to just someone who "did literature." Jim and I actually overlapped at Chicago, but it was only later that we got to know each other—and over the last quarter century or so, we've worked closely in a variety of contexts, including serving as co-editors of two books and of the *Theory and Interpretation of Narrative* series at Ohio

State University Press. Jim's long series of works—most recently, *Experiencing Fiction*—has significantly informed my own theory and practice.

2. What do you consider your most important contribution(s) to the field?

My most *enduring* work may well be my work as an editor, especially my work for the *Theory and Interpretation of Narrative* series, which has served as a lively forum for presentation of a wide variety of books with a wide variety of theoretical perspectives. I suspect, though, that the question is intended to get at the work I've written—and here, the answer, of course, depends on your definition of importance. My most widely cited work has probably been my work on audiences and on reading conventions; but there are times when I think that my work on music and narrative, while less familiar, is more provocative.

Audiences

To begin with audiences: Even as a young graduate student, I was struck by the multiple readerships implied in fiction—and by the multiple simultaneous roles we consequently need to take on as we experience those texts. "Truth in Fiction" developed that initial insight by distinguishing four levels of audience.

First, we have the *actual audience*, the flesh and blood people who pick up the text, and who have their own expectations, preferences, intellectual backgrounds, moral and political positions.

Authors can't know for sure just what qualities their actual audiences will have—but they can't make any rhetorical choices without making at least some assumptions about them. Authors thus write for what I call the *authorial audience*, a hypothetical set of readers with particular knowledge, particular values, particular expectations, etc. Thus, for instance, at one point in *The Big Sleep*, Chandler decides to add nuance to the characterizations and interactions of Philip Marlowe and Vivian Sternwood by giving them a brief and ironic exchange about Marcel Proust. In doing so, he banked on the assumption that his readers would know at least *something* about the French novelist. It's not only novels, though, that require this step. Even composing a text as simple as a family shopping list involves assumptions about the knowledge of who is reading it: I can write down "cottage cheese" only because I can assume that whoever ends up at the supermarket will know what brand and style of cottage cheese to buy. A given text may well have multiple authorial audiences. Many children's books are composed so that they will be simultaneously interesting, in different ways, to adults and children; works written under censorship are often aimed overtly at an "acceptable" audience and covertly at more anti-authoritarian readers. But whether the text is simple or complex, there's always a gap between actual and authorial audiences—as we know from hearing, on returning home from a shopping outing, such pained expressions as "Oh, I wanted *large curd* cottage cheese." Writers, in general, try to minimize that gap as much as possible, consistent with their purposes; one of the enduring battles among literary theorists is the degree to which readers of literary texts ought (either aesthetically or ethically) to try to join the authorial audience.

Fictional narratives, however, have narrators, implicit or explicit, single or multiple. A narrator, too, writes for a particular audience (which, like the authorial audience, may be multiple). I call this the *narrative audience*, an audience with beliefs, knowledge, and values that differ to a greater or lesser degree from those of the authorial audience. Generally speaking, the narrative audience accepts the "world of the text" as a real world. Thus, for instance, the narrative audience of Chekhov's story "The Lady with the Dog" believes that Anna and Gurov are "real people," even though the authorial audience knows they are invented; the narrative audience of *Mrs. Frisby and the Rats of NIMH* believes in talking rats. Different texts balance the authorial and narrative audiences in different ways: they may overlap to a greater or lesser extent (more on this later on), for instance, or we may be encouraged to emphasize one or the other. But whatever the balance, authors of fiction expect their readers to participate as both the authorial and narrative audiences at the same time. Thus, for instance, we are somehow failing as readers (strong words, there!) if we fail to sympathize with Anna and Gurov because they are invented constructs—but we are also failing if we get so caught up in the story that we try to track down the precise hotel room in which they first made love.

All fictional texts have at least these three audiences, some of which, as I've said, can be multiple. Ironic texts may also bring a fourth audience into play—the *ideal narrative audience*, the audience for which the narrator *wishes* he or she were writing, the audience that accepts uncritically the world as the narrator sees it. "Once a bitch always a bitch, what I say"—so Jason Compson launches his section of Faulkner's *The Sound and the Fury*. The ideal narrative audience shares the sentiment; the narrative audience believes that Jason exists, but doesn't share the sentiment; the authorial audience rejects the sentiment, too, but knows that Jason is an invented character and that Faulkner is rhetorically moving us in a particular direction through this ironic construction.

Two points should be emphasized here. First, this audience schema is purely pragmatic or heuristic: its purpose is not to show how fictional texts "are" in some essential way, but to offer one way of talking about them that is, under certain circumstances, useful. Many interpretive disputes—"Truth in Fiction" took off, for instance, from controversies about Nabokov's *Pale Fire*—can be profitably reframed by thinking more carefully about the relationship between the authorial and narrative audiences. This way of thinking is also useful as an entryway into certain theoretical debates, too. As I argue in "Shakespeare's Dolphin," the notion of the authorial audience provides a way to cut through some of the tangles surrounding questions about the degree to which authorial intention is a matter of private mental thoughts. Second, in a sense, fictionality is created by the reader. Texts can invite readers to read in a particular ways; they can be intended to be read in a particular way. But it is the reader who decides to read something *as fiction*. Fictionality, in other words, is not a formal quality in the way that iambic pentameter is.

Conventions

Much reader criticism has been rightly devoted to the experience of readers as they work their way through literary texts—but in a sense, much of the interpretive work involved in reading a text has been accomplished before the reader even picks up a book. That is, we approach a novel already armed with strategies for reading—strategies that, to a large extent, pre-shape the nature of the experience that we will have as we read. *Before Reading* was an attempt to clarify the nature of those strategies and to begin to talk about their consequences. The first half of the book charted out four classes of "rules of reading."

Whatever we were taught in school (especially those of us old enough to have been formed under the influence of the New Criticism), no one can pay equal attention to everything in a text, especially a narrative of some length. And no interpretation can account for everything. *Rules of notice* are conventional strategies that help us direct our attention. Some are called upon by a very broad set of texts (the rules that privilege beginnings and endings of texts, for instance); others apply more narrowly (in Robbe-

Grillet's *The Erasers*, apparently random lists and phrases like "or something of the kind" are signals of importance). But all of them serve to put textual details into some kind of hierarchy.

Once we've determined where to direct our attention, we need to figure out what to do with the details that we notice—and *rules of signification* help us do precisely that. These are the conventions that tell us, for instance, when to treat some textual detail as a metaphor (the conventions that tell us that the light at the end of Daisy's dock in *The Great Gatsby* is not simply a geographical marker), or when to treat it as a sign of some inner psychological state. Some rules of signification may well be the result of basic human cognitive architecture (Lisa Zunshine's work is especially instructive in this regard)—but good readers have learned many of their interpretive strategies from prior experience with books.

Reading narrative always involves the creation of appetites and expectations—and the effects of a narrative are profoundly dependent on their particular nature and the way in which they are resolved. Jane Austen's *Emma* has the effect it has only because we want and expect Emma and Mr. Knightley to get married; Faulkner's "A Rose for Emily" has the shock value that it has at least partly because we do *not* expect a revelation of necrophilia. Many of our expectations come from our "real life" experiences—but many come from literary experiences, too, through which we learn the *rules of configuration* that allow us to perceive emerging shapes and patterns and to make predictions about what will happen as the text moves along. From the beginning of *Bringing Up Baby* we know that Susan Vance and Doctor David Huxley will end up together. That's not because we live in a world where straight-laced paleontologists are usually united with zany members of the upper crust, but rather because our prior literary experience tells us that this is what is likely to happen *in this type of film* (that is, a screwball romantic comedy)—especially one starring Katharine Hepburn and Cary Grant.

Finally, once we have followed the route of the narrative (including its fulfillments and its non-fulfillments of our desires and expectations), we look back over the entire text and use *rules of coherence* to put it together in some coherent package, often by assigning general meanings (including thematic meanings).

As with the schema of audiences, this one is intended as a pragmatic tool—one of many that can be called in to help frame particular problems: theoretical, historical, interpretive. It's led me, for instance, to a reconceptualization of genre. I mentioned above, for instance, that we expect Susan and David to marry because they meet in a particular type of film; and this way of seeing narrative has provided a useful way of thinking about genres, not as particular textual forms, but as particular sets of reading activities that we are accustomed to performing *as a group*. In terms of history, this way of thinking about narrative has been useful in refining our understanding of canon formation, revealing in concrete fashion how texts that rely on less familiar interpretive strategies can be experienced as boring or inept. In terms of interpretation, it helps explain why readers—even readers trying to read "as the author intended"—so often miss the point. At the same time, recognition of the power of reader preconceptions shows some of the ways in which authors are hemmed in. In particular, I've written about what I've come to call "generic grip": since reading a text always involves reading it as an instance of a larger genre, authors who try to twist or resist generic patterns often find that their readers, accustomed to reading in a traditional way, fail to follow (see, for instance, Rabinowitz and Smith 1998, ch. 3)

Music and narrative

Parallel to my work on literature, I've been working on the application of narrative theory to music. The overlap between narrative and music, of course, is not virgin territory. On the contrary, over the past thirty years or so, Western musicologists have engaged in a spirited debate about the various ways in which music can be considered in narrative terms (see, for instance, McClary 1991). My own work has centered less on whether or not music "is" narrative than on the question of how techniques and concepts drawn from narrative theory might be useful in understanding musical meaning in the broad sense (including the attitudes it can convey and the ironies it can encode) and how they can illuminate the experience of listening. Thus, for instance, my analysis of the quotations in Shostakovich's Eighth Quartet suggests that rules of notice, signification, configuration, and coherence have their musical analogues, too, and that paying attention to them can help us understand Shostakovich's musical communication.

My earlier work, growing out of my interest in musical quotation in general and Charles Ives in particular, centered on what I call *fictional music*. Fictional music is music that imitates other music—specifically, some other performance of some other music. This category is similar to what is often called "diegetic music," but the conceptual framework is different, since thinking in terms of fiction puts the emphasis on the listener's choices (fictionality, as I've pointed out, is a way of perceiving, not a formal feature) and consequently on the listener's experience. There are a variety of conventions through which a composer can invite a listener to listen to music *as fiction*. Many of these are tied to textual elements (which explains why fictional music is found with so often in opera). But many—such as those involving quotation or apparently intentional ineptness—can work in the absence of words (which explains why composers like Ives and Mozart could produce untexted fictional instrumental music). But whether in opera or in absolute music, *listening to music as fictional*—like reading a text as fictional—puts us in a complex position where we're are engaging on several levels at once. Composers use that gap—that audience doubling—for a variety of rhetorical effects, not only taking positions but also encouraging us to share them. Thus, for instance, when we listen to Triquet's aria in *Eugene Onegin*, we are simultaneously hearing a piece composed by Tchaikovsky and "pretending" to be listening to a piece composed by Triquet for Tatyana's name day party; the music's humor emerges in the gap between those positions. Mahler, in his Sixth Symphony, uses fictionality to evoke the musical equivalent of our emotional response to tragedy (1981); Bizet, in *Carmen*, uses fictionality to reinforce his heroine's agency (1999); Kern, in *Show Boat*, uses fictionality to encourage particular attitudes toward sexuality (2004). But fictionality requires a particular perspective on the part of the listener.

My interest in musical fictionality has led me, in collaboration with composer Jay Reise, to chart a more general notion of musical rhetoric, starting out from the fundamental assumption that musical interpretation is not simply a matter of performance; the *listening* is intepretive, too. Specifically, listening is an active process that involves three separate strands. The technical strand consists of the actual notes on the page; the attributive stand consists of the conventional procedures—which involve such factors as harmonic conventions, conventional associations, and a repertoire of familiar music, among other things—for assigning meanings (in the broadest sense) to those notes; the synthetic consists of the application of particular attributive screens to the notes at hand. In other words, even at its most casual, listening is never unmediated interaction with sound; the sounds are always filtered through conventional ways of listening, parallel to the conventional ways of reading—conventional ways that often involve some kind of verbal component. Taking the attributive and synthetic seriously allows us to come to a better understanding, in particular, of why the "same" music has had such different effects in different historical and cultural environments.

3. What is the proper role of a narratology and narrative theory in relation to other academic disciplines?

My answers to the last three questions are going to appear evasive, since I'm a pragmatic pluralist. I'm pragmatic in the naïve, common-sense meaning of the term: to the extent that narrative theory is *useful* as people try to answer the questions that they themselves want to answer, fine; but to the extent that it serves to dictate the questions or distort the answers, then it ought to give way. I'm a pluralist in the common-sense meaning of the term, too: while not all perspectives are equal, there are more than enough valid perspectives to give us vertigo—and my interest in rhetorical narrative theory is a preference rather than an ideological commitment (which is not, of course, to suggest that it doesn't bring certain ideological implications along with it). That said, narrative is central to a wide range of human activities (from reading Tolstoy to explaining stock-market swerves to conducting internet dating); rhetoric is central to an even wider range of human activities. As a result, rhetorical narrative theory (the post-Chicago school with which I associate myself) is potentially valuable in a wide range of disciplines. (See, as but one example, the work of economist Deirdre McCloskey. Influenced by narrative theorists like Booth, one of her "staunch friends," she explores the ways in which the persuasion engaged in by science—economics in particular—can be analyzed using many of the same tools that rhetorical literary theorists use because, as she provocatively puts it, "Economics is literary" [xxi].) Ultimately, it's up to people in those disciplines to decide whether or not to make use of it.

4. What do you consider the most important topics and/or contributions in narratology?

Narrative theory—a more inclusive term than narratology—is an ever-changing field, in part because theorists consistently change their interests, in part because the kinds of books that people write and read change. Claims about importance are therefore always both extremely individual and historically variable—and looked at in retrospect, they're apt to seem quaint. That said, as a rhetorical narrative theorist, I'm personally most taken with work in a few neighboring fields that challenge the work that I do. The recent growth of interest in cognitive theory, represented by people like David Herman, Patrick Colm Hogan, Alan Palmer, and Lisa Zunshine, constantly forces me to think more clearly about the dividing line between universal cognitive processes and culturally determined conventions; the feminist narratology of theorists like Susan Lanser and Robyn Warhol forces me to think more clearly about the degree to which issues of race, gender, class, and sexuality inform even works that appear to ignore them; the work of Jan Alber, Henrik Skov Nielsen, and Brian Richardson on "unnatural narrative" and anti-mimetic fiction forces me to think more clearly about the degree to which my own theorizing is dependent on my preferences for a particular kind of mimetic narrative. Cause and effect are not easy to disentangle—and it's hard to know to what extent my intellectual interests stem from academic relationships, and to what extent I choose my academic friends according to my intellectual interests. In any case, I'm extremely fortunate to have been able to participate in a brain-sharpening joint project (*Core Concepts and Critical Debate*) with David Herman, Jim Phelan, Brian Richardson, and Robyn Warhol that, among other things, explores precisely these dividing lines.

5. What are the most important open problems in this field and what are the prospects for progress?

I don't believe that the progress-and-problems model suits literary study. Even if it did, prediction has never been my strong suit. Instead of being oracular, then, I'll be personal and reframe this as two questions: (1) What are the questions that most nag me in the way that the four-color problem nagged me as a teenager? (2) What's the most important area that we're currently tending to ignore?

(1) I remain fascinated by answered questions about fictionality. Despite excellent work by theorists like Richard Walsh, fiction remains a murky concept, in part because so many people use the term simply as a synonym for "crafted" or "emplotted." As a consequence, fictionality is often treated as a general quality shared by all narratives, and the line between fiction and non-fiction disappears. For me, however, that line is crucial. That doesn't mean (as it means for some of my colleagues, including Brian Richardson) that there's a sharp border between the "real world" and the fictional world within the text: I don't share Richardson's view that in fiction, "no description or event can be falsified by reference to nonfictional evidence" (Herman et al, *Practicing*). At the same time, of course, I don't believe that all descriptions and events can be tested in this way. So a key question emerges: how

do we know, as readers, *which* descriptions and events in particular can be tested by reference to nonfictional evidence? To put the question more broadly in terms of rhetorical narrative theory: how do we tell, *in any particular text*, what overlap there is between the authorial and narrative audiences? For instance, to what extent can we use our knowledge of how people operate in the real world to draw conclusions about fictional characters—conclusions for which there are no direct textual warrants? We've all been trained to believe that it's inappropriate to ask how many children Lady Macbeth had. But should we carry that prohibition over to questions about whether or not Hamlet and Ophelia had sex—or whether Octavian and Sophie are happy in their marriage after the curtain comes down on Strauss's opera *Der Rosenkavalier*? I don't believe that we can give an a priori answer that will work for all texts—but we don't yet have general rules that can help us determine the particular answers for particular texts.

(2) We need to do a better job of integrating our theorizing with the experiences of actual people—as, for instance, Janice Radway did in *Reading the Romance*. I'm particularly concerned about linking rhetorical narrative theory with the experiences of students, especially middle-school and high-school students. *Authorizing Readers*, which I wrote with Michael W. Smith, was an attempt to branch out to practical pedagogy—as was much of the work at the height of reader-response criticism. But that zeal, at least among literary theorists, seems to have diminished in the twenty-first century. It would be a major step forward if narrative theorists made a greater effort to communicate with high-school and even middle-school teachers.

27
Brian Richardson

Professor
English Department, University of Maryland

1. Why were you initially drawn to narratology or narrative theory?

I have always been interested in foundations. In high school, I began studying philosophy to get to the root of basic questions of ethics and metaphysics. When I started college, I slowly became fascinated by experimental literature. Soon, I was deep into the study of narrative theory in an attempt to get to basic components of narration, plot, and character. These were concepts I used every day and wanted to be able to define and comprehend, and then apply to the fascinating new literature that was being produced. It was an exciting time: I had just started getting interested in these issues as the following books were being published: Dorrit Cohn's *Transparent Minds*, Tzvetan Todorov's *The Poetics of Prose*, Roland Barthes' *Image-Music-Text*, Meir Sternberg's *Expositional Modes and Temporal Ordering in Fiction*, Seymour Chatman's *Story and Discourse*, the English translations of Wolfgang Iser's *The Act of Reading* and Gérard Genette's *Narrative Discourse*. The journal *Poetics Today* was just being established, there was an exceptional special issue on narrative in *Critical Inquiry*, and fascinating new studies were coming out of Paris each month. In the cafes in American college towns, young people were passionately debating temporality, voice, closure, and metafiction.

2. What do you consider your most important contributions to the field?

The most important contribution of my work is the identification of an entire area of literary narrative that has not been adequately theorized and the creation of alternative theoretical models to incorporate it. Virtually all types of narrative theory since Aristotle have a mimetic bias; most simply assume that a narrative is a story told by an individual about recognizable events involving human-like characters directed to a recognizable audience. The approach I have developed analyzes another category of narratives, what I call "antimimetic" or "unnatural" stories and offers theoretical formulations that attempt to do justice to this rich and exciting body of work. This approach eschews existing models derived from linguistics or logic and instead inductively works with the texts that innovative authors actually produce. Many others theorists, most notably Jan Alber and Henrik Skov Nielsen, have joined me in this project.

I am especially proud of my work in three areas. Concerning the first, narrators and narration, I have attempted to go beyond existing models of homo- and heterodiegetic or first-person, third-person, and figural narration to the new world of second-person, first-person plural, multiperson, and still more unusual forms of narration, exploring the range and functions of these extraordinary devices. I have tried to theorize the consequences of such unnatural modes of narration, showing where they defy existing models and moving to the point where we can transcend the idea of a unified, humanistic narrator altogether and explore narration after the "death" of the narrator.

My work on temporality discloses several significant unnatural forms of time that are impossible in the real world. It goes on to reconceptualize our concepts of fabula and sjuet in order to make them sufficiently flexible to incorporate narratives with infinite, dual, backwards, or contradictory chronologies. I have also worked to conceptualize the unnatural beginnings of authors like Beckett and Calvino and the many forms of outrageous endings. Of special interest are alternative forms of narrative progression; that is, how are events sequenced once the traditional forms of emplotment are transcended or even reversed, as in the case of what I have called "denarration." I identify allegorical, alphabetical, geometrical, and musical kinds of progression, as well as texts where events are generated by specific words or images.

In addition, I have also done related work on reader response theory, trying to expand its parameters to include multiple, divided, and antithetical readers. I'm especially interested in identifying the variety of multiple implied readers encoded in texts addressed to divergent or opposed audiences.

3. What is the proper role of a narratology and narrative theory in relation to other academic disciplines?

Narrative is increasingly being recognized as an important or foundational aspect of many disciplines, from history, philosophy, and anthropology to cognitive science, medicine, and theology. Because of this importance, it needs to be better known by those in other disciplines who necessarily draw on it, and those who do draw on it should be reasonably up to date and not relying on twenty-five or thirty year-old models.

4. What do you consider the most important topics and/or contributions in narratology?

It strikes me that the two most important topics in narrative theory, narration and plot, have been treated very differently. Since the 1920's, the related subjects of narrators, narration, and focalization have been widely discussed and continue to produce important new insights. On the other hand, the cluster of issues revolving around story, emplotment, narrative progression, and closure has received much less examination. And even here, we find asymmetries: much has been written about concepts of closure, while the study of narrative beginnings is still in its early stages. Theory of character has also lagged somewhat.

The more I continue to work in the field, the more I am impressed with the foundational insights of the Russian formalists, especially Viktor Shklovsky, the vision of Mikhail Bakhtin, and the system of Gérard Genette (and, to a somewhat lesser extent, that of Franz Stanzel). Unfortunately, much narrative theory continues to have a pronounced mimetic bias; this is particularly true of recent cognitive studies in narratology. A look back at Shklovsky, Tomashevsky, and Bakhtin is particularly pertinent now. Among more recent thinkers, the work of Peter Rabinowitz and Susan S. Lanser stands out as being especially penetrating, original, and enduring in addition to being rather undervalued. Feminist narrative theory, especially as developed by Lanser and Robyn Warhol, remains one of the most exciting developments of the last thirty-five years, and Marie-Laure Ryan's recent work on digital and electronic narratology is also extremely valuable.

5. What are the most important open problems in this field and what are the prospects for progress?

Since modern narrative began by focusing on a rather narrow range of European and North American works of fiction by authors from Fielding to the early Virginia Woolf, much territory remains understudied. Entire subfields are waiting to be included into a more comprehensive model of narrative. Postmodernism has many riches still to be explored and conceptualized. Minority and oppositional literatures would benefit tremendously from an analysis that employed unnatural narratology. This is especially true of African American, feminist, gay, and postcolonial narratives. Hyperfiction is another rich area just beginning to be theorized from this perspective. Classical Asian literature (especially that of India, China, and Japan) as well as Medieval European literature have many fascinating, nonrealist components that need to be studied and incorporated into a more comprehensive narratology. Drama needs to be studied much further as well. Applying unnatural narratology to folk, popular, and nonfictional narrative forms will also be a very rewarding endeavor.

28

Shlomith Rimmon-Kenan

Professor of English
The Hebrew University of Jerusalem

A Narratologist's Tale

"We cannot escape repeating", said the Israeli poet Avraham Shlonsky; "if we don't repeat others, we repeat ourselves" (my free translation). I am particularly aware of the latter danger in this interview-essay because in 2002 I wrote a new concluding chapter (entitled 'Towards') for my 1983 *Narrative Fiction*. That chapter was an attempt to account for changes in the discipline since my book first appeared, including modifications in my own views. As it happens, further changes have occurred in the eight years since then, and the five questions invite a re-thinking, so I console myself that, to the extent that this is a repetition, it is inhabited by difference (which is, incidentally, always the case as Borges' "Pierre Menard, Author of the *Quixote*" shows). Moreover, I have decided to focus this essay on my own itinerary, without eclipsing the larger framework, both because it seems to me a suitable mode for an interview and because, in my opinion, the objective/subjective is one of the axes on which changes in narratology have manifested themselves.

How to emplot these (retrospective) reflections? A dialectical, tripartite account seems appropriate to convey my experience of narratology as well as an aspect of its own trajectory. The dialectic I have in mind may be formulated as: development, crisis, re-emergence incorporating difference. Similar to this macro-structure, a micro-dialectic is thematized in my recent work on illness narratives, where it takes the form of: an assumption of continuity, disruption, continuity beyond disruption.

The Attraction of Narratology

I was originally drawn to narratology before it had a name (to the best of my knowledge, the name was given by Todorov in 1969). Ever since childhood, I loved reading stories and novels, and in my student-years I also became fascinated with conceptual questions concerning the specificity of narrative, or more precisely of literary narrative. I first studied Russian Formalism at the Hebrew University in a seminar conducted by Benjamin Hrushovski, who later founded what is now known as the "Tel-Aviv School of Poetics". As a Ph.D. student, I immersed myself in French Structuralism, with the help of a seminar taught by Frank Kermode at University College London. In both cases, I was attracted to the attempt to formulate a system of logically interrelated laws underlying the different manifestations of narrative. In other words, I was drawn to the endeavor to construct a theory. At the time, narratology was seen as a branch of poetics, both theoretical and descriptive, and as such, it carried connotations of 'objectivity', 'neutrality', even 'scientificity' (Todorov, 1969; Hrushovski, 1976) which also appealed to me. An amateurish exercise in retrospective self-analysis may explain my "rage for order" (Henry James's expression) and objectivity as the super-ego's attempt to control another aspect of myself that was spontaneous, impulsive, passionate and hence experienced as threatening. But this is as far as I allow a self-indulgent psychoanalysis by a non-expert to go public.

Development

The main influence on my work at the time was Genette's *Discours du récit* (1972; Eng. 1980). Genette's study brilliantly presents a system governing all literary narratives and shows its operation, including deviations from the system, in Proust's *A la recherche du temps perdu*. The most important contributions of this type of narratology, to my mind, are: 1) The distinction between the narrated events, abstracted from the story or novel and reconstructed in their chronological order, and their artistic organization in the text. This was the Russian Formalist distinction between *fabula* and *sjuet* (e.g. Tomashevsky 1965), the early French Structuralist differentiation between *histoire and discours* (Todorov 1966), and their Anglo-American rendering as 'story' vs. 'discourse' (Chatman 1978). Genette was the first to suggest a tripartite mapping: *'histoire'*, *'récit'*, *'narration'*, adding the act or process of production to the two"products". My own 'story', 'text', 'narration' (1983) as well as Bal's *'histoire'*, *'récit'*, *'texte narratif'* (1977) follow in his footsteps. 2) The study of temporal organization with its sub-categories: order, duration, frequency, and their sub-categories ('frequency' is Genette's original contribution, probably emerging from his engagement with Proust's work). Central to narratology's treatment of time is the assumption of its duality, i.e. an aspect of the distinction discussed in the previous item. 3) The distinction between narration and focalization, namely between the agent who sees (or through whose eyes the readers 'see', or experience the events), and the one who speaks or tells. This move dispels many of the confusions that characterized the earlier concept of 'point of view'. However, I believe that its general acceptance today invites a rethinking of the interrelations between the two activities. 4) The concept of narrative levels, enabling a systematic analysis of stories within stories as well as transgressions of their stratification, known as 'metalepses'. 5) The analysis of forms and degrees of the narrator's reliability or unreliability, the latter deriving mainly from limited knowledge, personal involvement, and problematic value-scheme. 6) The positioning of 'the implied author' as distinct from the real (biographical) author as well as from the narrator. Some saw the implied author as "the author's second self", others as a construct inferred and assembled by the reader from all the components of the text, representing its norms. Later developments sometimes led to an interrogation or modification of this concept, but we are not there yet.

One should not forget that there was another branch of narratology, interested not in the specificity of *literary* narrative but in that of narrative *tout court*, the latter conceived of as the succession of events that can be transposed from one medium to another (e.g. from the verbal to mime, dance, film, etc.). Theoreticians concerned with 'general narratology', as distinct from 'literary narratology' (Bal's distinction, 1977), often constructed 'story grammars' (Greimas, Bremond, early Barthes, Todorov), accounting for the ways in which an infinite number of stories can be generated from a relatively small number of "deep structures" and an equally small number of transformation rules.

My Early Contributions

My own contribution at this early period is threefold:

1) The Concept of Ambiguity, The Example of James (1977) defines 'ambiguity' as a conjunction of exclusive disjuncts, an operation classical logic does not recognize. It then defines 'narrative ambiguity' as a coexistence of mutually exclusive *fabulas* in one *sjuet*. At a more concrete level, narrative ambiguity manifests itself as the coexistence of two (or more) mutually exclusive gap-filling clues (and see Perry and Sternberg 1968). The second part of the book "appl[ies] the tools evolved in the theoretical part to four ambiguous works by Henry James" (p.76). I quote my own past formulation in order to emphasize the notion of an "application" of theory to literary works and—the other side of the coin—the use of literary works as examples which illustrate theoretical issues. This relationship between theory and literature will change at a later stage of my research, where theory will be derived from literature rather than applied to it.

2) *Narrative Fiction: Contemporary Poetics* (1983; with a new 'Afterword', 2002), often used as a textbook, systematizes, complements, and amends key approaches to narrative fiction, including New Criticism, formalism, structuralism, and phenomenology. However, it is not organized around 'schools' or individual theoreticians, but around issues such as events, time, focalization, characterization, narration, the text and its reading. The book does not offer a new narratological theory, but its integration of existing theories both implicitly and explicitly conveys my stand on the various issues. A broad range of literary examples illustrate the various aspects discussed.

3) Numerous essays on the manifestations of variegated narrative phenomena in specific works by Borges, Beckett, Brooke-Rose, Faulkner, James, Nabokov, Morrison.

Crisis

For me, the crisis came with deconstruction. For other theoreticians, it may have come with reader-oriented theories, feminism, more broadly—ideological critique, new historicism or cultural studies. And, of course, for some lucky scholars, there was no crisis. It is with glee that very early in the game Barthes rejects his own as well as his colleagues' structural analyses of narrative, celebrating plurality, writerliness, a play of multiple, undecidable networks of codes without closure (unfortunately, this literally dead author can no longer be asked whether his energetic glee covers up a less demonstrative crisis). *S/Z* (1970) is often considered a transition from structuralism to post-structuralism, although this 'post' is in fact simultaneous with the approach it wishes to supersede (as is Derrida's early deconstruction). Much later, and in retrospect, Herman (1999a, 1999b) formulates the felicitous distinction between classical and post-classical narratology, legitimizing a great variety of research activities under the umbrella of 'narratology'.

"Confessions of a Deconstructed Structuralist" is the title of a paper I read in a staff seminar at the Hebrew University but never published, a paper expressing (perhaps too dramatically from today's perspective) a deep distress caused by the interrogation of my "certain certainties". Deconstruction disarticulated the notion of science (or showed that it disarticulates itself) by pointing out contradictions and *aporias* which undermine the enterprise. It also challenged "the schematizing rationality devoted to intellectual mastery", celebrating, instead, the "expression" of the "experience of the failure of an attempt at mastery" (Hillis Miller 1980/81: 189). Objectivity and neutrality also came under skeptical critique, arguing that an element of subjectivity is necessarily implicated in every study, whether explicitly or implicitly, and an explicit statement of the theorist's position bespeaks greater integrity than its concealment behind the semblance of objectivity and neutrality. The critique of objectivity and its cognates undermines the narratological dream of pure description. Metalanguage was put in doubt, the possibility of distinguishing between the language of literature and language about literature pronounced as no longer tenable and all language seen as permeated by figurativity, indeterminacy, *aporias*. In many poststructuralist approaches, description has come to be conceived of as interpretation-bound and both activities have been said to depend on ideology, whether overtly or covertly. Perhaps most disturbing for narratology was the questioning of the very notion of '*differentia specifica*', stressing commonalities between discourses as well as the tendency they all share to subvert themselves. The presuppositions of narratology, and poetics in general, have thus been destabilized.

A quotation of the conclusion to my confessional unpublished paper may best convey my state of mind at the time:

> I often identify with the poignant lines you'll all remember from one of Shakespeare's best plays: "O, now forever/ Farewell the tranquil mind, farewell content! / [...] Othello's occupation's gone". Sometimes, in more sober or more indifferent moods, I console myself with Iago's answers: "Is't possible, my lord?", "Is't come to this?" And in rare moments of optimism I identify with the silent psychoanalyst who, at the end of *Portnoy's Complaint*, says to his patient: "So. [...] Now vee may perhaps to begin. Yes?"

Beyond Crisis, re-Emergence

To begin after a crisis was, for me, to continue, to integrate the doubt it entailed and re-think my positions, modify my approach, change direction. *A Glance beyond Doubt* (1996) is an attempt to reinstate representation and re-humanize subjectivity—not by returning to traditional humanist perspectives, but by incorporating the destabilization of these by deconstruction and other poststructuralist approaches and going beyond that destabilization. I suggest that it is the act or process of narration that both undermines representation and subjectivity and opens a way to a modified and qualified rehabilitation. Through a close analysis of five modern and postmodern novels, I show that the double-edged attitude to representation is dramatized mainly through a manipulation of narrative levels: their multiplication, analogies among them, and transgressions of the boundaries marking their separateness. The undermining cum rehabilitation of subjectivity takes the form of undecidability concerning the narrator's identity and structural position *vis-à-vis* the events narrated.

I have just said "through a close analysis of five modern and postmodern novels", and this marks another difference between *A Glance beyond Doubt* and my earlier books. The relation between theory and literature in my first two books was one of an application of a theoretical hypothesis to novels or—conversely—of a use of excerpts from novels to exemplify or corroborate a theoretical hypothesis. The third book, on the other hand, endeavors to theorize through literature, to use the novels as, in some sense, the source of theory.

The flourishing *interdisciplinarity* gave my research a new impetus. In many quarters, the concept of narrative has been transposed from narratology to historiography, psychoanalysis, anthropology, political science, legal studies, medicine. What I have in mind is not the study of 'story' and its grammar(s) that characterized one strand of early narratology, but a shift in the view of 'narrative' from something like "the narration of a succession of [fictional] events" (Rimmon-Kenan 1983) to a manner of perceiving, organizing, constructing meaning. When handled creatively, competently, and cautiously, interdisciplinarity enriches and interrogates both disciplines, although (or because?) it often involves a metaphoric transfer of concepts, terms, and methods from one to the other. It also encourages a defamiliarization of the "source discipline", now looked at from the perspective of another, thus inviting a re-thinking of the concept, term, or method within the discipline from which it was borrowed.

I have taught graduate seminars on "The concept of narrative in various disciplines", but have only published on the junctions with psychoanalysis and medicine. Leaving narrative medicine for a later stage in this essay, let me say something about my contribution to the interface between narratology and psychoanalysis. As a result of a year's seminar in the framework of the Center for Literary Studies of the Hebrew University, with participants from both psychoanalysis and literature, culminating in an international conference, I edited a collection of essays by eminent scholars in this interdisciplinary enterprise, *Discourse in Psychoanalysis and Literature* (1987). My own essay in that volume shows how important the encounter with psychoanalysis was for me in the period of crisis. I focus on the notion of 'repetition' in both repetition compulsion and transference, arguing that narration is a double-edged repetition. On the one hand, it repeats a story in the classical sense of reporting, representing, following through a line that is already there. On the other hand, it "performs", re-enacts, a story that is absent (at least to consciousness). Freud's view of repetition adds a further double-edgedness: As in the child's *fort/ da* game, it can serve the pleasure principle but it may also manifest a death instinct. The same seems to apply to narration-as-repetition: it may lead to a working through and an overcoming, but it may also imprison the narrative in a kind of textual neurosis, an issueless re-enactment of the events it both narrates and conceals. Such a detailed account of the main argument of this one essay may seem disproportionate, but its purpose is subordinate to the issue of crisis and re-emergence: I wish to show that the interdisciplinary dialogue between literature and psychoanalysis allowed me to grapple with something parallel to my attempt to incorporate the problematization of key notions in structuralism (and hence narratology) and go beyond it.

As a result of having become afflicted by a chronic neurological illness that affects my eyesight, I started exploring autobiographical narratives of serious illnesses. This exploration led me to a new interdisciplinary intersection, this time between psychology, sociology, anthropology, disability studies, the medical humanities or 'narrative medicine', their Columbia University variety (Charon 2006). While all these disciplines are concerned with illness narratives, they tend not to focus on their specifically *narrative* features. It is precisely here that my contribution to this interdisciplinary inquiry lies: The use of narratological concepts and tools to analyze first-person non-fictional illness autobiographies, while simultaneously investigating, sometimes problematizing, central notions in narratology and narrative theory through an exploration of a corpus that was not their initial basis. Interestingly, the dialectics structuring this interview-essay, as well as my academic trajectory as a whole, emerges as both a thematic concern and a structural principle in relation to time and identity in illness autobiographies. Our understanding of ourselves and the world begins with our reliance on the orderly functioning of our bodies (Becker 1999). Stories also rely on order, largely manifested in their handling of time and causality. In illness (and therefore in illness narratives) disruption becomes the rule, not the exception. What does this do to the assumption of order? In the light of this question, I re-think concepts like *fabula* and consider the possibility of defining narrative *via* contingency rather than order, or *via* an interplay between order and contingency (Rimmon-Kenan 2006). Just as disruption plays havoc with patients' sense of temporal order, so the rupture of continuity between past and present affects their sense of identity and hence also the structure of their narratives. I outline several ways in which illness narratives restructure the past so as to produce a new coherence between it and the present of the illness, and then interrogate both the concept of narrative identity and its dependence on continuity and coherence (Rimmon-Kenan 2002). One recurrent structure is: continuity—disruption—a new (though different) continuity. Although I argue—on ethical grounds—for the legitimization of patients' incapacity to cope with their predicament and its manifestation in fragmented narratives, my own work dramatizes continuity (*pace* my theoretical stance and my periods of inner collapse), if only in the very fact of going on with academic research. However, this post-disruption continuity embraces difference: in subject (closer to the bone) and in tone (much more personal than I could have dreamt of in the days of "this paper contends...").

The foregoing survey shows, I hope, that the personal in no way excludes general conceptual issues. Many of these involve an additional interdisciplinary junction that has become very popular these days, i.e. the intersection between narrative theory and ethics. This dimension is evident in my analysis of the social construction of illness (and patients' reactions to it), the interaction between doctors and patients, and the phenomenon of joint narration. In relation to the latter, I explore two questions: 1) whose life is it, anyway (an ethical question)? Is a person, here an ill person, the only owner of his/her life or does s/he have to let his/

her partner influence decisions, perhaps even appropriate his/her freedom? 2) Whose story is it, anyway (a narratological question with ethical implications)? To what extent can narration become an appropriation of the story of the other? How does this manifest itself structurally and stylistically? Is it possible to narrate the story of the other without turning it, in varying degrees, into self-narration? (Rimmon-Kenan 2005)

Not all contemporary narratologists are engaged in interdisciplinary work, and of those who are—not all are concerned with the junctions I have explored. Scholars adopt a variety of postclassical methods and perspectives, so that today we can speak of contextualist, marxist, feminist, postcolonial, "natural", postmodern, rhetorical, possible-worlds theoretical, cognitive, and computational narratologies. I imagine that the present volume will include representatives of most (if not all) of these.

This brings me to the last of the five questions: What are the most important open problems in this field and what are the prospects for progress? In principle, all the issues discussed in this essay are potentially open, since some theorist can always come along and disturb the consensus (to the extent that there is one) or suggest a new way of looking at an old problem. This is all to the good, emphasizing the status of narratology as an open-ended, ever changing process, rather than a series of problems with answers given once and for all.

The issues that I would be most interested in seeing developed are:

1) The relations between time and place/space

As is well known, classical narratology privileged time over space, considering space an element that is not specifically narrative, often relegating it to the status of background, setting, or "descriptive pause". In spite of earlier studies by seminal theorists like Bakhtin, Lotman, and Uspensky (who would not have called themselves narratologists), arguing for the generative role of space in literature and its inseparability from time, mainstream narratology has by and large focused on time. This position has recently been interrogated in postclassical narratology, resulting in a new exploration of the interaction between time and space and sometimes even in a reversal of the hierarchy between them (e.g. Herman 2000; Friedman 1993, 2005). As if to redress the balance, the October 2009 issue of *Narrative* returns to an emphasis on time. The focus here is not so much the organization of time, as in Genette, but its significance, and the perspective is clearly influenced by the current imperative to historicize. My own recent work has engaged with the time-space relationship (2009) and I am looking forward to further developments in this area.

2) Narrative medicine

Narrative medicine and its cousins (the medical humanities, literature-and-medicine) have become an integral part of the program of many medical schools and hospitals in the U.S and beyond. I believe that the attention it promotes in health care professionals to the stories of patients, as well as those of caregivers, has already contributed to making medical treatment more humane, empathic, and ethical, and will continue to do so as this new interdisciplinary enterprise expands. Narratology can make a conceptual contribution to these developments by providing theories and tools that can be (and are) translated into palpable influence in the world of medicine. It can also increase precision in the medical professions' borrowings from it, provide a greater awareness of the ramifications of the issues in the source discipline and yield a greater complexity of textual practices. But what lies in this encounter for narratology itself? This is where—as a narratologist—I expect further progress. As we read/ analyze more and more autobiographical illness narratives, we will encounter writings at the extremes of human experience. As a result, we will feel challenged to foreground aspects of narrative we have not sufficiently studied before. Such are, for example, the question of contingency as a governing principle; the centrality of space, brought home by the tendency of illness to confront the afflicted with a need to negotiate it and/ or accept its constriction; the tension between the resistance of embodied distress to language and its verbalization in narrative; the difficulty of narrating and reading about "repulsive" aspects of the body. Generic questions will also arise: Are there *differentia specifica* of illness narratives (in comparison, say, to trauma narratives)? Is "illness narratives" a genre? If so, is it defined only thematically, or can it be characterized by formal features, conventions, practices, or by a specific use of features, conventions, practices available to all narratives?

3) The limits of 'narrative'

In a sense, the present issue is a broadening of the foregoing questions from the case of 'illness narratives' to 'narrative' as such. With the plurality of approaches in postclassical narratology, the multiplicity of interdisciplinary junctions and the development of cultural studies, the term 'narrative' has become extremely widespread. This prevalence does yield new insights into phenomena we would not have previously considered from a narrative perspective, but it is also not free of risk. If everything is 'narrative', the concept may be emptied of any specific semantic content. In a discussion of technology-assisted narratives, an important as well as popular medium these days, H. Porter Abbot is impelled to ask the following question: "[...] when does something stop being narrative and start being something else?" (2005: 534). Similarly, I am tempted to query the notion of "life as narrative" or "storied lives", originating in constructivist approaches in the social sciences. Stories, one may wish to clarify, are not lived but told. In the last chapter of the 2002 edition of *Narrative Fiction*, I singled out 'narration' and 'dual temporality' as necessary characteristics of 'narrative'. Today, I would perhaps substitute "transmitting agency" for "narration" in order to be able to account for a complex of mediating factors, as in the cinema. In many cases, I would perhaps also prefer to speak about "narrative elements in X" instead of designating X a narrative, but I realize that this may be a somewhat evasive solution. My purpose at the closure of this interview-essay is not to provide solutions, but to invite a new generation of narratologists to re-think the object(s) of their discipline, as well as its methodologies, in a way that would preserve some kind of specificity within the sweeping "narrative turn".

28. Shlomith Rimmon-Kenan

29
Franz K. Stanzel

Professor Emeritus
Karl-Franzens-Universität

Narratology from Linnaean Taxonomy to Darwinian Evolution[1]

Darwin would not have been possible if he had not been preceded by Linnaeus, that is to say, if one had not already laid the theoretical and methodological bases permitting to describe and define the species which are subject to change. (Claude Lévi-Strauss)

It all started more than fifty years ago. The heated arguments for and against the 'legitimacy' of beginning a novel with an intrusive narrator saying things like "Eduard – so nennen wir einen reichen Baron im besten Mannesalter" (Goethe, *Wahlverwandtschaften*) profoundly irritated me. Retrospectively it appears that the question whether a narrator has the right to intrude into the story or not was more hotly debated in German criticism than in England and the United States. This state of things was perhaps my main motivation to plead for the recognition of several different narrative forms or styles. The history of the novel up to then demonstrated for me abundantly that in the mansion of fiction there are many rooms, some with a balcony from which the reader gets a breathtaking panoramic view not only of the scenery before him or her, but also glimpses of past and future events of the action. Other rooms offer more intimate vistas, of what happens in the house opposite or in the room next door, or even in the mind of one or several characters.

Some British and American critics long since had taken for granted that by definition narrative art requires a story and a story-

---

[1] This bio-bibliographical sketch is largely based on *Unterwegs. Erzähltheorie für Leser*, Göttingen, Vandenhoeck, 2002, which also reprints a selection of my articles on narrative studies. There, and in my main study of the novel, *Theorie des Romans*, Göttingen 1979, 8th Edition 2008 (*A Theory of Narrative*, CUP 1984) the reader will also find a more detailed bibliographical documentation than can be presented here.

teller and that the story-teller can assume different guises. But can he/she, as it were, refine himself/herself[2] out of existence for the eyes and ears of the reader? Followers of Henry James, Hemingway, Virginia Woolf and the early Joyce et al. would emphatically say, yes, he can. But admirers of Dickens, Balzac and followers of Wilhelm Raabe, Theodor Fontane, Thomas Mann et al. would reply, no, he cannot. This debate was additionally obfuscated by the terminological sloppiness which critics writing in English more often indulged in than the more philologically 'pedantic' critics writing in German. In the Fifties and even later, the terms 'author' and first-person narrator, as well as (authorial) narrator, were frequently used interchangeably, which had serious consequences for narrative criticism. Take for instance Joseph Warren Beach's, in those days, much quoted dictum: "Exit Author. In a bird's eye view of the English novel from Fielding to Ford, the one thing that will impress you more than any other is the disappearance of the author."[3] Echoes of this terminological confusion reverberate still in Wayne C. Booth's often reprinted, magisterial *Rhetoric of Fiction* (1961 ff).It is to the credit mostly of German critics like Wolfgang Kayser and others, that gradually this indiscriminate use of the terms author and (authorial) narrator was eliminated.

This clarification was perhaps helped in 1955 when, in a moment of Adamitic blissful innocence, I gave names to the different species of narrative animals. It was the birth of the three types of narrative situations, authorial, figural and first-person. That within a few years they became household words in German narrative criticism (their reception in English was delayed by circumstances which will be discussed later) shows that there was a wide demand for such a terminological distinction. In particular Kafka critics quickly adopted the term figural narrative situation. The general breakthrough of my concept of narrative situations on the critical front was achieved when in the late Fifties and the Sixties I joined the highly controversial debate over Käte Hamburger's *Die Logik der Dichtung* (1957, revised edition 1968, *The Logic of Literature* 1973). As a matter of fact it also had a profound effect on shaping my *Theorie des Erzählens*[4], as can be gathered from the many

---

[2] Future references to narrator etc. are to be understood as unspecific with regard to gender.

[3] Joseph Warren Beach, *The Twentieth Century Novel: Studies in Technique*, New York 1932, p.14.

[4] F.K.Stanzel, *Theorie des Erzählens*, Göttingen 1979, revised edition 1982, eighth reprint 2008, E-book forthcoming. *A Theory of Narrative*, Translation

references there to *Die Logik der Dichtung* and its critiques. The sentence with which Hamburger illustrated how, what she calle, the epic preterite can lose the meaning of pastness, "Morgen war Weihnachten/Tomorrow was Christmas" became the most often quoted sentence in the German narratological discussions of the Sixties and Seventies. It also became the classical paradigm for the much disputed "Erlebte Rede"/"Free Indirect Speech/Style". Dorrit Cohn, Roy Pascal and I can claim to have introduced the sentence into English and American discussions. Our efforts were not always met with success. At the end of a lecture I gave on Free Indirect Style, in which I quoted "Tomorrow was Christmas" as an example of FIS, my host, a native English speaker, rounded off the debate with "It's simply bad English". Dorrit Cohn was, as far as I am aware, the first American, and Roy Pascal the first British professor, to give the credit due to this seminal concept of narrative theory before French Structuralism began to dominate the debate.[5] Dorrit Cohn's very pertinent critique of my *Theory of Narrative* was extremely helpful for preparing the revised second edition of 1982.[6] Her critique also deserves mentioning because it discusses in detail the many parallels as well as some of the significant divergences between Gérard Genette's and my approach. The parallels are the more revealing since Genette and I had conceived our narrative systems entirely independently from one another[7].

After defining three types of narrative situation I consider the presentation of all possible narrative forms in the diagram of a typological circle to supplement or replace the prevailing diagrams of square boxes and stemmata for the visualizing of the narrative forms as perhaps my most significant contribution to the field of

---

by Charlotte Goedsche, Cambridge UP 1984.

[5] Dorrit Cohn, *Transparent Minds, Narrative Modes for Presenting Consciousness in Fiction*, Princeton, N.J., 1978, Roy Pascal, *The Dual Voice: Free Indirect speech and its functioning in the nineteenth century European novel*, Manchester 1977.

[6] Dorrit Cohn, "The encirclement of narrative. On Franz Stanzel's *Theorie des Erzählens*, Poetics Today 2, 1981, 157-82. Reprinted in F.K.Stanzel, *Unterwegs. Erzähltheorie für Leser*, Göttingen 202,365-390.

[7] Gérard Genette, *Narrative Discourse*, New York 1980 ("Discours du récit", *Figure III*, Paris 1972.) The wide international exchange of ideas in the field of narrative studies is indeed exceptional in the literary discipline. But there are also conspicuous omissions and delays, as Volker Schulz has painstakingly registered in his *A Structuralist-generative Model of Literary Narrative*, Frankfurt/M. 2005, 19ff.

narratology. The distinction of three types of narrative situations has helped to terminate the long lasting feud between the two narratological camps, the one insisting on the visible or audible presence of a personalized narrator and the other favouring the withdrawal of the narrator from the eyes or ears of the reader. Perhaps even more consequential in the long run, however, may have been be my insisting on a triadic system in place of the more commonly used dyadic one in imposing some kind of order on the variety of narrative forms. The triadic division between first-third PERSON, internal-external PERSPECTIVE and teller-reflector MODE, forms not only the structural basis for the three narrative situations, but also serves as the base for the three axes of the typological circle, which Genette once referred to - with tongue in cheek I suppose—as "rosace mirifique". The TRIAD offers, indeed, a decisive advantage over the dyadic square boxes and stemmata preferred by Doležel, Füger, Chatman, Genette et al. Its advantage is to be seen in the fact that it does not fix a particular novel or story in one definite classificatory box, but assigns it to a certain segment of the typological circle, thus occupying not only one spot but a whole sector of the formal continuum between two adjacent narrative situations. Not to fix a narrative text on a certain spot or in a box but rather to indicate the area within which the narrative situation in a story tends to shift or change suggests a certain analogy or affinity with Darwin's evolutionary concept of species, in contrast to the Linnaean taxonomy of boxes or stemmata.

I could justify my preference of circular presentation, suggesting continuity, gradual transition rather than strict categorization, by reference to Hemingway's "The Killers". Using the familiar boxes this story would have to be placed in a box labelled 'scenic presentation/dramatic dialogue/narrator withdrawn/ camera-eye'. Such a classification would indeed be correct for the main part of the story. It would, however, not take account of the significant shift from scenic-objective to figural perspective towards the end of the story, when the reader perceives the action exclusively from Nick Adams's point of view. On the typological circle, Hemingway's "The Killers" therefore appears halfway between the (third-person) scenic-dramatic and the figural sector. Such a diagrammatic definition of the text has particular heuristic value: It functions as a DISCOVERY TOOL, drawing the reader's attention to the significant shift towards the end of this highly dramatic story from objective/scenic to subjective/reflector-mode presentation. Hemingway's resorting to the reflector mode eases the reader's empathy with the main character Nick Adams, his confusion at being confronted with a kind of mysterious evil and his initiation into the stark reality of the world.

As the title of this article suggests the typological circle offers a chance once and for all to get rid of the approaches to visualizing the plurality of narrative forms by means of diagrams like boxes or stemmata which sooner or later must end as Linné in a taxonomic cul de sac.(Dolphin: fish or mammal? Etymology is more flexible than zoological taxonomy: Dolphin = porpoise/seahog, from lat. porcus+piscis). The design of the typological circle owes more to Darwin than Linné in two respects: The variant forms present themselves in their continuity, not even interrupted by the borderlines marking the predominance of one typical narrative situation from the other. In fact all boundaries on the circle are open. Narrative texts can be found at each boundary in which elements from both sides are combined.[8] The typological circle can, however, also be used to illustrate the historical of the novel

---

[8] Dorrit Cohn encountered an insurmountable "road block" at the boundary between third- and first person narration near the reflector pole of the circle. She had a point there as long as I used the Calypso-episode of *Ulysses* to demonstrate the unimpeded passage from third-to first person narration. In the revision of my Theory of Narrative for the second edition I substituted the Lestrygonians for the Calypso-episode which has removed the road block. See Dorrit Cohn, "The Encirclement of Narrative", *Poetics Today* 2.2 (1981), Reprinted in *Unterwegs*, 376-378.

29. Franz K. Stanzel

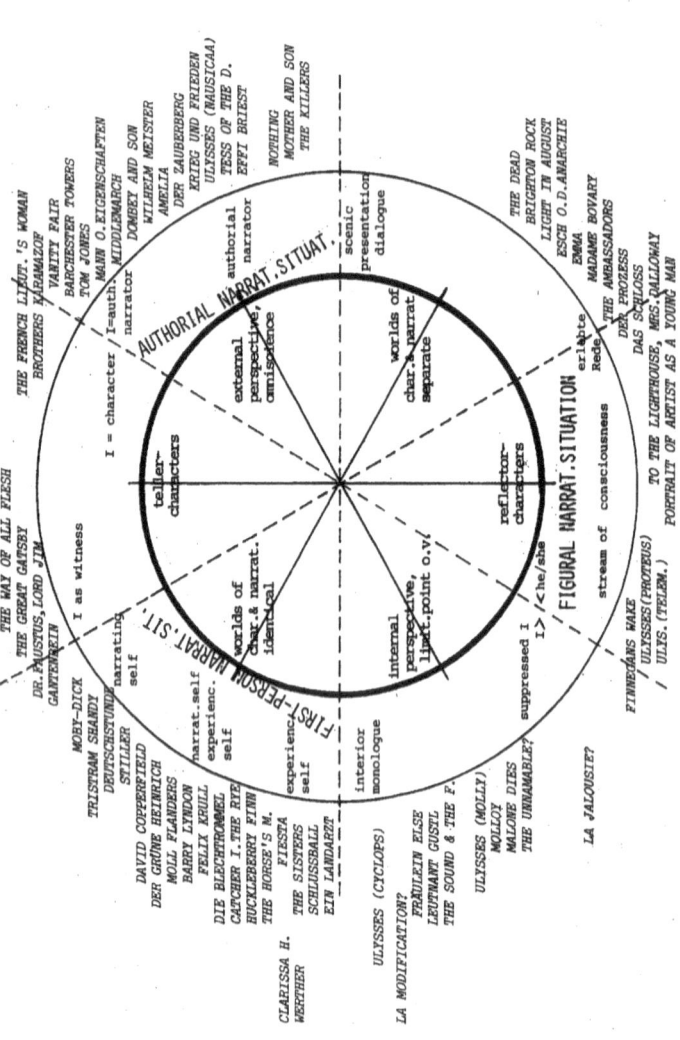

as an evolutionary process. During the 16/17 Century the circle would still be very sparsely populated. In the 18th century the first-person and the authorial narrative situation segments would gradually be filled. Only towards the end of the 19th Century the first novels would make their appearance around the reflector pole. In the 20th Century finally also the segments between the areas of the three main types of narrative situations are gradually being occupied by more experimental forms of narration. At the risk of laying myself open to the charge of succumbing to the mystique of circle and triad I would like to suggest that the typological circle looked at in that way reveals a certain analogy to Darwin's seminal concept of the "survival of the fittest". Why for instance, have those dinosaurs of the early novel like Roger Boyle's *Parthenissa,* and the even bulkier romances of La Calprenède and Mlle.de Scudéry left no traces behind and exist only as fossilized specimen on library shelves? They simply were not fit enough to compete with the much more sophisticated narrative structures of the novels of Defoe, Fielding, Sterne etc.

A Low Structuralist at Bay?[9]

In her review of my *Theory of Narrative in Times Literary Supplement* 1984, p.1508, Ann Jefferson writes: "In Stanzel's flexible world anything goes, since there is nothing normative about his categories, and adaptability and tolerance are the essence of his system". But then the reader is shown the other side of the coin: "But if this is good pedagogy, it does make for distinctly dull theory". This deserves quoting because it is symptomatic of a kind of critique, repeated by several other critics, the logic of which escapes me. How can a study of narrative be dull, that is to say uninspiring, and yet help the reader to new insights in understanding a story and the way in which it is told? W.C. Booth gives the same critique a slightly different twist. For him my *Narrative Situations in the Novel* as well as similar other studies, mostly of German provenience, pursue phantom problems of little relevance for the interpretation of novels. Such a phantom problem in his eyes, for instance, is our exaggerated emphasis on the difference between first-person and third-person narration: "Perhaps the most overworked distinction is that of person".[10] It took Booth more than

---

[9] Cf. "A Low Structuralist at Bay? Further Thoughts on *A Theory of Narrative*", in *Poetics Today* 11 (1990), pp.805-816 and reprinted in *Unterwegs*, 219-230.

[10] Wayne C. Booth, *Rhetoric of Fiction*, 1961, p.150 and „Distance and

twenty years and as many reprints of his *Rhetoric of Fiction* before he had second thoughts about this. In the "Afterword" to the second edition (1983) we read the laconic self-rebuttal of this pet idea of his: "Plain wrong", which is, however, not followed by a revision of the pertinent passages in his book.

It is true that German critics developed very early on a special interest in the narrative distinctness of first-person narration (K. Forstreuter, *Die deutsche Ich-Erzählung*, 1924), whereas English-American critics have always paid more attention to the "telling-showing" distinction (Percy Lubbock, following in the footsteps of Henry James, Norman Friedman et al.) Recently these 'national' differences have virtually disappeared. In 1973 K. Hamburger's *The Logic of Literature*, the in-depth treatment of the first/third person distinction, appeared in an English translation-perhaps this was the proverbial last straw to bring down the high and mighty disdain of PERSON in Booth's otherwise meritorious *Rhetoric of Fiction*.[11]

Critique and Further Development of the Concept 'Narrative Situation'

Let us begin with an important supplementation of the system of three basic narrative situations: Monika Fludernik's "Second Person Fiction: Narrative *You* As Addressee And/Or Protagonist" (Fludernik 1993b). In my *Theory* I mention you-narration only in passing. M. Fludernik's article supplies what could be considered a missing link in my system. Such a supplement is doubly welcome, because it also provides further evidence for the smooth transition from teller-mode to reflector-mode and vice versa. This aspect of transition receives a more detailed discussion in M. Fludernik's comprehensive study *The Fictions of Language and the Languages of Fiction* (1993a), which also presents a critical comparison with Ann Banfield's *Unspeakable Sentences*. (1992) Here Fludernik shows that "unspeakable sentences" can appear only in narrative texts presented in what in my terminology is called the reflector-mode.[12]

From the early days of conception and elaboration of my narrative theory, James Joyce's *Ulysses* turned out to be the most resistant, at the same time revealing text for the practical applic-

---

point of view", in: *Essays in Criticism*, 11 (1961), 60-79.

[11] See his "Afterword" to the second edition of *Rhetoric*, 1981

[12] M. Fludernik, *The Fictions of Language*, p. 64. See also Stanzel, *Unterwegs*, 102 ff.

ation and textual verification of my typology, because many of its episodes defy definition according to my original typology or require decisive modifications. I made a first, still somewhat rudimentary, attempt to take account of this in the final chapter of *Typische Erzählsituationen* in 1955. More to the point are those sections in chapter 6 (teller/reflector mode) of my *Theory of Narrative* which deal with Joyce's narrative innovations. The close analysis of passages from *Ulysses* produced the admittedly somewhat unwieldy term "Reflektorisierung", which in English became "figuralization". This concept served M. Fludernik as a starting point for further, quite provocative differentiations between reflector-characters who appear in person on the narrative stage and reflector-characters whom the reader perceives only as 'voice'.[13] For further comments on critiques concerning my *Theory of Narrative* see the articles reprinted in *Unterwegs. Erzähltheorie für Leser*, Teil I.

If Ann Jefferson meant it as a compliment "In Stanzel's flexible world anything goes" it was a somewhat backhanded one as was already pointed out.[14] It does, however, hint at the aspect of my narrative theory which can perhaps best explain its popularity on different educational levels from final year in grade-school to academic courses, introductions and seminars in narratology. It has been in demand now for almost fifty years as can be gathered by the sale of *Typische Formen des Romans*, first published in 1964, now in its 12th reprint, as well as *Theorie des Erzählens* (1979, 8th reprint 2008). Of its many translations, including a Japanese one, the English one had to be reprinted several times by Cambridge UP. I suppose that it was its very flexibility and openness, visualized in the diagram of the Typological Circle, combined with its handiness as a critical tool for imposing a first tentative classificatory order on the richness and variety of the textual material offered within the narrative genre, which can explain the wide reception of my typology by the interpretative community. And there are signs indicating that the latest reprints will not have to be remaindered in the near future. Thus prominent narratologists have devoted space to extensive critical discussions of my narrative theory in recent studies: Christoph Bode in *Der Roman. Eine Einführung* (Tübingen 2005), Volker Schulz, *A Structuralist-generative Model of Literary Narrative*, (Frank-

---

[13] See M. Fludernik, *Towards a 'Natural' Narratology*, 1996.
[14] *Times Literary Supplement,* Dec. 28 1984, 1508

furt/M. 2005); Monika Fludernik, *Einführung in die Erzähltheorie*, (Darmstadt 2006); Silke Lahn/Jan Christoph Meister, *Einführung in die Erzähltextanalyse*, (Stuttgart 2008); Monika Fludernik, *An Introduction to Narratology*, (Abingdon and New York 2009).

What Future Narratology?

No other branch of literary criticism and theory has developed with such rapid speed and opened up so many new fields of inquiry as narratology. I want to make no prognosis but it seems that further explorations will follow the currently very attractive methods characterized by prefixes like 'post-, inter- meta'-etc to their titles. Following the time-proven maxim to stray far from the 'madding crowd', I would like to suggest that one of the most pressing tasks for narrative studies lies in the field stretching from historiography, in particular historical biography, to fiction. The vexing question of what are facta and what are ficta, is posed most pointedly by biographical confessions of contemporaries, witnesses etc. of the ill-fated recent past, like Sebastian Haffner's *Defying Hitler*, (2000), Ralf Dahrendorf's *Über Grenzen. Lebenserinnerungen* (2002), Marcel Reich-Ranicki's *Mein Leben* (2003), Joachim Fest's *Ich Nicht. Erinnerungen an eine Kindheit* (2006), Günter Grass' *Peeling the Onion* (2007), and Imre Kertész, *Dossier K.* [File ‚K'] (2006). Of this plethora of life-stories produced by time-witnesses, the final two provoke their readers to compare the later autobiographical with the earlier fictional treatment of, for instance, one and the same episode: G. Grass in the novel *Dog Years* (1965) and I. Kertész in *Fateless* (1992).

In the years to come we shall have to take a closer look at the transformation of historical facts into fictional matter as is occurring in an ever increasing number of books published under the signum 'Novel' and in so-called documentary films. With our critical sense sharpened by the these handy tools of narrative theory without straying too far into the rarified air of post-, super-,meta-, trans-, inter- etc. projects could perhaps do to modern narrative studies what Addison wished to achieve with his *Spectator*-Essays: "to bring Philosophy out of Closets and Libraries, Schools and Colleges, to dwell in Clubs and Assemblies, at Tea Tables and in Coffee Houses." *(Spectator* No. 10).

30
Peter Stockwell

Professor of Literary Linguistics
University of Nottingham

---

1. Why were you initially drawn to narratology or narrative theory?

Fundamentally I am a stylistician: I inherit the millennia-old tradition of rhetoric and poetics that has been so badly ignored by literary scholars in the second half of the 20th century, but which is now re-emerging in a startling new form as a cognitive poetics. When I set out, the notion that the language of literary texts should be the primary focus of research was still regarded as anomalous. Intellectually at least, my entire career could be seen as an attempt to appear less anomalous by engaging in argument and discussion to persuade scholars in my field to recognise along with me that an interest in language form, feature and structure is central rather than peripheral to literary study.

My initial training was in stylistics, or 'literary linguistics', in the British tradition of pioneering scholars like Roger Fowler, Mick Short, Geoffrey Leech, Walter Nash, Ron Carter, Katie Wales and Henry Widdowson. Paul Simpson guided my doctoral studies at Liverpool University in the 1980s, at a time when literary linguistics was turning towards models from pragmatics and sociolinguistics—in fact my first academic post was as a lecturer in sociolinguistics, since lectureships in stylistics did not really exist then. This move from text-bound to contextual analysis began to draw social relations, communicativeness, and 'natural' narrative within the sphere of interest of literary stylisticians.

The prospect of being able to examine longer prose texts in a principled and systematic way led to an explosion of studies in narrative fiction, adapting work by earlier narratologists of literature from Vladimir Propp to Gérard Genette, and of course from the sociolinguistic work of William Labov on oral narratives. As part of the broad field of applied linguistics, stylistics also drew on emerging work in the education and acquisition of narrative competence, in which social psychology and social theory were equally important. The work at this time of Monika Fludernik, Peter Verdonk and Michael Toolan in their different ways represented for me the exciting possibilities of a literary linguistic approach to narrative fiction.

My own interests in literature featured science fictional texts, with the prototype of the genre being the magazine short story (see Stockwell 2000). Cast in a realist mode but constructing a fantastical, futuristic or alternate universe, science fiction is primarily a narrative genre that has the potential to test the limits of any narratological framework. Its primary trope is one of metaphorical projection, mapping the fictional scene with the reader's own state of knowledge and expectations, so it requires a narratology of both ontology and epistemology (Stockwell 2003). And since science fiction readers are generally not high-brow academics but wide-eyed seekers after wonder, the scholarly explorer of science fiction needs to be interested also in the emotional effects of action, pace, resolution, wild extrapolation, and enlightenment, through the defamiliarising essence of SF. For me then, science fiction was Literature, but more so, and if models for its analysis worked in the SF domain, they could surely work in what SF scholars slyly call all other 'mundane' fiction.

It is clear to me now that my continuing interest in narrative and its rigorous account derives from this formative collision of literariness, readerliness, communicativeness, and the three classical domains of information, emotion and socio-ideological positioning, as elaborated below.

2. What do you consider your most important contribution(s) to the field?

The 'cognitive turn' in language and literature scholarship over the last two decades has resulted in a wide-ranging reconstruction of what I like to see as the rational impulse in literary studies, and I am pleased and proud to have been a part of it (Stockwell 2002). My development of cognitive poetics as a major force within stylistics has narrative fiction at its core. Narratology has a longstanding tradition of rationality and the production of evidence, as opposed to the impressionism and untested intuition that has generally characterised literary criticism. The post-classical evolution of narratology has largely not fallen into the self-regarding obscurantism of other post-structuralist approaches, but has developed a strong methodology in cognitive narratology (Herman 2003). Very generally speaking, an American tradition is emerging in which insights into consciousness and mind at the global level are being applied to the processes and effects of literary reading. Meanwhile (again, very generally), the European flavour of the cognitive revolution has maintained its text-focused and stylistic sense. My own work in cognitive poetics reflects this continuing attachment to the stylistic texture of literary works.

It has been observed (by Louwerse and van Peer 2009) that cognitive poetics—in spite of its popularity amongst stylisticians—has drawn more on cognitive psychology than on cognitive linguistics. An emphasis on the text-readerly construction of fictional worlds, on conceptual framing, and on episodic tracking and scene-maintenance in cognitive poetics has certainly prioritised narrative texts. It is perhaps unsurprising that literary scholars even of a stylistic persuasion have been initially excited by the possibilities of generating analyses across large swathes of discourse, and it should be recognised that the influence of cognitive science in literary studies has occurred simultaneously with major innovations in computational methods to produce a powerful corpus stylistics—a discipline which also offers the possibility of whole-text analysis.

However, recently researchers in cognitive poetics—including myself—have been turning towards more central cognitive linguistic sources for application to literary reading. This has not entailed an abandonment of narrative in favour of lyric or meditative or contemplative poetic forms, but rather a recognition of the fractally narrativised nature of micro-level linguistic structures. In other words, matters of grammar are often modelled in cognitive linguistics as mini-narratives, with key notions such as participant role, prominence, perspective, action chain, force dynamics, summary and sequence, and construal (these terms developed or adapted by Langacker 2008) all serving to signal the narrativising paradigm that informs the framework.

For example, in some of my own recent work, I have tried to develop Langacker's Cognitive Grammar—one of several different cognitivist approaches to grammatical description—in order to effect a stylistically-sensitive and psychologically-grounded account of both lyric and narrative literary texts (see Stockwell 2009a). Most simply, CG models a clause as an action chain in which an element which is given some sort of attentional prominence is understood as moving—either physically or virtually—in relation to other, backgrounded material. All clauses in CG are basically teleological, drawing on the fundamental and universal human experience of the perception of motion. The prominent element (a 'trajector' in CG) describes a trajectory through a clause, with a readerly sense of pace or stasis being produced by the stylistic nature of the clause and the perspective in terms of which the reader generates a construal of the clause. In this sense, the sequences 'It was a bright cold day in April', 'a boot stamping on a human face forever' and 'he loved Big Brother', for example, can be understood to generate different foregrounds and backgrounds, different perspectives, different senses of pace, and different emotional effects. These are narrative in essence. Going beyond the current capacities of CG, the internal force dynamics of the clause can then be regarded as part of a chain operating across clauses, producing text and discourse. The ultimate aim here is a rich cognitive discourse grammar: it would be ideal but not essential if there were a stable, fractal structure between clause and discourse in the model, but in any case at the centre of the project is a continuity based around sequence, significance and viewing position that is essentially narratological.

3. What is the proper role of a narratology and narrative theory in relation to other academic disciplines?

Narrative is foundational to all human thinking and therefore all human inquiry. This is true not only in the grammatical sense set out above that narrative sequencing is a fractal feature of all language, but also in the more global sense that all representative thinking and expression involves perspective, sequential organisation and reception, and degrees of significance or "tellability". Canonical social and ideological paradigms are grand narratives; scientific theories, data and proofs are narrated representations of the otherwise ineffable material universe; arts and expression from the everyday to the institutional originate from narrators who are either prominent or pointedly obscured and deflected. Even the most determinedly non-narrative forms of meditation, or entrancement, or a moment of emotional impact, or a lyrical contemplation all require a narrative substrate that is the prototypical essence of human communication.

Of course, it is for practitioners in all the different disciplines to recognise the narratological fabric of their own enterprises. For those of us working with literary discourse, the significance of narratology and narrative theory is immediate and tangibly self-evident. Two decades ago (as I recorded in Stockwell 2008b), it was not outlandish for critical theorists to pronounce narratology dead, a victim of its own achievement in having successfully answered all of its original research questions, a discipline mined out and with nowhere to go. Instead, the field has been revivified, largely by a shift in emphasis towards communicativeness. Where earlier theorists could set their faces against discussion of intention or effect, modern narrative theorists are happy to engage with matters of authorial choice and readerly impact again. It is a move of course that coincides reflexively with the greater pragmatic and cognitive concerns mentioned above, but it also in my opinion begins to shift our academic and scholarly pursuit towards a contact with our non-academic fellows once again. The communicative concerns of modern narratology in the effects of plot and the nature of character and the social significance of what authors are trying to get across to readers are all the sorts of things that 'civilians' (i.e. non-academics) think about and discuss when they read literature. There is a democratisation impulse at the heart of much modern narratology that is to be welcomed and nurtured, while the discipline itself should maintain its principles and rigour.

4. What do you consider the most important topics and/or contributions in narratology?

The most important characteristic of narratology is its interdisciplinary confluence. It is this attribute that has generated the most valuable insights and innovations in the field. For example, the recognition that narrative is central to human experience could not have happened nor been explored without cross-disciplinary influences between discourse analysis, critical theory, sociolinguistics and anthropology. The reinvigoration of the field has happened because those accustomed to classical narratology were open to new ideas emerging from cognitive science and linguistics. Conversely, the powerful evolutionary arguments presented within cognitive science (Turner 1996, 2006, Lakoff and Johnson 1999, Johnson 2007) rely very heavily—though often without acknowledgement—on insights developed within narrative theory.

Of course, cross-disciplinarity brings its own problems. From the researcher's perspective, it is very difficult to keep abreast of the very latest developments across several fields simultaneously and to the same degree of detail. Inevitably, narratologists therefore lean towards one cross-discipline or another, as I lean towards linguistics. Furthermore, the insights that are regarded as most useful to be adapted tend to be those that are becoming paradigmatic, just behind but not on the cutting-edge of the source disciplines. There can be a virtue in this necessity, in that the resulting work in narratology has a more stable and more consensual foundation, but the impression that can be given to our colleagues working in the source disciplines is that narratology is adaptive rather than innovative.

There is a tendency, still, in narrative study to establish rules, norms and universals—a legacy of the field's highly successful structuralist past. While of course generalisation, abstraction, idealisation and the discovery of patterns and protocols in narrative text and reading processes are essential elements of narratology (as in every form of human inquiry), there is a particular need for narrative researchers to be aware of what Attridge (2004) calls the 'singularity' especially of literary works and the uniqueness of readers' experiences. This is particularly a risk requiring diligence in my own cognitive poetic analyses. Literary critics can easily point to the reductiveness of narratological theory, in which literary works are treated only as exemplars of a recurring pattern, or are forced into generic categories without regard to the ways in which different readers find different configurations of value in them.

The solution in this regard, for me, is to insist permanently on an account of text-drivenness in any narratological model. Analyses which are more interested in 'the mind' rather than the particular experience of a reading based on cognitivist principles risk appearing as poor imitations of disciplined cognitive psychology or as merely another loose critical theory (see Stockwell 2007). Empirical testing of readers either in lab conditions or in the wild (in the form of book groups or seminars) represent one form of validity, but close and principled stylistic analysis represents another equally valuable form.

Naturally, then, my favourite forms of analysis are those which combine a narratological account with a detailed stylistic sense. There are a number of frameworks where cognitive poetics and narratology overlap which allow for both the schematic global level and the micrological texture of reading, most convincingly 'text world theory' (Werth 1999, Gavins 2007). Drawing on other, prior worlds theories in both the philosophy of language and cognitive psychology, text world theory provides a means of tracking the ontological status of narrativised situations, including authorly and readerly roles, and character representation in a single principled fractally repeating structure. Crucially—and unlike other models of schematic mental projection—it retains a stylistic impulse at its heart. I have found the methods of TW theory most useful in trying to describe the emotional and aesthetic experiences of reading literature (Stockwell 2009a, 2009b, 2010b). Along the way, I am finding that my analytical sense of the reader is moving towards a cognitive psychological model of personality as plastic, provisional, contingent and soft-assembled for each narrative encountered.

Largely as a result of the narratological enterprise, we have developed quite a good account of meaningfulness across text and discourse. My own recent work has attempted to describe the aesthetics of texture, and I have come to realise that the third dimension of the classical rhetorical domain—ethics—is primed for systematic investigation (Stockwell 2010a). The basis of modern ethics in cognitive narratology lies not in precepts for moral action but in an applied linguistic account of the respective positioning of author, character and reader (Phelan 2005, 2007b). Crudely, ethics is the difference between what is and what should be, and both states-of-affairs are expressed narrationally and through alternativity. Narratology, especially informed by a worlds-based analysis, offers for me the best way of exploring this aspect of human experience.

5. What are the most important open problems in this field and what are the prospects for progress?

From my own perspective, the principled accounts of authorial choice and of readerly reception of narrative are the key to further advances in the field. In both cases, innovations here are dependent on further insights into the workings of the embodied mind and its expressions (see Stockwell 2008a). The narratological understanding of communicativeness has progressed far beyond the codification model of earlier periods, but we have yet to settle on a paradigmatic account of how an author and a reader models the intentions and effects of the other, and uses those impressions to build and recognise narratives.

Given that the cognitive revolution is touching most fields of inquiry, and given narratology's cross-disciplinary nature, the prospects for narrative research being super-charged by exciting progress in other fields is real and immediate. I am optimistic for its future.

31

Reuven Tsur

Professor Emeritus of Hebrew Literature
Tel Aviv University

Poetic Structures and Poetic Qualities

Why was I initially drawn to Cognitive Poetics?

When I was a nine-year-old boy, my sister and I were listening to Schubert's Forellenquintett on 78 rpm records. I asked my sister, four years older than me, why was it called "The Trout"? She answered with a strange smile indicating pleasure: "Don't you feel the Trout-quality of this music?" I felt I was excluded from a great secret known only to the grown-ups. (Only years later I discovered the real reason: that the quintette contained a series of variations on Schubert's Lied "The Trout"). Then I determined that I must fathom the secret of these mysterious qualities and experiences associated with works of music and poetry. When I became professionally involved in these questions I discovered that there *is* such a thing as "aesthetic qualities" to which one may refer by "aesthetic concepts" (cf. Sibley 1962). Consider the adjective "sad". When you say "My sister is sad", and "The music is sad", you use it in two different senses. In the first sentence you refer to some mental process of a person. In the second sentence you do not refer to a mental process of the sound sequence, nor to a mental process it arouses in you. One may be perfectly consistent when saying: "That sad piece of music inspired me with great happiness". You refer to a perceptual quality generated by the interaction of the particular melodic line, rhythm, harmony, minor scale, and timbre of the music. In other words, you report that you have detected some structural resemblance between the sound patterns and emotions. When you say "This poem is sad", you use the adjective in the second sense. In this sense "sad" becomes an *aesthetic quality* of the music or the poem.

As an undergraduate I was exposed to "New Criticism", and espoused its techniques to explore the verbal subtleties of poetry. These explorations were guided by my intuitions concerning those aesthetic qualities of poems. But then I realized that I needed an additional stage in my argument: to justify the attribution of those aesthetic qualities to precisely those verbal structures. This required to invoke psychological processes of the reader. Ehrenzweig (1965) claims in his seminal book that depth psychology may explain much about the contents of art; but to account for artistic form one needs Gestalt Psychology. Gestalt psychology is a branch of Cognitive Psychology; and I found other branches of Cognitive Psychology too very helpful in accounting for aesthetic qualities. That is how Cognitive Poetics came into being.

My early work was devoted to close readings of individual poems. Later I attempted to generalize my findings in various domains: interpretation, metaphor, rhyme, rhythm, expressive sound patterns, the critic's decision style, witty and emotional style, and so forth. But I did not dream of elaborating a coherent and comprehensive theory of poetics. It was Dr. Kees Michielsen of North Holland Publishers who suggested to me that I had reached a stage in my research into Cognitive Poetics in which I should at-tempt to integrate the various aspects of my work, not as a collection of essays, but into a coherent whole. That is how my book *Toward a Theory of Cognitive Poetics* was born.

Beardsley (1958: 465-469) expounded three general canons with reference to which one may justify evaluative statements: unity, complexity, and some intense human quality. Analytic criticism, such as New Criticism, Structuralism, Russian Formalism, have created very effective tools to account for unity and complexity. Cognitive Poetics, as I understand it, has contributed tools that may account in a principled manner for intense human qualities. Human language is conceptual and logical; my research has explored how does it sometimes convey such illogical and nonconceptual experiences as emotions or mystic insights. Some poems convey emotional or mystic contents; but some readers sometimes have an impression that a poem not only *tells* us that it contains emotional or mystic experience, but allows to perceive some emotional or mystic quality.

Cognitive Poetics as I understand it differs from Cognitive Poetics as the *Cognitive Linguists* understand it. The latter is meaning-oriented, the former gestalt-oriented. Regarding deixis, for instance, meaning-oriented Cognitive Poetics investigates point of view in a text, or the speaker's placement in his environment in time and space; whereas gestalt-oriented Cognitive Poetics explores such elusive perceptual qualities as atmospheres or supersensory presences felt to arise in a poem from, e.g., a combination of deixis and gestalt-free or thing-free qualities (see below).

The other day I had a very special experience. A student from an American university received a grant to come to Israel and discuss with me her projects in Cognitive Poetics. She was engaged in two different projects, trying to apply the principles of Cognitive Poetics to Biblical poetry, and to a piece of modern dance. We met for five consecutive days, three and a half hours each time. Of all the arts to which I have been exposed, I am least qualified to comment on dance. But it was pretty clear that her discussion was very much meaning-oriented. She had elaborated an ingenious system of gestures and symbolic meanings, but didn't know how to handle the more elusive emotional qualities. Even from my unprofessional comments she understood that I was missing in her discussion something that might be of great significance, but I didn't have the tools to make it clear to her what it was. So I decided to attack the problem from my own home ground, poetry. I presented her with certain problems in semantic structures and perceived emotional qualities. Then I extended this to problems regarding the sound dimension and performance of poetry, such as enjambment, where the syntax demands continuity, whereas the line ending demands discontinuity. Can we imagine or secure a vocal performance in which both the demands for continuity and discontinuity are satisfied? After a brief thought-experiment, I showed her my work in computer-aided analysis of actual vocal performances. After the fourth meeting she said that our dealings with the sound and vocal performance of poetry helped her to understand what it was I was missing in her discussion, and it has fundamentally changed her conception of dance analysis. Next morning she brought a rudimentary revision of her analysis which gave, indeed, ample evidence that she had understood and internalized what she found difficult to realize in our first meeting.

Her problem appeared to be this. In our everyday use of signs we tend to identify the signifier with the signified. In art, this relationship tends to be loosened to some degree or other. The most elementary step in this direction is to notice associations of certain signifiers (or patterns of signifiers) with certain types of signifieds. My student was stuck at this stage of critical functioning. In art, however, signifiers undergo sometimes patternings of great sophistication which may display certain aesthetic qualities which, in turn, may interact with the signifieds in a variety of ways. The mental ability required for following those more sophisticated processes involves an ability to dissociate the signifier from the signified to a greater degree. When my student realized that such a dissociation of the phonetic signifier from the semantic signified was possible, she couldn't help applying this newly acquired ability, with the necessary changes, to dance too.

Some of my Main Contributions to Cognitive Poetics

The Sound Effects of Poetry

One of my most important contributions to poetics concerns the handling of the aesthetic effects of the sound patterns of poetry (that is, of the phonetic signifier). Most critics and professors of literature agree that the sound patterns of poetry are of crucial importance in the total aesthetic effect, but poetic theory does not even have a vocabulary to refer to them, let alone properly handle them. Cognitive Poetics as *I* understand it accounts in a principled manner for sound effects, by having recourse to gestalt theory on the one hand and experiments in speech research and instrumental phonetics on the other—creating tools to account for what our ear tells our mind.

Speech sounds are transmitted by a stream of rich precategorial auditory information, which is immediately recoded into phonetic categories, and excluded from awareness. We only perceive a unitary, discrete phonetic category as [i] or [u]. Some of the precategorial auditory information, however, lingers on subliminally in active memory, and is available for certain cognitive tasks and aesthetic purposes. Such lingering auditory information normally serves to preserve verbal material in active memory for efficient processing. It is active, usually, in the background, unnoticed; but rhyme and alliteration may direct attention to it, turning it to aesthetic end in that it is perceived as musicality. This information may account for our intuition that, e.g., [i] is somehow higher and brighter than [u]; and that [s] can be perceived as imitating noises, whereas [l] is somehow perceived as musical, harmonious. Vowels are uniquely determined by concentrations of overtones called formants. The second formant of [i] is higher than that of [u]; that's why it is perceived as higher, even if uttered at the same fundamental pitch. The first two formants of [u] are nearer to one another than those of [i], and more difficult to discriminate; that is why [u] is perceived as darker, [s] consists of random noises, [l] of periodic tones; that's why the former is perceived as noise-like, the latter as more musical, harmonious.

The same speech sounds are sometimes perceived as reverberating in active memory, and sometimes as exhibiting some kind of "opacity", blocking the reverberation of overtones, sounding like compact units. This difference may be accounted for with reference to mental sets, speech research and gestalt theory. Consider Tennyson's notorious verse line "And murmuring of innumerable bees". It contains the sound cluster *mər* three times: twice in *murmuring*, and once in *innumerable*. One of its consonants is nasal, one liquid. *Innumerable* contains an additional liquid and nasal, [l] and [n]. Acoustically, both liquids and nasals are periodic (frequently perceived as "harmonious"). Periodic speech sounds are relatively "unencoded", that is, relatively much of their rich precategorial auditory information may reach awareness in certain circumstances. The meaning of *murmuring* may activate a mental set that directs attention to the rich precategorial auditory information reverberating in acoustic memory. Now, consider John Crowe Ransom's transcription of this line: "And murdering of innumerable beeves"—the reverberating acoustic information disappears. Ransom's transcription contains the sound cluster *mər* only twice; the rich precategorial information associated with it still could reverberate in acoustic memory, but it doesn't. The semantic component of the words *murdering* and *beeves* directs attention away from the reverberating precategorial information, to a unitary phonetic category, and does not activate the relevant features of the *mər* clusters. It is most illuminating to note that even [b] in "bees" and "beeves", and the sound sequence [bl] (in "innumerable") is perceived differently in the two phrases. [l] is a liquid, [b] a voiced stop. Liquids are voiced, continuous, and periodic. Stops are acoustically abrupt, and highly encoded (that is, little or no precategorial auditory information reaches awareness); voicing is periodic. The [b] is perceived in the "murdering" context as a unitary event. The "murmuring" context, by contrast, separates the periodic "voiced" feature in [b] and activates it, blending its voiced, periodic element with that of [l].

Experimental literature suggests three possibilities in the perception of successive speech stimuli. If a subsequent stimulus is very similar to the preceding stimulus, it may generate an enhanced response, because of integration with the lingering auditory information; if it is moderately similar, it will be reduced, inhibiting the lingering auditory information; if there is no similarity, it will be unaffected. In ordinary verbal communication usually one of the latter two possibilities is the case. The repetition of the sound cluster mur may, in some performance, activate and enhance their periodic feature, which, in turn, would be perceived as the imitation of the sounds bees make. One of my papers is called "Musicality in Verse and Phonological Universals". It took me months before I realized that all the sounds of "verse" are included in "universals", in the same order. The same sequence of sounds is usually uttered as shorter in a polysyllable than in a monosyllable; and the same sound sequence bears different pitch in the utterance. Thus, the two sound sequences are only moderately similar, therefore lateral inhibition seems to occur. If I want to *hear* the alliteration, I must assign the two sound sequences the same duration and the same pitch. As to gestalt theory, when versification organizes the sound patterns into strong gestalts, they exert "tight" control over the reverberation of overtones; the weaker the gestalts, the "looser" that control becomes, and the freer the reverberation and interaction of lingering overtones (this phenomenon has precedent in "color interaction" in visual perception, and overtone interaction in polyphonic music).

When the rhyming words do not occur in close succession, the interaction of acoustic features generates musical *fusion*; when they occur in close succession, it may result in acoustic con*fusion*, especially when the syntactic relation between the items is not unambiguous (Gerald Manley Hopkins systematically exploits the latter effect in his brilliant sound plays, as in *"dapple-dawn-drawn Falcon"*).

Convergent and Divergent Structures

Meaning-oriented Cognitive Poetics frequently explores iconic resemblances between form and content. This approach, however, allows the critic to handle only those instances in which the similarity between form and content exists, or else compels him to read the similarity into them. Cognitive Poetics as *I* understand it replaces this dichotomy by the materials-and-structures dichotomy proposed by Wellek and Warren (1956: 129). It regards both the contents and the formal elements of versification as aesthetically neutral *materials* that can be combined into aesthetic structures. According to this model, a wide range of elements (which are independent variables) may occur in any combination; consequently, a set of critical tools must be offered that may describe any unforeseen combination of elements in a poem. Unforeseen combinations may display unforeseen gestalt qualities, and cognitive poetics may systematically account for them. When we say "The poem is sad", we may refer *either* to the mere contents of the poem, *or* to an aesthetic quality arising from a configuration

of divergent structure, low energy level, slow motion, sad contents.
It is the structure of such an aesthetic whole that may resemble
the structure of a human emotion.

Contents, "projected world", word meanings, syntactic units,
metaphor, speech sounds, meter, rhyme, alliteration, are all materials. Structures are their various combinations. Poetic effects
arise from the subtle interaction of a great variety of materials.
The sequence of stressed and unstressed syllables may converge
with or diverge from the sequence of strong and weak metric positions; syntactic units may coincide with verse lines, or may run
on from one line to another; alliteration may work in conjunction with, or against, meter; and so forth. Briefly, they may act in
convergence reinforcing each other, yielding exceptionally strong
gestalts, sometimes with a pervasive witty quality as in Alexander Pope, sometimes suggesting simplified mastery of reality, as
in nursery rhymes. Or they may act in divergence blurring each
other, so as to yield an exceptionally weak gestalt with a pervasive emotional or subtle ironic quality as in Milton. "Hypnotic"
poetry typically involves exceptionally regular meter–stress mappings, end-stopped lines but unpredictable groupings of lines, alliterations that work both in conjunction with and against meter,
frequent repetition of key phrases, high energy level, the irruption
of the irrational in the world stratum, as in "Kubla Khan".

On the world stratum, focusing on objects that have stable characteristic visual shapes may reinforce the effects arising from the
strong gestalts of convergent structures. Focusing on the *spatial
relationships* between the objects or on abstract nouns in a landscape defined here and now may enhance the emotional qualities
arising from the divergent structures. Abstract nouns in generalized settings tend to be perceived as compact concepts. Consider
the following two quotes from Wordsworth: "For all good poetry
is the spontaneous overflow of powerful feelings", and "O listen!
for the Vale profound / Is overflowing with the sound". In both
quotes *overflow* occurs in a metaphorical construction with an
abstract noun. The former phrase, however, is perceived as expressing compact concepts, even though it contains the phrase
"powerful feelings"; whereas the latter as expressing some diffuse,
engulfing percepts generating a "powerful feeling". One may account for this difference with reference to two principles: (1) the
different mental sets demanded by the expository prose and the
lyric poem; (2) the generalized setting of "spontaneous overflow of
powerful feeling" suggested by "*all* good poetry" and the absence

of particular circumstances, as opposed to the concrete setting of "overflowing with the sound" suggested by the particular circumstances, and the strong deictic element in the imperative verb.

Poetic Rhythm

Some of my most original contributions to Cognitive Poetics are in the domain of poetic rhythm. In a recent controversy I was accused of prescribing in some of my work "a set of criteria for the 'best' performance of poetry read aloud by actors". This is a gross misrepresentation of my position. Stricter prescriptive norms prevail in metrics than in any other area of literary research. Far from pursuing a prescriptive agenda, the distinctive feature of my work in prosody is, precisely, an all-out opposition to those strict prescriptive norms. I argue that some of the most musical poets, like Milton and Shelley (but Shakespeare too) consistently violated all the criteria for metricalness hitherto proposed. The existence of such lines, however, cannot refute the normative theories in metrics, precisely because the verse lines that contain those violations are "unmetrical". Rather, proponents of those theories claim that one of the virtues of their respective theory is that it can distinguish between a metrical and an unmetrical line. Thus the traditional theories as well as the generative theories are irrefutable. I claim (with Wittgenstein, 1968) that we draw a boundary for a special purpose. I translated the normative conceptions into descriptive terms: in departures from the paradigmatic line, scales of difficulty, or of "unnaturalness" can be constructed, on which various poets and theorists may draw the utmost boundary of metricalness at different points. Instead of relying on authoritative rules, according to which a stress maximum in a weak position or a polysyllable with its stressed syllable in a weak position render the line unmetrical, I define the boundary in terms of its purpose: to mark the utmost limit of the performer's willingness or ability to perform the verse line rhythmically. I have given a descriptive definition to "rhythmical performance": one in which the conflicting patterns of language and versification can be perceived at the same time. This limit varies with the performer's cognitive and vocal skills, as well as aesthetic conception. If the performer of a line with a stress maximum in a weak position cannot render its patterns of language and versification perceptible at the same time, it falls apart; if he succeeds, exceptionally high tension is generated.

In my 2007 paper I write among other things: "As to the first six lines of Paradise Lost, the issue at stake is not which one of the many possible performances is the right one, but whether we can secure a performance that may convey its fluid structure". Later on I write: "There are one thousand ways to perform such a line. Opting for the performance suggested here is not meant to disqualify the other nine-hundred-ninety-nine readings. It merely insists that there should be at least one reading that conforms with the foregoing 'divergent', 'suspensive', 'fluid', construal of the passage".

Owing to recent software developments, I can "doctor" now recorded readings manipulating the rhythmic solutions they offer; and that's what I am doing in some of my recent publications. It is an empirical way to probe into the question whether a performance can be imagined or secured that allows to perceive the conflicting linguistic and versification patterns at the same time. There are almost insurmountable difficulties in eliciting rhythmicality judgments. But such a doctored performance, not as an imagined performance, can be put—in principle, at least—to empirical test. One could submit a genuine and a doctored version of a line to flesh-and-blood listeners and ask them judge whether any one of them does offer a solution to the conflict of language and versification.

Briefly, nobody knows what rules govern English metre from Chaucer to Yeats, but all agree that they yield admirable results. All the rules proposed by traditional metrists were blatantly violated by the greatest English poets. In my 1977 book I worked out a theory with a radically different conception, including a theory of rhythmical performance. In my 1998 book I provided empirical support to that theory of performance.

Decision Style

When critics speak of the affective fallacy, they focus on what the text does to readers; what attitudes or emotions it succeeds or fails to arouse in them. Cognitive Poetics too focuses on the text–reader relationship, but asks what the reader does to the text; how he makes sense of it, how he derives an aesthetic (or intense human) quality from the poetic structure. Norman Holland speaks of a reader-active and a text-active approach. An extreme text-active approach falls back upon the reader whose response is determined by the text. This is obviously false. On the other hand, an extreme reader-active approach ends up with the assumption that anything goes. This is obviously as untenable as the opposite position. I have adopted an *interactive* conception of the process: the reader's (I mean the *real* reader's) activity is constrained by his cognitive style on the one hand, and, on the other, by the text and prevailing aesthetic norms. Participants of the two symposia in 1948–1950 (Bruner and Kretch1968; Blake and Ramsey 1951) integrated two fields in which research began independently: "perception" and "personality". They established that one's perceptions are crucially influenced by one's personality and information-processing style. In a paper devoted to the critic's possible decision styles (Tsur 1975, [reprinted in Tsur 2008: 511–529]; see also Tsur 2006: 11–77, 115–141), I have elaborated on two critical attitudes. They can be defined relative to each other as ranking higher or lower on a scale, one end of which may be marked as what Keats called *negative capability*, the other as *positivism* or *factualism* or *quest for certitude*. One end of the spectrum may be characterized, then, by Keats's description of the quality "which Shakespeare possessed so enormously—I mean *Negative Capability*, that is when man is capable of being in uncertainties, Mysteries, doubts, without any irritable reaching after fact and reason"; the other end by the lack of it. This dichotomy, of *Negative Capability* and *Quest for Certitude*, based on "literary" formulations in Keats's letters, is astonishingly similar to dichotomies formulated by psychologists about 80-100 years later, such as: liberal vs. authoritarian personality; open vs. closed mind; flexibility vs. rigidity; tolerance vs. intolerance of ambiguity; abstract vs. concrete personality; "leveler" vs. "sharpener", and so forth.

Now consider the following description of just one of these dichotomies: "The leveler is more anxious to categorize sensations and less willing to give up a category once he has established it. Red is red, and there's an end on't. He levels (suppresses) differences and emphasizes similarities in the interest of perceptual stability. For him the unique, unclassifiable sensation is particularly offensive, while the sharpener at least tolerates such anomalies, and may actually seek out ambiguity and variability of classification" (Ohmann, 1970: 231). It suggests that levelers, or people intolerant of ambiguity or, simply, who lack negative capability would be less receptive to elusive aesthetic qualities or diffuse precategorial semantic and auditory information discussed above, and will tend to produce a kind of criticism that avoids them. That is what I call "the implied critic's decision style".

To sum up. In a top-down perspective, I have explored how language—that is conceptual and logical by nature—may generate poetic qualities that are nonconceptual and illogical. In a bottom-up perspective, I have explored how poetic structures may induce the cognitive system to perceive diffuse precategorial percepts behind unitary phonetic and semantic categories; how structures at the sound stratum, units of meaning stratum and the world stratum of a poem may act in convergence or divergence, giving rise to a wide variety of aesthetic qualities. The qualities perceived in those interacting structures crucially depend on the readers' individual modes of perception. Poetic structure does not determine uniformly the readers' response; but this does not mean that anything goes. I invoked research on perception-and-personality to account in a principled manner for the contribution of the readers' cognitive style to the resulting effect.

Richard Walsh

Senior Lecturer
Department of English and Related Literature, University of York

Ruminations in response to five questions

What makes a narrative theorist? My own training has been literary, but I have always had a rather scientific turn of mind, and it would be possible to give an account of my interest in narrative theory as a personal renegotiation of the "two cultures" debate inaugurated by C. P. Snow just over fifty years ago. I suspect that many narratologists could say the same, though in most cases this intellectual temperament manifests itself in a desire to ground the study of narrative in a scientific methodology; its symptoms include a rage for typology and an inflated sense of the explanatory power of diagrams (I sometimes think you cannot be said to have truly arrived as a narratologist until your name is attached to some eminently reproducible diagrammatic figure, and I've played around with a few myself; the playfulness has always been to the fore, though, and my susceptibility to the solace of diagrams is tempered by an awareness that they usually conceal and distort as much as they clarify). Most fundamentally, of course, the scientific aspirations of narratology are those of the structuralist tradition to which it owes so much; to conceive of the system of narrative as an object of scientific inquiry, and the interpretation of specific narratives as a secondary application of the conceptual toolbox that results. This methodology was originally modelled upon the structuralist pilot-science of linguistics, but as structuralism fell out of favour the narratological response was often to look for firmer foundations elsewhere—cognitive science now being the discipline of choice. While I share aspects of this predisposition, my own journey has been somewhat different, and I see the relation between narrative and science in terms both more reciprocal and more irreducibly antithetical than the mainstream view would have it. But in fact the question of science itself has been mostly subterranean in my work until quite recently, and my disposition towards it has only appeared by proxy, manifested in a more than usually analytical intellectual orientation.

At a symposium on narrative held at the University of Chicago in 1979, Ursula Le Guin's irreverent contribution included the lines:

The *histoire* is the what
and the *discours* is the how
but what I want to know, Brigham,
is *le pourquoi*.
Why are we sitting here around the campfire?
(*On Narrative*, 188)

That pretty well articulates the nub of my intellectual curiosity, and the question more or less directly motivates all my work. What is it about stories—often stories that we know are not true—that makes them such a ubiquitous and privileged feature of human culture? In one form or another it was this question that drew me to literary theory at the peak of post-structuralism, and to the innovative fictions of postmodernism. In both respects I was interested in continuities, though the agonistic idiom of theory tended to obscure the crucial respects in which structuralism was a premise as well as an object of critique for post-structuralism, just as postmodernism was all too readily glossed as anti-modernism, or the postmodern novel as the anti-novel. In *Novel Arguments* (1995) I was concerned to demonstrate the theoretical and empirical inadequacy of such antithetical accounts of innovative fiction, grounding my claims in close readings of an eclectic but exemplary group of texts by Donald Barthelme, Ishmael Reed, Robert Coover, Walter Abish and Kathy Acker. I wanted to look beyond the superficial perception of these fictions as in some sense anti-mimetic, and show that they were manifestly engaged and significant works of narrative representation which shared some fundamental objectives with the novel tradition. The important and enduring point, for me, was that understanding these fictions required a more inclusive concept of what fiction is and what it does; it relativized many of the features of broadly realist fiction that were too often taken as normative in criticism and narrative theory. Mimesis, from this perspective, was no longer conceived as a representational end but as a rhetorical means, alongside other less familiar resources for narrative communication. My point in advancing the concept of the "argument" of fiction was very much to affirm the view that fictions are not just representational products, but communicative acts; processes to be worked through. The formal invention of innovative fiction was not something to be thematicised, much less flattened into a kind of immanent content, but read for its rhetorical force.

In truth the narrative theory in this work was all very implicit; there's some Roland Barthes, some Jean-François Lyotard, some Mikahil Bakhtin, but they're not invoked in primarily narrative terms, and the idiom throughout is literary-critical rather than theoretical. The narratological implications of the approach I had taken to fiction were quite radical, however, and needed explicit formulation; the attempt to do so led me along the research trail that culminated in *The Rhetoric of Fictionality* (2007). In a certain key respect my perspective upon narrative through the lens of fictionality was analogous to my perspective upon fictions in general through the lens of the most innovative examples; the supposedly anomalous particular case turns out to be a powerful way of defamiliarising our unexamined assumptions about the general category. This is also, for me, the justification for the privileged place of literary narrative in the history and continuing practice of narrative theory. Hard cases may make bad law, but they make good theory. Gérard Genette's *Narrative Discourse* has been, for me, the single most important contribution to narrative theory (I say that whilst dissenting from most of its arguments), and much of its power and subtlety comes from the fact that it takes the gloriously anomalous *À la recherche du temps perdu* as its test case. It was the aesthete in Roland Barthes, not the pseudo-scientist, whose literary sensibilities enabled *S/Z* (Barthes 1990) to break out so brilliantly from the too static structuralist paradigm he had himself helped to establish. Franz K. Stanzel's typological circle (Stanzel 1984) was important less for its categories in themselves than for the way its mapping of the literary canon encapsulated the fluidity of narrative techniques within and across conceptual boundaries. And while I'm incanting the names of the august, I'll put in a word for Henry James, whose prefaces repeatedly amaze me as demonstrations of his ability to balance the demands of generalisation with the complexity and nuance of the particular case. These are all instances of the way our most elaborate narrative forms can stimulate theoretical reflection that, in rising to the challenge of the literary, also elaborates a rich conceptual framework with the capacity to continually re-inflect and even transform our understanding of narrative in general and how it functions in the broadest cultural and cognitive terms. Narrative theory continues to be productive within the discipline of literary study, of course, but even for theorists like me, who have come to see narrative as a topic of massively interdisciplinary scope, there is still a lot to gain from attending to the rhetorical complexities of its literary manifestations.

Innovative fiction led me to fictionality itself, then; I thought the issue had not been well served, and that in fact narrative theory had conspired with philosophy in various ways to evade it. Fictive narration was made safe for theory by being framed or disavowed: it was a pretended speech act; it was no kind of assertion, but a prop in a game of make-believe; it did in fact refer, but to a fictional world; the narration was itself contained within the fictional frame. A wariness about the truth status of fictive narration so dominated these discussions that there seemed to be no room for an account of its real-world discursive efficacy. On the other hand, post-structuralist scepticism about truth claims as such had given currency to a view in which fictionality was synonymous with narrativity in general. I have a lot of sympathy with Hayden White's important work on historiography in this respect, but ultimately it is a conceptual impoverishment to efface the distinct rhetorical gesture that characterizes fictive storytelling. I staged a confrontation between these two broad camps in "Fictionality and Mimesis" (2003), where I found Paul Ricoeur's ideas to be extremely helpful, both because *Time and Narrative* assumes an essentially post-structuralist concept of narrativity, and because his reworking of mimesis foregrounds process in a way that lent itself to the pragmatic model of fictive communication I was elaborating. Here and elsewhere in *The Rhetoric of Fictionality*, fictional worlds theory was a focus of my critique in part because it seemed to me the most fully worked out defence of a referential model of fictionality, and in this connection (as in others) I have found Marie-Laure Ryan's work (notably in *Possible Worlds, Artificial Intelligence and Narrative Theory*, 1991) an enormously productive foil to my own thinking.

This was not the fulcrum of my work on fictionality, however. That was "Who Is the Narrator?" (1997), in which I mounted an argument against the legitimacy of a keystone of narrative theory, the concept of an agent of narration distinct from both author and character. This was my point of leverage, and it's a tight argument because I believed then, and still believe, that if you accept it (and it is by no means generally accepted) then the whole edifice of the orthodox representational model of narrative tumbles down. It is the function of this concept of the narrator, above all, to reduce fictive narrative acts to fictional narrative acts, and in doing so to entirely foreclose the question of the real-world rhetorical force of fictionality. Demonstrating the incoherence of the concept of the narrator was a crucial first step in opening up that question; it soon became clear that the logic of the argument would call into question a wholes series of other core narratological concepts, beginning with the implied author (though this has been under more or less constant attack from several quarters for decades). In "Fabula and Fictionality" (2001) my target was the fabula-syuzhet distinction and its Anglophone equivalent, the story-discourse distinction given currency by Seymour Chatman's influential exposition of a discourse-oriented structuralist narratology; here the point was to reclaim the intuitive value of this distinction, given that none of the extant rationalizations of it made sense without the representational paradigm I had rejected. In a similar spirit, the ramifications of my argument extended to a critique of the medium-independence of narrative in "The Narrative Imagination across Media" (2006); of narrative authorship as the transmission of a somehow prior concept, vision or intent in "The Novelist as Medium" (2000); and of the presumption that suspension of disbelief—or some more current equivalent formula for imaginative relocation within the representational frame—is a precondition for the reader's emotional involvement with fiction in "Why We Wept for Little Nell" (1997). The argument also entailed drawing out the multiple concepts lurking within the metaphor of voice in narrative theory, and calling into question the logical coherence of the orthodox notions of person and level in narration—this last darkly hinted at in *The Rhetoric of Fictionality* itself, but elaborated more fully in "Person, Level, Voice" (2010). Throughout these arguments I was at pains not only to demonstrate the inadequacy of received narratological concepts in their own terms, but also to show how a pragmatic and rhetorical theory could better account for the narrative phenomena concerned. Nevertheless, there is a risk attached to such broad revisionism, which is that each successive critique is not perceived as the incremental elaboration of a coherent alternative position, but rather as the repeated performance of a gad-fly role in relation to narrative scholarship; a nuisance, to be sure, but implicitly conceding the value of what it attacks. This is difficult, not only because in fact I am far from dismissive of the legacy of narrative theory, but also because there is some appeal to the role, and I suspect myself of having, on occasion, played up to such a perception of my work. Nonetheless, the alternative position, a concept of fictive narration as a rhetorical resource directly exploited as part of the pragmatics of communication, does pervade all these critical analyses, and is solidly established in the essay that became the opening chapter of *The Rhetoric of Fictionality*, "The Pragmatics of Narrative Fictionality" (2005). There the foundations of my position are most substantially and explicitly laid upon the tradition of speech act theory that passes from H. P. Grice to the relevance theory of Dan Sperber and Deirdre Wilson (1995). The importance of this work for narrative theory has not been fully recognized, I think, because scholars (including Sperber and Wilson themselves) have tended to subordinate it to a representational paradigm when addressing fictional narrative.

I have already affirmed the value of literary narrative as a focus for theoretical reflection upon narrative in general, but I would also want to urge the complementary view that serious attention to the full range of narrative's manifestations is an essential counterbalance to the potential for parochialism in literary narratology. I was mindful of this accountability to a larger frame of reference throughout *The Rhetoric of Fictionality*, and consideration of narratives in other media was an important part of several of the key arguments of that book. The fact that the narrative mode can be articulated through various semiotic channels is not only important for the way it throws into relief some of the linguistic bias of narrative theory, but also because it requires us to think of narrative understanding as a much more fundamental cognitive faculty than the scope of literary narratology has generally implied. From my point of view the cognitive turn in narrative theory is above all a recognition that narrative is an elemental part of how we think—the implications of which seem far more significant than the relatively prosaic idea that the business of literary criticism can be rejuvenated by approaching it through the concepts and idiom of the cognitive sciences. A cognitive frame of reference does help to elucidate issues in narrative theory that are particularly germane to literary study, and I have explored certain aspects of that relation myself, for instance in "Dreaming and Narrative Theory" (2010); but the real interest, I think, lies in pursuing the matter in the other direction. The literary grounding of narrative theory is an excellent point of departure for a really far-reaching inquiry into the role of narrative across the full range of human sense-making activities.

Just as the narrative mode features in a range of media, the topic of narrative is of increasing interest across disciplines. Here again there are different conceptions of the role of narrative theory, and in fact disciplines also work with markedly different conceptions of what constitutes narrative. So while many disciplines have experienced a "narrative turn" in recent decades, the effects of this boom in transdisciplinary narrative scholarship have often been reductive with respect to both narrative theory itself and the discourses of the disciplines concerned. The result, in sociology, musicology, philosophy of mind and computer game studies, to name a few, has been an entirely understandable backlash against the perceived narrative imperialism of such approaches. At the root of the problem, I think, is a mistaken premise that underwrites most attempts at interdisciplinary collaboration, which is an expectation that the encounter between disciplinary perspectives will produce synthesis (unfortunately, I suspect that this same premise is the basis of the privileged status interdisciplinary study enjoys among the criteria of research funding councils). In many cases the expectation of synthesis itself creates a climate in which collegiate discussion can quickly degenerate into a territorial struggle of disciplinary annexation, or else an entrenched intellectual stalemate which never attains the status of meaningful communication.

I am convinced that narrative is of fundamental importance not just in the humanities and social sciences, but across the full range of academic disciplines; but I do not believe it follows that narrative theory should therefore aspire to the status of a master-discipline or transdisciplinary paradigm. Interdisciplinary dialogue is of enormous value, and narrative theory is ideally placed to facilitate such dialogue; the model of interdisciplinary dialogue I advocate, however, includes no presumption of consilience between disciplinary perspectives, and its goal is not theoretical synthesis but the kind of insight that arises when we triangulate the incommensurability between discourses. Narrative theory has such interdisciplinary scope because unlike the disciplines, which are typically defined in relation to an object of knowledge, it can be defined in relation to a mode of knowledge—one that is fundamental to consciousness and to our apprehension of the world around us. My current research is very much concerned with the relation between this privileged way of knowing and other ways in which we model our environment, which may be spatial (images, maps, graphs), abstract (mathematics) or systemic (simulations). These kinds of modelling have great representational or predictive power, and can capture information that eludes narrative representation; yet the indebtedness of the human perspective to narrative is such that these kinds of modelling do not attain the full status of understanding until they are brought into relation with a narrative account. This is unproblematic when they are consistent with narrative representation, or entirely heterogeneous to it (lacking significant temporality, for example); but there are well-defined, discrete temporal developments that are incompatible with narrative representation, for example the phenomenon of emergence in complex systems, which has been the focus of my recent work, for example, "Emergent Narrative in Interactive Media" (2011).

Narrative theory in an interdisciplinary context can approach the condition of a theory of everything—narrative is universal, ubiquitous, inescapable, to the extent that it loses specificity as an object of study and its conceptual apparatus is trivialized by dilution; on the other hand, there are objects of knowledge that are obscured or traduced by conceptualization in narrative terms. It would be possible to say, in a conciliatory spirit, that there is a negotiable middle ground between these extremes which can demarcate the appropriate scope of narrative theory; but I think that response is fundamentally mistaken. Emergent phenomena are refractory to narrative conceptualization—but they are just as ubiquitous and inescapable as narrative itself. A consideration of narrative in relation to emergence, then, squeezes out that comfortable middle ground entirely, and requires us to reconceive the relation between narrative's scope and its limits. My current work is fundamentally concerned with the limits of narrative understanding, but does not take this as any restriction upon its scope. My hunch is that by exploring the conceptual mismatch between emergence and narrative within the context of a model of interdisciplinary dialogue that can accommodate such incommensurability we can gain insight not only into the nature of emergence and narrative, but also into the pragmatics of knowledge.

33
Robyn Warhol

Arts & Humanities Distinguished Professor of English
University of Ohio State University

---

1. Why were you first drawn to narratology?

In graduate school I was one of "Ian's boys." That meant it was so unusual for Ian Watt to have a research assistant who was anything other than male, I could not possibly be doing that job and be a girl. I found the moniker amusing. Inspired by having read Watt's *The Rise of the Novel* (Watt 1957) and Wayne Booth's *The Rhetoric of Fiction* (Booth 1961) for an Oxford tutorial during my undergraduate semester abroad, I went from my B. A. at Pomona College to the doctoral program at Stanford University specifically to work with Watt. I didn't think it was so funny when, having worked many quarters as his research and teaching assistant, I asked Watt to direct my dissertation. "But I thought you were *Tom's* girl," he said, alluding to my having T.A.'d first for Thomas Moser and invoking a discourse of dating that in the late 1970s was already pretty dated. I learned a lot from Ian Watt, particularly the empiricist-historicist methodology I still practice and teach: look at the text, identify patterns, and then look into historical and cultural factors that may account for them. Evidently I *was* more Tom's girl than Ian's boy, though, because Moser was to direct my thesis while Watt became my second reader, even though the work I was doing on narrators in 19th-century fiction was more up Watt's alley. When I later explained my topic to him, he remarked, "Oh, I see. It's to be a sort of a footnote to *The Rhetoric of Fiction*." Until I luckily fell in with some narratologists in the mid-1980s, that's what I thought I was writing.

My dissertation proposed a distinction between the earnest "engaging narrator" and the playful "distancing narrator" in the 18th- and 19th-century realist novel. Both kinds of narrator interrupt their storytelling for passages of direct address to "you," the reader. I observed that while direct address disturbed "the illusion of reality," as Anglo-American humanist critics still working in the tradition of James, Forster, and Lubbock used to call it, it could disrupt formal realism without undermining the emotional impact of the novel as long as the "narrative intrusions" were earnest ones. I could attest to that emotional impact, because whenever I re-read Elizabeth Gaskell's *Mary Barton* or Harriet Beecher Stowe's *Uncle Tom's Cabin*, the device would make me cry, despite my critical awareness that the passages of sincere direct address were supposed to be aesthetic flaws at best, sentimental drivel at worst. My engaging narrators came from the early George Eliot as well as Stowe and Gaskell; the novels with distancing narrators—the ones who fooled around with metaleptic direct address for frankly metafictional purposes—ranged from Henry Fielding and Laurence Sterne to W. M. Thackeray. It never crossed my liberal-humanist mind that one category contained only men and the other only women.

Beginning my first academic job at the University of Vermont, I fortunately showed my work to Philippe Carrard, a professor of French and a professional narratologist who had trained in Switzerland. Carrard did not call my dissertation a footnote to anything. He gave me a copy of Genette's *Narrative Discourse* and a xerox of Gerald Prince's "Introduction to the Study of the Narratee," (Prince 1980d) and said (in his inimitable *Vaudois* accent) "You have a point! These guys will help you make it." My first publication, an essay using Prince to frame my categories of direct address, got accepted at *PMLA*; the reviewers were Barbara Johnson and Peter Brooks, both of them–like Prince and Carrard–specialists at that time in French literature and theory. Both agreed with my thesis that engaging narration invites the actual reader to identify with the narratee by creating an implied reader that is indistinguishable from the narratee, while distancing narrators maintain ironic divisions between narratee, implied reader, and reader. In an offhand comment at the end of her review, Johnson—god rest her brilliant soul!—wondered why I had not made anything of the gender divide between my female-authored engaging narrators and my male-authored distancing ones. I had a lot of make-up work to do, in order to learn the feminist literary theory that had been entirely absent from my graduate education. That was in 1986, for me the year feminist narratology was born. Soon I was corresponding with Susan Sniader Lanser, who had just placed her foundational essay on feminist narratology in *Style*, and who was looking for an ally to agree that feminism and narrative analysis were not mutually exclusive. We have been reading and learning from each other ever since. Once my primary influences switched from Watt, Booth, and Moser to Johnson, Lanser, Elaine Showalter, Nancy K. Miller, Jane Gallop, Helena Michie, and D. A. Miller, I began to see how narrative forms are inflected by discursive constructions of gendered and sexual difference. Narratology, I argued then and still do now, provides a vocabulary for describing narrative structures that may have been originally conceived as "universal," but that are nonetheless useful for communicating differences in narrative forms born of their authors' and audiences' historical contexts.

2. What do you consider your most important contributions to the field?

The introduction to my first book, *Gendered Interventions* (1989), painstakingly spells out the reasons "Why Feminists Don't 'Do' Narratology." In its quest for universals, structuralist narratology was relentlessly Eurocentric and "phallocentric" as we feminists used to say, purposely putting aside marks of cultural differences among texts. That meant marginalizing every text that did not happen to follow the narrative conventions of a Western white-male-authored canon. By 1986 Anglo-American feminism was firmly positioned against structuralism. Resolutely anti-essentialist, anti-universalist, and pro-poststructuralist, feminist literary criticism eschewed the binary oppositions that structured culture hierarchically by sorting everything into male/female, public/private, straight/gay, high culture/low culture, and so forth. The logic of feminism had moved—again to invoke Johnson—from a focus on "the difference between" the sexes to an awareness of "the difference within." While many scholars have acknowledged my book's identification of engaging narrators with female authors of the mid-nineteenth century, thus getting my point about the "difference between" engaging and distancing narration, not everyone recalls that the main point of *Gendered Interventions* was to look not at the difference between male and female authors, but to look at the *difference within* narrators created by both sexes. I argued that styles of narrative, like all cultural productions, bear signs of both masculinity and femininity—that is, features that a particular culture considers appropriate to men or appropriate to women. Although my book begins by showing how feminine engaging narrative strategies dominate a "woman's text" like *Mary Barton*, the later chapters are more important because they discuss how authors like Stowe and Charles Dickens "cross genders," strategically drawing on narrative devices that were coded masculine and devices that were coded feminine in their day. In this way I detached the gendering of narration from the sex of the author who created it. This I think was an important step in connecting feminist narratology with the post-structuralist understanding of gender as a performative process and not a stable category, though I did not have the vocabulary in 1986 to put it that way.

Having a Good Cry (2003) was my attempt to get more technical in my narratological analysis of gender-as-process. If masculinity and femininity are not essential traits but are constructed by culture, then cultural artifacts must somehow be constructing them for individuals who perform across the range of possible genders. I suggested that the narrative forms of popular texts in gendered genres (soap opera, chick flicks, serialized fiction) rehearse gendered feelings for their fans, thus partly *constituting* gender in readers and audiences. I used narratology to identify patterns that certain formula-narratives follow, and argued that their affective impact goes a long way toward reinforcing masculine or effeminate subjectivity through their emotional impact on people's bodies. I said "effeminate" instead of "feminine" in order to avoid the binary opposition with "masculine," and also to embrace the gender performance of those gay men who are fans of pop cultural forms that are marketed to (feminine) women. For a model of affect I looked to Silvan Tomkins, but unlike the cognitive narratologists who have also been interested in his psychophysiological theories, I did not trace his insights on the connection between body and feeling to the universal experience of all humans. Instead I thought about how the bodies of people who consume contemporary popular culture go through repeated and predictable patterns of crying, of excitement, of embarrassment— and I argued that these patterns of affect inscribe gender on those responsive bodies. Re-reading it now in the context of all the cognitive and neurological narrative work on emotion and empathy that was written around the same time, I can see why *Having a Good Cry* has not made the impact I hoped it would upon narrative theory. The book does not address cognition at all. With its focus on embodiment, *Having a Good Cry* asserts that bodies in this culture are gendered, sexed, raced, and classed; with its grounding in feminist theory, the book also insists that gender matters. As cognitive narrative theorists like David Herman now turn their attention in the direction of embodiment, I will be interested to see whether the issues of gender and sexuality raised in *Having a Good Cry* begin to enter the cognitive conversation.

3. What is the proper role of a narratology and narrative theory in relation to other academic disciplines?

Speaking as a feminist, I would never use the word "proper" in the context of literary theory. Twenty-first-century feminism is not much invested in what is supposed to be suitable, appropriate, correct or prescribed. I do think the example feminist narratology sets for the other disciplines is the method it models for analyzing identity positions as constructs, rather than as essences or stable categories. To be more general I would say that wherever narrative theory can be useful in unveiling the received wisdom of dominant ideology, wherever it can help to uncover social or cultural formations that contribute to the oppression not just of women, but of queer people, people of color, working-class and under-class people, disabled people, the very young and the very old, all academic disciplines are welcome to it!

Indeed, once history had identified the record of women's inferiority as only a story; once economics had recognized the narratives driving consumer culture as nothing more than useful fictions; once biological science had acknowledged the human-centric teleology of traditional models of evolution, narrative theory had already begun to do its work outside of literary studies. As interdisciplinary practitioners of narrative theory learn from us, we also have much to learn from them about the extradiegetic world that produces and receives the narrative texts we study.

4. What do you consider the most important topics and/or contributions in narratology?

I would not presume to identify the most important topics in all of narratology—the field is too large and too diverse in its priorities. For me the most important topic is still narrative poetics, the continuing project that colleagues like Brian Richardson, Brian McHale, Emma Kafalenos, and others are carrying forward as they seek to describe how the huge variety of narrative forms and strategies work. Because I find narratology most useful for its creation of a vocabulary for pointing out narrative structures that may carry significance for the construction of gender and sexuality, I am grateful to those scholars who are pushing out the boundaries of the kinds of texts narratology can account for. I think particularly here of McHale's energetic forays into genres like lyric or science fiction, which were absent from the corpus of the original narratologists, and of Richardson's indefatigable cataloguing of devices to be found in the "unnatural narratives" of post-modern fiction and drama.

I have always been fascinated in particular by narrators and narration. That may just be an idiosyncracy, but I don't believe it's coincidental that narration has featured prominently in Lanser's research as well as mine. As feminists we are interested in the workings of text on the extradiegetic world, which is another way of saying we are indebted to the project of rhetorical narratology. Though they are sometimes maddeningly gender-blind in their conception of the "authorial audience," the theoretical models developed by Peter Rabinowitz and James Phelan make the work of feminist narratology possible. The rhetorical narrative theorists inherited from Wayne Booth a focus on the ethical impact of narratives which is very similar to feminist narrative theory's emphasis on the politics of the narrative act. Thinking about narrative as an act of communication, a rhetorical transaction, or a conversation between producers and receivers of texts is central to the feminist approach because feminist criticism, whether narrative-centered or not, always looks at the relationship between representation and the "real world." From rhetorical narrative theory we extrapolated our conviction that narrative *matters* in the material sense of that word. The communication model of narrative transmission (the scheme that distinguishes narrator from narratee, implied author from ideal reader or authorial audience, and flesh and blood author and reader from their textually created avatars), introduced by Seymour Chatman and elaborated by James Phelan, is for me the single most important analytic tool that narrative theory has to offer.

5. What are the most important open topics in this field and what are the prospects for progress?

To me the most pressing open topic is a meta-question about the field itself. Can historically oriented narrative theorists (those who take feminist, queer, race-centered, and/or postcolonial approaches) and cognitive/neuroscientific narrative theorists talk to one another? At present the scholarly interactions between those who see narrative as a universal activity and those who think more locally and historically about narrative form range from mutual condescension to outright hostility. For the conversation to move forward, feminist and queer narrative theorists would have to get over our ingrained reaction against the category of "the human." We assume that "the human" means the white, the male, the privileged, the straight, the "normal," because that is what we have shown it to have meant in classical structuralist narratology. Thirty years of feminist and anti-racist scholarship have demonstrated the material damage real people suffer when their identity categories get marginalized by the discourses that structure their lives. Narrative theory, peripheral as its place in the larger world of the academy might look to those of us who do it, contributes to that dominant discourse. Cognitive and neuroscientific narrative theorists appear to position themselves as having moved past the imperatives of identity, as in Frederic Luis Aldama's calling his approach "post-ethnic." "Post" implies that this is the newest, the latest, the up-to-date surmounting of a problematic past. The real problem is, though, that although identity categories *should* not matter, they still *do* matter in the production and reception of narratives as in all aspects of a racist, homophobic, and misogynist culture. If the cognitive and neuroscientific narrative theorists could more explicitly acknowledge this in their pursuit of an experimentally verifiable understanding of what narrative is, the conversation between them and the historically oriented narrative theorists would not have to break down. As evidenced by the tenor of the annual International Conference on Narrative, the diversity of approaches represented on the faculty of Project Narrative at the Ohio State University (the Mother Ship of U.S. narrative theory, where Phelan, McHale, Herman, Aldama and I all make our academic home), and the contributions to this volume, narrative theory has for twenty-five years been friendly to innovation and difference. Keeping the lines of communication open among all kinds of narrative theorists is crucial to the continuing growth and influence of the field.

General Bibliography

Abbott, H. Porter. 1980. Letters to the Self: the Cloistered Writer in Nonretrospective Fiction. *PMLA* 95: 23-41.
– 1984. *Diary Fiction: Writing as Action.* Ithaca: Cornell University Press.
– 1988. Autobiography, Autography, Fiction: Toward a Taxonomy of Literary Categories. *New Literary History* 19: 597-615.
– 1992. Writing and Conversion: Conrad's Modernist Autography. *Yale Journal of Criticism* 5.3: 135-163.
– 1996. *Beckett Writing Beckett: The Author in the Autograph.* Ithaca: Cornell University Press.
– 2003. Unnarratable Knowledge: the Difficulty of Understanding Evolution by Natural Selection. David Herman (ed.), *Narrative Theory and the Cognitive Sciences.* Stanford: CSLI Publications: 143-162.
– 2005. The Future of All Narrative Futures." James Phelan & Peter Rabinowitz (eds.), *Blackwell Companion to Narrative Theory.* Oxford: Blackwell: 529-541.
– 2008a. Unreadable Minds and the Captive Reader. *Style* 42.4: 448-467.
– 2008b. "Narrative and Emergent Behavior. *Poetics Today* 29.2: 227-244.
– 2008c. *The Cambridge Introduction to Narrative*, 2nd Edition. Cambridge University Press.
– 2009. Immersions in the Cognitive Sublime: The Textual Experience of the Extratextual Unknown in García Márquez and Beckett. *Narrative* 17.2: 131-142
Alber, Jan. 2002. The 'Moreness' or 'Lessness' of 'Natural' Narratology: Samuel Beckett's "Lessness" Reconsidered. *Style* 36.1: 54-75. Reprinted in *Short Story Criticism* 74 (2004): 113-24.
– 2004. Bibliography of 'German' Narratology. *Style* 38.2: 253-72.
– 2005. Natural' Narratology. In David Herman, Manfred Jahn, and Marie-Laure Ryan (eds.), *The Routledge Encyclopedia of Nar-*

rative Theory. London: Routledge: 394-5.
– 2009. Impossible Storyworlds – And what to Do with Them. *Storyworlds: A Journal of Narrative Studies* 1.1: 79-96.
– 2010. Hypothetical Intentionalism: Cinematic Narration Reconsidered. In Jan Alber and Monika Fludernik (eds.), *Postclassical Narratology: Approaches and Analyses*. Columbus: Ohio State University Press. 163-85.
– (forthcoming). The Diachronic Development of Unnaturalness: A New View on Genre. In Jan Alber and Rüdiger Heinze (eds.), *Unnatural Narratology*. Berlin and New York: de Gruyter.
– 2011. Cinematic Carcerality: Prison Metaphors in Film. *The Journal of Popular Culture* 44.2: 217-32.
Alber, Jan, and Monika Fludernik. 2009. Mediacy. In Peter Hühn, John Pier, Wolf Schmid, and Jörg Schönert (eds.)., *Handbook of Narratology*. Berlin and New York: de Gruyter. 174-89.
– 2010a. Introduction. In Jan Alber and Monika Fludernik (eds.), *Postclassical Narratology: Approaches and Analyses*. Eds.. Columbus: Ohio State University Press. 1-31.
– (eds.). 2010b. *Postclassical Narratology: Approaches and Analyses*. Columbus: Ohio State University Press.
Alber, Jan, Stefan Iversen, Henrik Skov Nielsen, and Brian Richardson. 2010. Unnatural Narratives, Unnatural Narratology: Beyond Mimetic Models. *Narrative* 18.2: 113-36.
Aldama, Frederick Luis. 2003. *Postethnic Narrative Criticism: Magicorealism in Oscar "Zeta" Acosta, Ana Castillo, Julie Dash, Hanif Kureishi, and Salman Rushdie*. Austin: University of Texas Press.
Ankersmit, Frank. 2001. *Historical Representation*. Stanford, CA: Stanford University Press.
Aristotle. *Poetics*. Oxford: Clarendon Press,1968.
Attridge, Derek. 2004. *The Singularity of Literature*. London: Routledge.
Auerbach, Erich. 2003. Mimesis: The Representation of Reality in Western Literature. Fiftieth Anniversary Ed. Trans. Willard Trask. Princeton: Princeton University Press, **2003.**
Bakhtin, Mikhail. 1981. *The Dialogic Imagination*. Edited by Michael Holquist, translated by Caryl Emerson and Michael Holquist. Austin: Univ. of Texas Press.
– 1984. *Problems of Dostoevsky's Poetics*. Translated by Caryl Emerson. Manchester: Manchester University Press.
Bal, Mieke. 1977. *Narratologie. Essais sur la signification narrative dans quatre romans modernes*. Paris: Klincksieck.

– 1985. *Narratology: Introduction to the Theory of Narrative.* Trans. Christine van Boheemen. Toronto: University of Toronto Press; 2nd printing 1988; 3rd printing 1992; 4th printing 1994; 2nd rev. and exp. ed. 1997; 3rd rev. and exp. ed. 2009.

– 1988. *Death and Dissymmetry: The Politics of Coherence in the Book of Judges.* Chicago: University of Chicago Press.

– 1991a. *On Story-Telling: Essays in Narratology.* Ed. David Jobling. Sonoma: Polebridge Press.

– 1991b. *Reading "Rembrandt": Beyond the Word-Image Opposition.* Cambridge, UK, and New York: Cambridge University Press.

– 1994. *On Meaning-Making: Essays in Semiotics.* Sonoma: Polebridge Press.

– 1996. Double Exposures: The Subject of Cultural Analysis. London and New York: Routledge

– 1997. *The Mottled Screen: Reading Proust Visually.* Trans. Anna-Louise Milne. Stanford, CA: Stanford University Press.

– 1999. *Quoting Caravaggio: Contemporary Art, Preposterous History.* Chicago: University of Chicago Press.

– 2001. Looking In Norman Bryson (ed.), *The Art of Viewing.* Amsterdam: G & B Arts International.

– 2002. *Travelling Concepts in the Humanities: A Rough Guide.* Toronto: University of Toronto Press.

– 2006. *A Mieke Bal Reader.* Chicago: University of Chicago Press.

– 2008a. 2MOVE: Video, Art, Migration. Murcia, Spain: Cendeac (with Miguel Á. Hernández-Navarro).

– 2008b. *Loving Yusuf: Conceptual Travels from Present to Past.* Chicago: University of Chicago Press.

– 2010. Of *What One Cannot Speak: Doris Salcedo's Political Art.* Chicago: University of Chicago Press.

Bally, Charles. 1912. Le *style indirect libre en français moderne. Germanisch-Romanische Monatsschrift* 4: 549-556, 597-606.

Banfield, Ann. 1973. Narrative Style and the Grammar of Direct and Indirect Speech. *Foundations of Language* 10: 1-39.

– 1982. *Unspeakable Sentences: Narration and Representation in the Language of Fiction.* London: Routledge and Kegan Paul.

– 1985. Grammar and Memory. *Proceedings of the Berkeley Linguistic Society* 11: 387-397.

– 1987. Describing the Unobserved: Events Grouped Around an Empty Center. In Nigel Fabb, Derek Attridge, Alan Durant and Colin MacCabe (eds.), *The Linguistics of Writing.* Manchester:

Manchester University Press: 265-285.

– 1998. The Name of the Subject: the 'il'. In Tom Pepper (ed.), *The Place of Maurice Blanchot. Yale French Studies* 93, fall:133-174.

– 2000. Tragic Time: The Problem of the Future in Cambridge Philosophy and *To the Lighthouse*. *Modernism/ Modernity* 7.1: 43-75.

– 2002. A Grammatical Definition of the Genre 'Novel'. *Polyphonie—linguistique et littérature/Lingvistisk og litterær polyfoni*, Documents de travail/arbejdspapirer No. IV, Les polyphonistes scandinaves/De skandinaviske polyfonister, Samfundslitteratur Roskilde : 76-100.

– 2005. Tense and Narrative. In David Herman, Manfred Jahn, Marie-Laure Ryan (eds), *Routledge Encyclopedia of Narrative Theory*. London: Routledge: 592-4.

Baroni, Raphaël. 2007. *La Tension narrative. Suspense, curiosité et surprise*. Paris: Seuil.

– 2010. Juste une question de *timing*. Du schéma quinaire à la conception postclassique de l'intrigue. In Sylvie Patron (ed.), *Théorie, analyse, interprétation des récits / Theory, analysis, interpretation of narratives*, Bern: Peter Lang, pp. 189-214.

Barry, Jackson G. 1990. Narratology's Centrifugal Force: A Literary Perspective on the Extensions of Narrative Theory. *Poetics Today* 11.2: 295–308.

Barthes, Roland. 1966. Introduction à l'analyse structurale des récits. *Communications* 8: 1-27. English version: An Introduction to the Structural Analysis of Narrative. *New Literary History* 6 (1975): 237-72.

– 1990. Barthes, Roland. *S/Z*. New York: WileyBlackwell.

Bartlett, Frederic. 1932. *Remembering: A study in experimental and social psychology*. Cambridge: Cambridge University Press.

Becker, Gay. 1999. *Disrupted Lives: How People Create Meaning in a Chaotic World*. Berkeley: University of California Press.

Beach, Joseph Warren. 1932. *The Twentieth Century Novel: Studies in Technique*, New York: The Century Company.

Beardsley, Monroe C. 1958. *Aesthetics: Problems in the Philosophy of Criticism*. New York & Burlingame: Harcourt, Brace & World.

Bell, Alice. 2010. *The Possible Worlds of Hypertext Fiction*. Basingstoke: Palgrave-Macmillan.

Benveniste, Emile. 1966. *Problèmes de linguistique générale*, 1. Paris: Gallimard.

Betti, Emilio. 1954. *Zur Grundlegung einer allgemeinen Auslegungslehre. Ein hermeneutisches Manifest.* Tübingen: J.C.B. Mohr.
– 1955. *Teoria Generale della Interpretazione.* Milan: Giuffrè Editore.
Blake, Robert R. and Glenn V. Ramsey (eds.). 1951. *Perception — An Approach to Personality.* New York: Ronald Press.
Bode, Christoph. 2005. *Der Roman. Eine Einführung.* Tübingen: Francke. English translation: *The Novel: An Introduction.* Wiley-Blackwell.
Bonheim, Helmut. 1982. *The narrative modes : techniques of the short story.* Cambridge: Brewer.
– 1990. *Literary Systematics.* Cambridge: Brewer.
Booth, Wayne C.. 1961. *The Rheotric of Fiction.* Chicago: The University of Chicago Press.
– 1988. *The Company We Keep.* Berkeley: Univ. of California Press.
Bordwell, David. 1985. *Narration in the Fiction Film.* London: Routledge.
Bortolussi, Marisa & Peter Dixon. 1996. The Effects of Formal Training on Literary Reception. 1996. *Poetics* 23.6:471-89..
– 1998. Science and the study of literature. *Spiel* Jg. 16.1-2.
– 2003. *Psychonarratology: Foundations for the Empirical Study of Literary Response.* Cambridge: Cambridge University Press.
Bortolussi Marisa, Peter Dixon, P. and P Sopcak, P. 2010. Gender and reading. *Poetics* 38.3.
Bremond, Claude. 1958. Etude d'un matériel filmique thématique (with G. Cohen-Séat and J.-F. Richard). *Revue Internationale de Filmologie* 8.30-31:105-134.
– 1964. Le message narratif. *Communications* 4, 1964: 4-32.
– 1966. La logique des possibles narratifs', *Communications* 8: 60-76.
– 1973. *Logique du récit* , Paris: Seuil, 1973.
Brooks, Peter. 2006. Narrative Transactions. Does the Law Need a Narratology? *Yale Journal of Law and the Humanities* 18: 1-28.
Bruner, Jerome. 1986. *Actual Minds, Possible Worlds.* Cambridge, MA: Harvard University Press.
– 1990. *Acts of Meaning.* Cambridge, MA: Harvard University Press.
Bruner, Jerome S. and David Kretch (eds.). 1968. *Perception and Personality.* New York: Greenwood Press.
Chafe, Wallace. 1973. Language and Memory. *Language* 49: 261-281.

– 1980. *The Pear Stories: Cognitive, Cultural, and Linguistic Aspects of Narrative Production.* Norwood, NJ: Ablex.

– 1986. Beyond Bartlett: Narratives and Remembering. In Elisabeth Gülich and Uta M. Quasthoff (eds.), *Narrative Analyisi: An Interdisciplinary Dialogue.* Special Issue of *Poetics*, vol. 15.

– 1994. *Discourse, Consciousness, and Time: The Flow and Displacement of Conscious Experience in Speaking and Writing.* Chicago: The University of Chicago Press.

– 2007. *The Importance of Not Being Earnest: The Feeling Behind Laughter and Humor.* Amsterdam/Philadelphia: John Benjamins.

– 2010. Literature as a Window to the Mind. *Acta Linguistica Hafniensia* 42: 51-63.

Chafe, Wallace, and Jane Danielewicz. 1987. Properties of Spoken and Written Language. In Rosalind Horowitz and S. J. Samuels (eds.), *Comprehending Oral and Written Language.* New York: Academic Press: 83-113.

Charon, Rita. 2006. *Narrative Medicine: Honoring the Stories of Illness.* Oxford and New York: Oxford University Press.

Chatman, Seymour. 1978. *Story and Discourse: Narrative Structure in Fiction and Film.* Ithaca and London: Cornell University Press.

– 1990a. *Coming to Terms: The Rhetoric of Narrative in Fiction and Film.* Ithaca: Cornell University Press.

– 1990b. What can we learn from contextual narratology? *Poetics Today*, 11.2.

Cohn, Dorrit. 1978. *Transparent Minds: Narrative Modes for Presenting Consciousness in Fiction.* Princeton, NJ: Princeton University Press.

– 1981. The encirclement of narrative. On Franz Stanzel's *Theorie des Erzählens. Poetics Today* 2: 157-82.

– 1999. *The Distinction of Fiction.* Baltimore: The Johns Hopkins University Press.

Coleridge, S. T. 1983. *Biographia literaria*, 2 Vols. J. Engell & W. J. Bate (eds.). London: Routledge & Kegan Paul. (Original work published 1817.)

Collier, Gordon. 1992. *The Rocks and Sticks of Words: Style, Discourse and Narrative Structure in the Fiction of Patrick White.* Amsterdam: Rodopi

Culler, Jonathan. 1974. *Flaubert: The Uses of Uncertainty*, London: Elek Books, and Ithaca: Cornell University Press; expanded edition, Cornell University Press, 1985.

– 1975. *Structuralist Poetics: Structuralism, Linguistics, and the Study of Literature*, London: Routledge; Ithaca: Cornell University Press, 1975, revised edition: Routledge Classics, 2002).
– 1980. Fabula and Sjuzhet in the Analysis of Narrative: Some American Discussions. *Poetics Today* 1.3.
– 1981. *The Pursuit of Signs*, London: Routledge, and Ithaca: Cornell University Press.
– 1997. *Literary Theory: A Very Short Introduction*, Oxford: Oxford University Press; revised and expanded edition, 2011
– 2004. Omniscience. In *Narrative* (2004), substantially revised for publication as chapter 8 of Culler 2007.
– 2007. *The Literary in Theory*, Stanford: Stanford University Press, 2007.
Cupchik, G. C., Keith Oatley, and P. Vorderer. 1998. Emotional effects of reading excerpts fromshort stories by James Joyce. *Poetics* 25: 363-377.
Dannenberg, Hilary P. 2008. *Coincidence and Counterfactuality: Plotting Time and Space in Narrative Fiction*. Lincoln: University of Nebraska.
Darnton, R. 1995. *The Forbidden Best-Sellers of Pre-Revolutionary France*. London, New York: W.W. Norton & Company.
De Sousa, Ronald. 1987. *The Rationality of Emotion*. Cambridge, MA: MIT Press.
Dick, Philip K. 1995. *The Collected Stories of Philip K. Dick, Volume 1: The Short Happy Life of the Brown Oxford*. New York: Carol Publishing Group.
Dixon, Peter and Marisa Bortolussi. 2001. Text is not communication: A challenge to a common assumption. *Discourse Processes*, 31.1: 1-25.
– 2010. *Textual and extratextual determinants of literary evaluation*. Paper presented at the International Society for the Empirical Study of Literature, Utrecht, Netherlands
Doležel, Lubomír. 1973. *Narrative Modes in Czech Literature*, Toronto and Buffalo: University of Toronto Press.
– 1998. *Heterocosmica: Fiction and Possible Worlds*. Baltimore and London: The Johns Hopkins University Press.
Eakin, Paul John. 1999. *How Our Lives Become Stories: Making Selves*. Ithaca: Cornell Unviersity Press.
Ehrenzweig, Anton. 1965. *The Psychoanalysis of Artistic Vision and Hearing*. New York: Braziller.
Emmott, C., A.J. Sanford, A. J., and L. I. Morrow. 2006. Capturing the attention of readers? Stylistic and psychological

perspectives on the use and effect of text fragmentation in narratives. *Journal of Literary Semantics* 35: 1-30.
Fauconnier, Gilles, and Mark Turner. 2002. *The Way We Think: Conceptual Blending and the Mind's Hidden Complexities.* New York: Basic Books.
Fleischman Suzanne. *Tense and Narrativity : From Medieval Performance to Modern Fiction*, Austin: University of Texas Press, 1990.
Fludernik, Monika. Fludernik, Monika 1991. The Historical Present Tense Yet Again: Tense Switching and Narrative Dynamics in Oral and Quasi-Oral Storytelling. *Text* 11.3: 365-98.

– 1993a. *The Fictions of Language and the Languages of Fiction. The Linguistic Representation of Speech and Consciousness.* London/New York: Routledge.

– 1993b. Second Person Fiction: Narrative *You* As Addressee And/Or Protagonist. *Arbeiten aus Anglistik und Amerikanistik* 18: 217-247.

– 1994a. Introduction: Second-Person Narrative and Related Issues." *Style* 28.3: 281-311.

– 1994b. Second-Person Narrative: A Bibliography. *Style* 28.4: 525-48.

– 1996. *Towards a 'Natural' Narratology.* London and New York: Routledge.

– 1998. (Ed.), *Hybridity and Postcolonialism: Twentieth-Century Indian Literature.* Tübingen: Stauffenburg.

– 2003a. The Diachronization of Narratology. *Narrative* 11.3: 331-48.

– 2003b. Natural Narratology and Cognitive Parameters. In David Herman (ed.), *Narrative Theory and the Cognitive Sciences.* Stanford, CA: CSLI Publications. 243-67.

– 2003c. (Ed.), *Diaspora and Multiculturalism: Common Traditions and New Developments.* Readings in the Post/Colonial Literatures in English, 66. Amsterdam: Rodopi.

– 2005. Histories of narrative theory (II): From structuralism to the present. In James Phelan & Peter J. Rabinowitz (eds.), *A Companion to Narrative Theory.* Maldlen, Oxford & Victoria: Blackwell Press:36-60.

– 2006. *Einführung in die Erzähltheorie.* Darmstadt: Wissenschaftliche Buchgesellschaft.

– 2009. *An Introduction to Narratology.* Abingdon and New York: Routledge.

– 2010. Naturalizing the Unnatural: A View from Blending Theory. *Journal of Literary Semantics* 39.1: 1-27.

– 2011. (Ed.) *Beyond Cognitive Metaphor Theory: Perspectives on Literary Metaphor.* Routledge

Fludernik, Monika & Greta Olson (eds.). 2004). *In the Grip of the Law: Prisons, Trials and the Space Between.* Frankfurt/New York: Peter Lang.

Forster, E. M. 1927. *Aspects of the Novel.* New York: Harcourt, Brace, & World.

Friedman, Susan Stanford. 1993. Spatialization: A Strategy for Reading Narrative. *Narrative* 1: 12-23.

– 1995. Spatial Poetics and Arundhati Roy's *The God of Small Things*. In James Phelan and Peter J. Rabinowitz (eds.), *A Companion to Narrative Theory.* Oxford: Blackwell Publishing, 192-203.

– 1998. *Mappings.* Princeton: Princeton University Press.

Frye, Northrop. 1957. *Anatomy of Criticism, Four Essays.* Princeton: Princeton University Press.

Galbraith, Mary. 1995. Deictic Shift Theory and the Poetics of Involvement in Narrative. In Judith F. Duchan, Gail A. Bruder and Lynne E. Hewitt (eds.), *Deixis in Narrative: A Cognitive Science Perspective,* Hillsdale: Lawrence Erlbaum Associates: 19-59.

Gavins, J. 2007. *Text World Theory.* Edinburgh: Edinburgh University Press.

Genette, Gérard. 1972. *Figures III.* Paris: Seuil.

– 1980. *Narrative Discourse: An Essay in Method* [1972]. Transl. Jane E. Lewin Ithaca, NY: Cornell University Press.

– 1988. *Narrative Discourse Revisited* [1983]. Transl. Jane E. Lewin. Ithaca, NY: Cornell University Press.

– 1993. A Logic of Literature. Preface to Käte Hamburger, *The Logic of Literature*, trans. Marilynn J. Rose, Bloomington and Indianapolis: Indiana University Press, 1993 (2nd ed.): vii-xix. Reprinted in Gérard Genette, *Essays in Aesthetics*. Trans. Dorrit Cohn, Lincoln: University of Nebraska Press, 2005: 108-115.

Graesser, A., N. Person and G. Scott Johnston. 1996. Three obstacles in empirical research on aesthetic and literary comprehension. In R. J. Kreuz & M. S. MacNealy (eds.), *Empirical approaches to literature and aesthetics.* Norwood, NJ: Ablex: 3-22.

Graesser, Arthur C, Millis, Keith K., and Zwaan, Rolf A., 1997. Discourse comprehension. *Annual Review of Psychology* 48: 163-189.

Graesser, Arthur C., Murray Singer, Murray and Tom Trabasso. 1994. Constructing inferences during narrative text

comprehension. *Psychological Review* 101: 371-395.
Green, Christopher. 1998. The thoroughly modern Aristotle. *History of Psychology* 1: 8-20.
Greimas, Algirdas Julien. 1971. Narrative Grammar: Units and Levels, *Modern Language Notes* 86: 793-806.
Gu, Ming Dong. 2006. *Chinese Theories of Fiction: A Non-Western Narrative System*. Albany: State University of New York Press.
Hakemulder, Jèmeljan. 2000. *The moral laboratory: Experiments examining the effects of reading literature on social perception and moral self-concept*. Amsterdam / Philadelphia: John Benjamins.
Hale, Dorothy J.. 1989. "*As I Lay Dying*'s Heterogeneous Discourse," *Novel: A Forum on Fiction* 23: 5-23.
– 1994. "Bakhtin in African American Literary Theory". *ELH* 61: 445-471.
– 1988. "Profits of Altruism: Caleb Williams and Arthur Mervyn". *Eighteenth-Century Studies* 22: 47-69.
– 1998a. "Henry James and the Invention of Novel Theory". In Jonathan Freedman (ed.), *The Cambridge Companion to Henry James*. NY: Cambridge University Press: 79-101.
– 1998b. *Social Formalism: The Novel in Theory from Henry James to the Present*. Stanford: Stanford University Press. Introduction to "*Social Formalism*", translated by editors into Danish for special issue of *Kultur & Klasse* 35 (2007): 17-33.
– 2006. Ed. and author.*The Novel: An Anthology of Criticism and Theory: 1900-2000*. Oxford: Blackwell.
– 2007. "Fiction as Restriction: Self-Binding in New Ethical Theories of the Novel." *Narrative* 15: 187-206.
– 2009a. Aesthetics and the New Ethics: Theorizing the Novel in the Twenty-First Century. *PMLA* 124.3: 896-905. Reprinted in Henrik Skov Nielsen (ed.), *Why Study Literature?*, forthcoming from Aarhus University Press.
– 2009b. "An Aesthetics of Alterity: The Art of English Fiction in the Twentieth Century." In Robert Caserio (ed.),*The Cambridge Companion to the Twentieth-Century English Novel*. Cambridge: Cambridge University Press: 10-22.
– forthcoming. "*On Beauty* as Beautiful? The Problem of Novelistic Aesthetics by Way of Zadie Smith." In Andrzej Gasiorek and David James (eds.), special issue of *Contemporary Literature*.
Hamburger, Käte. 1957. *Die Logik der Dichtung*. Stuttgart: Klett-Cotta. *The Logic of Literature*. Trans. Marilynn J. Rose,

Bloomington and Indianapolis: Indiana University Press.
Heinze, Rüdiger. 2008. Violations of Mimetic Epistemology in First-Person Narrative Fiction. *Narrative* 16.3: 279-97.
Herman, David. 1997. Scripts, Sequences, and Stories: Elements of a Postclassical Narratology. *PMLA* 112.5: 1046-59.
– 1998. Limits of Order: Toward a Theory of Polychronic Narration. *Narrative* 6.1: 72-95.
– 1999a. Introduction. In David Herman (ed.), *Narratologies: New Perspectives on Narrative Analysis*. Columbus: Ohio State University Press: 1-30.
– 1999b. Ed. *Narratologies: New Perspectives on Narrative Analysis*. Columbus: Ohio State University Press.
– 1999c. Toward a Socionarratology: New Ways of Analyzing Natural-Language Narratives. In David Herman (ed.), *Narratologies: New Perspectives on Narrative Analysis*. Columbus: Ohio State University Press: 218-46.
– 2001. Sciences of the Text. *Postmodern Culture* 11.3. http://www.iath.virginia.edu/pmc/text-only/issue.501/11.3herman.txt.
– 2002. *Story Logic: Problems and Possibilities of Narrative*. Lincoln: University of Nebraska Press.
– 2003. (Ed.), *Narrative Theory and the Cognitive Sciences*. Stanford, CA: CSLI [Center for the Study of Language and Information] Publications.
– 2004. Toward a Transmedial Narratology. In Marie-Laure Ryan. (ed.), *Narrative across Media: The Languages of Storytelling*. Lincoln: University of Nebraska Press: 47-75.
– 2005b. "Quantitative Methods in Narratology" In Jan Christoph Meister, ed. (in cooperation with Tom Kindt, Wilhelm Schernus, and Malte Stein), *Narratology Beyond Literary Criticism*. Berlin: de Gruyter: 125-49.
– 2007a. "Storytelling and the Sciences of Mind", *Narrative* 15.3 (2007): 306-34.
– 2007b. (Ed.), "Narrative and Drama", Cambridge Companion to Narrative Theory, Cambridge UP: 142-56.
– 2008. "Narrative Theory and the Intentional Stance" *Partial Answers* 6.2 (2008): 233-60.
– 2009a. "Beyond Voice and Vision: Cognitive Grammar and Focalization Theory" *Point of View, Perspective, Focalization: Modeling Mediacy*. Eds. Peter Hühn, Wolf Schmid, and Jörg Schönert. Berlin: de Gruyter: 119-42.
– 2009b. *Basic Elements of Narrative*. Oxford: Wiley-Blackwell.

– 2009c. "Storied Minds: Narrative Scaffolding for Folk Psychology" *Journal of Consciousness Studies* 16.6-8 (2009): 40-68.
– 2010a. "Narrative Theory and the Second Cognitive Revolution" In Lisa Zunshine, ed., *Introduction to Cognitive Cultural Studies*. Baltimore: Johns Hopkins University Press: 155-75.
– 2010b. "Directions in Cognitive Narratology: Triangulating Stories, Media, and the Mind" In Jan Alber and Monika Fludernik, eds., *Postclassical Narratology: Approaches and Analyses*. Columbus: Ohio State University Press: 137-62.
– 2011a. "1880-1945: Re-minding Modernism." In David Herman, ed., *The Emergence of Mind: Representations of Consciousness in Narrative Discourse in English*. Lincoln: U of Nebraska: 243-72
– 2011b. "Introduction." In David Herman, ed., *The Emergence of Mind: Representations of Consciousness in Narrative Discourse in English*. Lincoln: U of Nebraska P: 1-40
– 20011c. Ed. *The Emergence of Mind: Representations of Consciousness in Narrative Discourse in English*. Lincoln: University of Nebraska Press, 2011.
Herman, David, Manfred Jahn, and Marie-Laure Ryan (eds.). 2005. *The Routledge Encyclopedia of Narrative Theory*. London: Routledge.
Herman, David, Brian McHale, and James Phelan (eds.). 2010. *Teaching Narrative Theory*. New York: MLA Publications.
Herman, David, James Phelan, Peter Rabinowitz, Brian Richardson, and Robyn Warhol 2012. *Narrative Theory: Core Concepts and Critical Debates*. Columbus: Ohio State University Press.
Herman, Luc, and Bart Vervaeck. 2005. Postclassical Narratology. In David Herman, Manfred Jahn, and Marie-Laure Ryan (eds.), *The Routledge Encyclopedia of Narrative Theory*. London: Routledge: 450-51.
Herrnstein Smith, Barbara, and Arkady Plotnitsky, (eds.). 1997. *Mathematics, Science, and Postclassical Theory*. Durham: Duke University Press.
Hirsch, E.D.. 1967. *Validity in Interpretation*. New Haven: Yale University Press.
–1976. *The Aims of Interpretation*. Chicago: University of Chicago Press.
Hogan, Patrick Colm. 1997. Literary universals. *Poetics Today* 18: 223-249.
– 2003a. *The mind and its stories: Narrative universals and*

human emotion. Cambridge: Cambridge University Press.
– 2003b. *Cognitive Science, Literature, and the Arts: A Guide for Humanists.* New York: Routledge, 2003.
–(forthcoming). *Affective Narratology: The Emotional Structure of Stories.* Lincoln: University of Nebraska Press.
Hrushovski, Benjamin. 1976. Poetics, Criticism, Science: Remarks on the Fields and Responsibilities of the Study of Literature', *Poetics and Theory of Literature* 1: iii-xxxv.
Hühn, Peter, John Pier, Wolf Schmid & Jorg Schönert (eds.). 2009. *Handbook of Narratology.* Narratologia 19. Berlin/New York: de Gruyter.
Hutto, Daniel D. (2008). *Folk Psychological Narratives: The Sociocultural Basis of Understanding Reasons.* Cambridge, MA: MIT P.
Ingarden, Roman. 1973. *The Literary Work of Art.* tr. George G. Grabowicz. Evanston: Northwestern University Press.
– 1981. *Spór o istnienie $\frac{1}{2}$wiata [Controversy over the Existence of the World]*, vol. III. Warsaw: Pañstwowe Wydawnictwo Naukowe.
– 1987. *Spór o istnienie $\frac{1}{2}$wiata [Controversy over the Existence of the World]*, vol. I-II/1-2, 3rd revised ed. Warsaw: Pañstwowe Wydawnictwo Naukowe.
Iser, Wolfgang. 1978. *The Act of Reading: A Theory of Aesthetic Response.* Baltimore: Johns Hopkins University Press.
– 1980. The reading process: A phenomenological approach. In Jane P. Tompkins (ed.), *Reader response criticism: From Formalism to Post-structuralism.* Baltimore: Johns Hopkins University Press: 50-69.
– 1989.*Prospecting: From reader response to literary anthropology.* Baltimore: Johns Hopkins University Press.
Jackson, Tony E. 2002. *Issues and problems in the blending of cognitive science, evolutionary psychology, and literary study.* Poetics Today 23: 161-179.
Jakobson, Roman. 1990. *On Language.* Edited by Linda R. Waugh and Monique Monville-Burston. Cambridge, MA: Harvard University Press.
Jahn, Manfred. 1996. Windows of Focalization: Deconstructing and Reconstructing a Narratological Concept. *Style* 30.2: 241-67
– 1997. Frames, preferences and the reading of third person narratives: Towards a cognitive narratology. *Poetics Today* 18.4: 441-68.
– 1999. 'Speak, friend, and enter': Garden Paths, Artificial Intel-

ligence, and Cognitive Narratology. In David Herman (ed.), *Narratologies: New Perspectives on Narrative Analysis*, Ohio: Ohio State University Press: 167-94.
– 1999b. More Aspects of Focalization: Refinements and Applications. *GRAAT: Revue des Groupes de Recherches Anglo-Américaines de L'Université François Rabelais de Tours* 2: 85-110.
– 2001. Narrative Voice and Agency in Drama: Aspects of a Narratology of Drama. *New Literary History* 32: 659-79.
– 2004. Foundational issues in teaching cognitive narratology. *European Journal of English Studies*. 8.1: 105-27.
– 2004. 'Awake! Open your eyes!' The Cognitive Logic of External and Internal Stories. In David Herman (ed.), Narrative Theory and the Cognitive Sciences, Stanford: CSLI Publications: 195-213.
– 2005. Cognitive Narratology. In David Herman, Manfred Jahn, and Marie-Laure Ryan (eds.), *The Routledge Encyclopedia of Narrative Theory*. London: Routledge. 67-71.
– 2005. *PPP: Poems, Plays, Prose: A Guide to the Theory of Literary Genres*. http://www.uni-koeln.de/~ame02/ppp.htm.
James, Henry. 1962. *The Art of the Novel: Critical Prefaces*. Ed. Richard P. Blackmur. New York: Scribner's, 1962.
Johnson, Mark. 2007. *The Meaning of the Body: Aesthetics of Human Understanding*. Chicago: University of Chicago Press.
Kafalenos, Emma. 2006. *Narrative Causalities*. Columbus: Ohio State University Press
Kafetsios, Konstantinus, and Eric LaRock. 2005. "Cognition and Emotion: Aristotelian Affinities with Contemporary Emotion Research", *Theory of Psychology* 15: 639-657.
Kawashima, Robert. 2004. *Biblical Narrative and the Death of the Rhapsode*, Bloomington: Indiana University Press.
Kearns, M. 1999. *Rhetorical Narratology*. Lincoln: University of Nebraska Press.
Keen, Suzanne. 2007. *Empathy and the novel*. Oxford: Oxford University Press.
Kellner, Hans. 1989. *Language and Historical Representation: Getting the Story Crooked*. Madison: University of Wisconsin Press.
Kermode, Frank. 1966. *The Sense of an Ending: Studies in the Theory of Fiction*. Oxford: Oxford University Press.
Kindt, Tom & Hans-Harald Müller (eds.). 2003. *What is Narratology? Questions and Answers Regarding the Status of a Theory*. Narratologia 1. Berlin/New York: de Gruyter.
Kintsch, Walter. 1998. *Comprehension*. Cambridge: Cambridge

University Press.
Kintsch, Walter and E. Greene. 1978. The role of culture-specific schemata in the comprehension and recall of stories. *Discourse Processes.* 1:1-13.
Kozloff, Sarah. 1988. *Invisible Storytellers: Voice-over Narration in American Fiction Film.* Berkeley: U of California Press.
Kuiken, Don, Miall, David S., and Shelley Sikora. 2004. Forms of self-implication in literary reading. *Poetics Today* 25: 171-203.
Kuroda, S.-Y. 1973. Where Epistemology, Style and Grammar Meet: A Case Study from the Japanese. In Stephen R. Anderson and Paul Kiparsky (eds.), *A Festschrift for Morris Halle.* New York: Holt, Rinehart and Winston: 377-391.

– 1976. Reflections on the Foundations of Narrative Theory — from a Linguistic Point of View. In Teun A. van Djik (ed.), *Pragmatics of Language and Literature.* Amsterdam and New York: North-Holland Publishing Company: 107-140.

– 1979. Some Thoughts on the Foundations of the Theory of Language Use. *Linguistics and Philosophy* 3.1: 1-17.

Labov, William. 1972a. *Language in the Inner City.* Philadelphia: University of Pennsylvania Press.

– 1972b. The Transformation of Experience in Narrative Syntax. In *Language in the Inner City.* Philadelphia: University of Pennsylvania Press: 354-96.

Labov, William, and Joshea Waletzky. 1967. Narrative Analysis: Oral Versions of Personal Experience. In June Helm (ed.), *Essays on the Verbal and Visual Arts: Proceedings of the 1966 Annual Spring Meeting of the Amertican Ethnological Society.* Seattle: University of Washington Press.

Lahn, Silke and Jan Christoph Meister. 2008. *Einführung in die Erzähltextanalyse.* Stuttgart: J.B. Metzler.

Lakoff, George and Johnson, Mark. 1999. *Philosophy in the Flesh: The Embodied Mind and Its Challenge to Western Thought.* New York: Basic Books.

Langacker, Ronald. 2008. *Cognitive Grammar: A Basic Introduction.* Oxford: Oxford University Press.

Lanser, Susan S. 1981. *The Narrative Act: Point of View in Prose Fiction.* Princeton: Princeton University Press.

– 1986. Toward a Feminist Narratology. *Style* 20: 341-63.

– 1988. Shifting the Paradigm: Feminism and Narratology. *Style* 22:1: 52-60.

– 1989. Feminist Criticism, "The Yellow Wallpaper," and the

Politics of Color in America. *Feminist Studies*, 15.3: 415-41.
– 1992. *Fictions of Authority: Women Writers and Narrative Voice*. Ithaca: Cornell University Press.
– 1995. Sexing the Narrative: Propriety, Desire, and the Engendering of Narratology. *Narrative* 3.1: 85-94
– 1996. Queering Narratology. In Kathy Mezei (ed.), *Ambiguous Discourse: Feminist Narratology and British Women Writers*. Chapel Hill: University of North Carolina Press: 250-61.
– 2001. (Im)plying the Author. *Narrative* 9.2: 153-60.
– 2003. The Author's Queer Clothes: Authority and Sex/uality in *The Travels and Adventures of Mademoiselle de Richelieu*. In Robert Griffin (ed.), *The Faces of Anonymity 1500-1900*. London: Palgrave Press: 81-102.
– 2005a. The Novel Body Politic. In Paula Backscheider and Catherine Ingrassia, (eds.) *The Eighteenth-Century Novel: Companion to Literature and Culture*. Oxford: Blackwell: 481-503.
– 2005b. The 'I' of the Beholder. *The Blackwell Companion to Narrative Theory*. Oxford: 206-219.
– 2010. Sapphic Dialogics: Historical Narratology and the Sexuality of Form. In Monika Fludernik and Jan Alber (eds.), *Postclassical Narratology: Approaches and Analyses*. Columbus: Ohio State University
Lavocat, Françoise and Anne Duprat (eds.). 2010. *Fiction et cultures*. Collection Poétiques comparatistes. Paris: SFLGC.
Le Guin, Ursula. 1981. It Was a Dark and Stormy Night, Or, Why Are We Huddling about the Campfire? In W. J. T. Mitchell (ed.), *On Narrative*. Chicago: University of Chicago Press: 187-95.
Lintvelt, Jaap. 1981. *Essai de Typologie narrative: le "point de vue"*. Paris: Corti.
Lips, Marguerite. 1924.*Le Style Indirect Libre*, Paris: Payot
Lodge, David. 1977. *The Modes of Modern Writing: Metaphor, Metonymy and the Typology of Modern Literature*. London: Edward Arnold.
Lord, Albert. 1960. *The Singer of Tales*, Cambridge, MA: Harvard Univ. Press.
Lothe, Jakob, Jeremy Hawthorn, and James Phelan, (eds.). 2008. *Joseph Conrad: Voice, Sequence, History, Genre*. Columbus: Ohio State Univ. Press.
Lothe, Jakob, Susan R. Suleiman, and James Phelan. (forthcoming). *After Testimony: The Ethics and Aesthetics of Holocaust Narrative*. Columbus: Ohio State University Press.
Louwerse, Max and van Peer, Willie. 2009. How cognitive is

cognitive poetics? Adding a symbolic approach to the embodied one. In Geert Brône and Jeroen Vandaele (eds.), *Cognitive Poetics: Goals, Gains and Gaps*, Berlin: Mouton de Gruyter, pp.423-54.

Magliano, Joseph P., and Arthur C. Graesser. 1991. A three-pronged method for studying inference generation in literary text. *Poetics* 20: 193-232.

Mani, Inderjeet. 2010. *The Imagined Moment: Time, Narrative and Computation*. Lincoln: University of Nebraska Press.

Margolin, Uri. 1984. Narrative and Indexicality: A Theoretical Framework. *Journal of Literary Semantics* 13,: 181-204.

– 1986-7. Decentering/Voiding the Subject: A Narratological Perspective. *Texte* 5/6: 181-201.

– 1990. Narrative 'You' Revisited. *Language and Style* 23.4:425-46.

– 1991. Reference, Co-reference, Referring and the Dual Structure of Literary Narrative. *Poetics Today* 12.3: 517-42.

– 1992. Singulars, Splits, Multiples: The Theme of the Double and Fictional Worlds Semantics. *Journal of Literary Semantics* 21.3: 175-203.

– 1995. Changing Individuals in Narrative: Science, Philosophy, Literature. *Semiotica* 106.3-4: 373-92.

– 1996a. Telling Our Story: On 'We' Literary Narratives. *Language and Literature* 5.2: 115-33.

– 1996b. Characters and their Versions." In Calin-Andrei Mihailescu and Walid Hamarneh (eds.), *Fiction Updated*. University of Toronto Press: 113-32.

– 1999. Of What Is Past, Is Passing or To Come: Temporality, Aspectuality, Modality and the Nature of Literary Narrative. In David Herman (ed.), *Narratologies: New Perspectives on Narrative Analysis*. Ohio State University Press: 142-66.

– 2000. Telling in the Plural: From Grammar to Ideology. *Poetics Today* 21. 3: 591-618.

– 2002. Naming and Believing: Practices of the Proper Name in Narrative Fiction. *Narrative* 10.2, 2002: 107-22.

– 2005. Character. In *Routledge Encyclopedia of Narrative Theory*. Routledge: 52-7.

– 2007. Character. In David Herman (ed.), *The Cambridge Companion to Narrative*. Cambridge University Press, 2007: 66-79.

McHale, Brian. 1987. *Postmodernist Fiction*. New York and London: Methuen & Co. Ltd.

– 1991. Weak Narrativity: the Case of Avant-Garde Narrative

Poetry. *Narrative* 9: 161-67
- 1992. *Contructing Postmodernism.* London and New York: Routledge.
- 2009. Beginning to Think about Narrative in Poetry. *Narrative* 17.1: 11-30.
McClary, Susan. 1991. *Feminine Endings: Music, Gender, and Sexuality.* Minneapolis: University of Minnesota Press.
McCloskey, Deirdre. 1998. *The Rhetoric of Economics.* 2nd Edition. Madison: University of Wisconsin Press.
Meister, Jan Christoph. 2009. Narratology. In Peter Hühn, John Pier, Wolf Schmid and Jorg Schönert (eds.). 2009. *Handbook of Narratology.* Narratologia 19. Berlin/New York: de Gruyter: 329–350.
Miall, David S. 1976. Aesthetic unity and the role of the brain. *Journal of Aesthetics and Art Criticism* 35: 57-67.
- 1989. Beyond the schema given: Affective comprehension of literary narratives. *Cognition and Emotion* 3: 55-78.
- 1990. Readers' responses to narrative: Evaluating, relating, anticipating. *Poetics* 19. 323-339.
- 2008. Feeling from the perspective of the empirical study of literature. *Journal of Literary Theory vol. 1*: 377-393.
- 2010. *A neurophysiological approach to the elements of literariness.* Paper presented at the conference of the International Society for the Empirical Study of Literature and Media (IGEL). July, 7-11, University of Utrecht.
- Forthcoming. Enacting the Other: Towards an Aesthetics of Feeling in Literary Reading. In Peter Goldie and Elisabeth Schellekens (ed.), *The Aesthetic Mind: Philosophy and Psychology.* Oxford: Oxford University Press.
Miall, David S., and Don Kuiken. 1994. Foregrounding, defamiliarization, and affect: Response to literary stories. *Poetics* 22: 389-407.
- 1999. What is literariness? Three components of literary reading. *Discourse Processes* 28: 121-138.
- 2001. Shifting perspectives: Readers' feelings and literary response. In Willie van Peer and Seymour Chatman (eds.), *New perspectives on narrative perspective.* Albany, NY: State University of New York Press: 289-301.
Miller, Hillis J. 1980/81. A Guest in the House. Reply to Shlomith Rimmon-Kenan's Reply. *Poetics Today* 2.1b: 189-191.
Milner, Jean-Claude. 1978. *De la syntaxe à l'interprétation. Quantités, insultes, exclamations.* Paris: Seuil

Mitscherling, Jeff. 1997. *Roman Ingarden's Ontology and Aesthetics.* Ottawa: University of Ottawa Press.
− 2010. *Aesthetic Genesis: The Origin of Consciousness in the Intentional Being of Nature.* Lanham: University Press of America.
Mitscherling, Jeff, DiTommaso, Tanya, and Nayed, Aref. 2004. *The Author's Intention.* Lanham: Lexington Books.
Mukařovský, J. 1964. Standard language and poetic language. In P. L. Garvin (ed.), *A Prague School reader on esthetics, literary structure, and style.* Washington, DC: Georgetown University Press: : 17-30. (Original work published 1932.)
Nelles, William. 2001. Beyond the Bird's Eye: Animal Focalization. *Narrative* 9.2: 188-94.
Nielsen, Henrik Skov. 2004. The Impersonal Voice in First-Person Narrative Fiction. *Narrative* 12.2: 133-50.
Nünning, Ansgar. 1995. *Von historischer Fiktion zu historiographischer Metafiktion. Bd. 1.: Theorie, Typologie und Poetik des historischen Romans. Bd. 2.: Erscheinungsformen und Entwicklungstendenzen des historischen Romans in England seit 1950.* [*From Historical Fiction to Historiographic Metafiction. Vol. 1: Theory, Typology, and Poetics of the Historical Novel. Vol. 2: Kinds and Developments of the Historical Novel in England since 1950*]. 2 vols. Trier: Wissenschaftlicher Verlag Trier
− 1998a. (Ed.), *Unreliable Narration: Studien zur Theorie und Praxis unglaubwürdigen Erzählens in der englischsprachigen Erzählliteratur.* [*Unreliable Narration: Studies on the Theory and Use of Unreliable Narration in English Fiction*]. Trier: Wissenschaftlicher Verlag Trier 1998.
− 1998b. (Ed.), *Metzler Lexikon Literatur- und Kulturtheorie: Ansätze − Personen − Grundbegriffe.* [*Metzler Encyclopedia of Literary and Cultural Theory: Approaches - Theorists - Technical Terms*]. Stuttgart, Weimar: J.B. Metzler Verlag, 4th ed. 2008.
− 2003. Narratology or Narratologies? Taking Stock of Recent Developments, Critique and Modest Proposals for Future Usages of the Term. In Tom Kindt and Hans-Harald Müller (Eds.), *What is Narratology?* Berlin: de Gruyter. 239-75.
− 2004. Where Historiographic Metafiction and Narratology Meet: Towards an Applied Cultural Narratology. In Monika Fludernik and Uri Margolin (eds.), *Recent Developments in German Narratology, Style* 38.3: 352-375.
− 2005a. Reconceptualizing Unreliable Narration: Synthesizing Cognitive and Rhetorical Approaches. In James Phelan and Peter

J. Rabinowitz (eds.), *A Companion to Narrative Theory*. Oxford: Blackwell: 89-107.

– 2005b. On Metanarrative: Towards a Definition, a Typology, and an Outline of the Functions of Metanarrative Commentary. In John Pier (ed.), *The Dynamics of Narrative Form. Studies in Anglo-American Narratology*, Narratologia 4. Berlin, New York: de Gruyter: 11-57.

– 2007. Distinguishing and Historicizing Different Kinds of (Meta-)Description: Forms and Functions of Description in Realist, Modernist, and Postmodernist Fiction. In Werner Wolf and Walter Bernhart (eds.), *Description in Literature and Other Media*, Amsterdam: Rodopi: 91-128.

– 2008. Diegetic and Mimetic Narrativity: Some Further Steps towards a Narratology of Drama. In John Pier and José Angel García Landa (eds.), *Theorizing Narrativity*, Narratologia 12. Berlin, New York: de Gruyter: 331-354 (with Roy Sommer).

– 2009. Surveying Contextualist and Cultural Narratologies: Towards an Outline of Approaches, Concepts and Potentials. In Sandra Heinen and Roy Sommer (Eds.), *Narratology in the Age of Cross-Disciplinary Narrative Research*, Narratologia 20. Berlin, New York: de Gruyter: 48-70.

– 2010. Making Events – Making Stories – Making Worlds: Ways of Worldmaking from a Narratological Point of View. In Vera Nünning, Ansgar Nünning & Birgit Neumann (eds.), *Cultural Ways of Worldmaking: Media and Narratives*. New York: de Gruyter: 191-214.

Nünning, Ansgar and Birgit Neumann. *Introduction to the Analysis of Narrative Fiction*. Stuttgart: Klett 2008.

Nünning, Ansgar & Vera Nünning (eds.). 2000. *Multiperspektivisches Erzählen: Zur Theorie und Geschichte der Perspektivenstruktur im englischen Roman des 18. bis 20. Jahrhunderts*. [*Multiperspectival Narration: On the Theory and History of the Perspective Structure of English Novels from the 18th to the 20th Century*]. Trier: Wissenschaftlicher Verlag Trier.

– 2002a. *Neue Ansätze in der Erzähltheorie*. [*New Approaches in Narrative Theory*]. WVT-Handbücher zum literaturwissenschaftlichen Studium, Bd. 4. Trier: Wissenschaftlicher Verlag Trier.

– 2002b. *Erzähltheorie transgenerisch, intermedial, interdisziplinär*. [*Transgeneric, Intermedial, Interdisciplinary Narrative Theory*]. WVT-Handbücher zum literaturwissenschaftlichen Studium, Bd. 5. Trier: Wissenschaftlicher Verlag Trier.

– 2004. *Erzähltextanalyse und Gender Studies*. [*Analysing Nar-

rative Fiction and Gender Studies]. Sammlung Metzler, Bd. 344. Stuttgart: J.B. Metzler Verlag.
Nussbaum, Martha. 1990. *Love's Knowledge: Essays on Philosophy and Literature.* New York: Oxford Univesity Press.
Oatley, Keith. 2002. Emotions and the story worlds of fiction. In Melanie C. Green, Jeffrey J. Strange, & Timothy Brock (eds.), *Narrative impact: Social and cognitive foundations.* Mahwah, NJ: Lawrence Erlbaum: 39-69.
Ochs, Elinor, and Lisa Capps. 2001. *Living Narrative: Creating Lives in Everyday Storytelling.* Cambridge, MA: Harvard University Press.
Ohmann, Richard. 1970. Modes of Order. In Donald C. Freeman (ed.), *Linguistics and Literary Style,* 209-242. New York: Holt, Rinehart & Winston [1962].
Olson, Greta, (Ed.), (Forthcoming). *Current Trends in Narratology.* Narratologia. Berlin/New York: de Gruyter.
– 2011 (Ed.), "Endings in Drama and Performance: A Theoretical Model" Current Trends in Narratology, Berlin: de Gruyter, 2011: 181-99.
Page, Ruth. 2006. *Literary and Linguistic Approaches to Feminist Narratology.* New York: Palgrave.
Palmer, Alan. 2004. *Fictional Minds.* Lincoln: University of Nebraska Press.
– 2010. *Social Minds in the Novel.* Columbus: Ohio State University Press.
Patron, Sylvie. 2005a. Le narrateur et l'interprétation des termes déictiques dans le récit de fiction. In Daniele Monticelli, Renate Pajusalu, Anu Treikelder (eds.), *De l'énoncé à l'énonciation et vice-versa. Regards multidisciplinaires sur la deixis / From utterance to uttering and vice-versa: Multidisciplinary views on deixis.* Tartu: Tartu University Press, "Studia Romanica Tartuensia", vol. VI: 187-202
– 2005b. Describing the Circle of Narrative Theory: a Review Essay. *Style* 39.4: 479-488.
– 2005-2006. Sur l'épistémologie de la théorie narrative (narratologie et autres théories du récit de fiction). *Les Temps modernes* 635-636: 262-285.
– 2006/2008. On the Epistemology of Narrative Theory: Narratology and Other Theories of Fictional Narrative. Trans. Anne Marsella. In Matti Hyvärinen, Anu Korhonen and Juri Mykkänen (eds.), *The Traveling Concept of Narrative, COLLeGIUM: Studies across Disciplines in the Humanities and Social Sciences,* URL :

http://www.helsinki.fi/collegium/e-series/volumes/volume_1/index.htm, 2006: 118-133; reprinted in Robert Kawashima, Gilles Philippe and Thelma Sowley (eds.), *Phantom Sentences: Essays in Linguistics and Literature presented to Ann Banfield*. Berne: Peter Lang: 43-65.

– 2009. *Le Narrateur. Introduction à la théorie narrative*. Paris: Éditions Armand Colin, "U".

– 2010a. La mort du narrateur et l'interprétation du roman. L'exemple de *Pedro Páramo* de Juan Rulfo. In Sylvie Patron (ed.), *Théorie, analyse, interprétation des récits / Theory, analysis, interpretation of narratives*. Bern: Peter Lang: 149-185.

– 2010b. The Death of the Narrator and the Interpretation of the Novel: The Example of Pedro Páramo by Juan Rulfo. Trans. Susan Nicholls. Journal of Literary Theory, 4.2: 253-272.

– 2010c. Enunciative Narratology: a French Speciality. Trans. Anne Marsella,. In Greta Olson (ed.), *Current Trends in Narratology*. Berlin: Walter de Gruyter. Narratologia: 267-289.

– 2011d. (Ed.), *Théorie, analyse, interprétation des récits / Theory, analysis, interpretation of narratives*, Bern: Peter Lang.

– forthcoming *a*. Homonymie chez Genette ou la réception de l'opposition histoire/discours dans les théories du récit de fiction. In Émilie Brunet and Rudolf Mahrer (eds.), *Relire Benveniste. Actualité des recherches sur l'énonciation*, Louvain-la-Neuve: Academia-Bruylant.

– forthcoming *b*. Homonymy, Polysemy, and Synonymy: Reflections on the Notion of Voice. Trans. Susan Nicholls. In Stefan Iversen, Per Krogh Hansen and Henrik Skov Nielsen (eds.), *Strange Voices*. Berlin: Walter de Gruyter. Narratologia.

– forthcoming *c*. Narrative Fiction Prior to 1850: Instances of Refutation for Poetic Theories of Narration? Trans. Susan Nicholls. Amsterdam International Electronic Journal for Cultural Narratology (ACJN) 6. Proceeedings of the 2nd Conference of the European Narratology Network.

Pavel, Thomas. 1976. *La Syntaxe narrative des tragédies de Corneille: Recherches et propositions*. Paris: Klincksieck & Ottawa: Editions de l'Université d'Ottawa.

– 1985. *The Poetics of Plot: The Case of English Renaissance Drama*. Minneapolis: University of Minnesota Press ("Theory and History of Literature", vol. 18)

– 1989. *Fictional Worlds*. Cambridge, MA: Harvard University Press, 1986. Paperback edition, Spring 1989.

– 1996. *L'Art de l'éloignement. Essai sur l'imagination classique*.

Paris: Gallimard.

– 1998a. (With Claude Bremond). *De Barthes à Balzac. Fictions d'un critique et critiques d'une fiction*. Paris: Albin Michel.

– 1998b. Freedom, from Romance to the Novel: Three Anti-Utopian American Critics. *New Literary History* 29: 579-598.

– 2000. Fiction and Imitation. *Poetics Today* 21.3: 521-541.

– 2001 *The Spell of Language. Post-Structuralism and Speculation*, University of Chicago Press. Revised edition of *The Feud of Language*, Oxford & New York: Basil Blackwell, 1989.

– 2003. *La Pensée du roman*, Paris: Gallimard

– 2006. *Comment écouter la littérature*, Paris: Fayard, Leçons inaugurales du Collège de France.

Pellauer, David. 2007. *Ricoeur: A Guide for the Perplexed*. London: Continuum.

Perry, Menachem. 1979. Literary Dynamics: How the Order of a Text Creates its Meanings. *Poetics Today* 1-2: 35-64; 311-61.

Perry, Menachem and Meir Sternberg. 1968. The King through Ironic Eyes: The Narrator's Devices in the Biblical Story of David and Bathsheba and Two Excursuses on the Theory of the Narrative Text (in Hebrew). *Hasifrut* 1: 263-292. English Abstract 449-452.

Phelan, James. 1981. *Worlds from Words: A Theory of Language in Fiction*. Chicago: University of Chicago Press.

– 1989a. *Reading People, Reading Plots: Character, Progression, and the Interpretation of Narrative*. Chicago: University of Chicago Press.

– 1989b. (Ed.), *Reading Narrative: Form, Ethics, Ideology*. Ed. Columbus: Ohio State University Press, 1989.

– 1996. *Narrative as Rhetoric: Technique, Audiences, Ethics, Ideology*. Columbus: Ohio State University Press.

– 2005. *Living to Tell about It: A Rhetoric and Ethics of Character Narration*. Ithaca, NY: Cornell Univ. Press.

– 2007a. Estranging Unreliability, Bonding Unreliability, and the Ethics of *Lolita*. *Narrative* 15: 222-38.

– 2007b. *Experiencing Fiction: Judgments, Progressions, and the Rhetorical Theory of Narrative*. Ohio State Univ. Press, 2007.

Phelan, James and Peter J. Rabinowitz (eds.). 1994. *Understanding Narrative*. Columbus: Ohio State University Press, 1994

– 2005. *A Companion to Narrative Theory*. Oxford: Blackwell, Publishing.

Phelan, James and David H. Richter (eds.). Forthcoming. *Fact, Fiction, and Form: Selected Essays of Ralph W. Rader.*

Columbus: Ohio State University Press.
Philippe, Gilles. 2002. *Sujet, verbe, complément. Le moment grammatical de la littérature française 1890-1940*. Paris: Gallimard.
Pichert, J. W. & Anderson, R. C. 1977. Taking different perspectives on a story. *Journal of Educational Psychology* 69: 309-315.
Pier, John. 2003. On the Semiotic Parameters of Narrative Discourse: A Critique of Story and Discourse. In Tom Kindt and Hans-Harald Müller (eds.), *What is Narratology? Questions and Answers Regarding the Status of a Theory*. Narratologia 1. Berlin/New York: de Gruyter: 73–97.
– 2004a. Narrative Configurations. In John Pier (ed.), *The Dynamics of Narrative Form. Studies in Anglo-American Narratology*. Narratologia 4. Berlin/New York: de Gruyter: 239–268.
– 2004b. (Ed.), *The Dynamics of Narrative Form. Studies in Anglo-American Narratology*. Narratologia 4. Berlin/New York: de Gruyter.
– 2007. (Ed.), *Théorie du récit. L'apport de la recherche allemande*. Trans. Thierry Gallèpe et al. Villeneuve d'Ascq: Presses universitaires du Septentrion.
– 2008. After this, therefore because of this. In John Pier and José Ángel García Landa (eds.), *Theorizing Narrativity*. Narratologia 12. Berlin/New York: de Gruyter.: 109–140.
– 2010. Gérard Genette's Evolving Narrative Poetics. *Narrative* 18.1: 376–386.
– forthcoming a. Intermedial Metareference: Index and Icon in William Gass's *Willy Masters' Lonesome Wife*". In Werner Wolf (ed.), *The Metareferential Turn: Forms, Functions, Attempts at Explanation*. Studies in Intermediality 5. Amsterdam/New York: Rodopi.
– forthcoming b. Is There a French Postclassical Narratology? In Greta Olson (ed.), *Current Trends in Narratology*. Narratologia. Berlin/New York: de Gruyter.
Pier, John and Jean-Marie Schaeffer (eds.). 2005. *Métalepses. Entorses au pacte de la représentation*. Recherches d'histoire et de sciences sociales 108. Paris: Éditions de l'EHESS.
Pier, John and José Ángel García Landa (eds.). 2008. *Theorizing Narrativity*. Narratologia 12. Berlin/New York: de Gruyter.
Pier, John and Francis Berthelot (eds.). 2010. *Narratologies contemporaines. Approches nouvelles pour la théorie et l'analyse du récit*. Paris: Éditions des Archives Contemporaines.

Prince, Gerald. 1971. Notes Towards a Preliminary Categorization of Fictional 'Narratees'. *Genre* 4.1: 100-06
- 1973a. *A Grammar of Stories*. Mouton: The Hague, 1973.
- 1973. Introduction a l'étude du narrataire. *Poétique* 14: 178-96. English translation "Introduction to the Study of the Narratee", in Jane Tompkins (ed.), *Reader-Response Criticism*. Baltimore: Johns Hopkins University Press, 1980: 7-25
- 1977. Remarques sur les signes métanarratifs. *Degrés* 11-12: e1-e10.
- 1978. Le Discours attributif et le récit. *Poétique* 35: 305-13
- 1980a. Notes on the Text as Reader. In Susan R. Suleiman and Inge Crosman (eds.), *The Reader in the Text*. Princeton: Princeton University Press: 225-240.
- 1980b. Attributive Discourse in *Madame Bovary*. In Robert Mitchell (ed.), *Pretext/Text/Context*. Columbus: Ohio State University Press: 268-75.
- 1980c. Aspects of a Grammar of Narrative. *Poetics Today* 1.3: 49-63.
- 1980d. Introduction to the Study of the Narratee. In Jane Tompkins (ed.), *Reader-Response Criticism*. Baltimore: Johns Hopkins University Press: 7-25
- 1981a. On Metanarrative Signs. In Béla Köpeczi and Gyorgy M. Vayda (eds.), *Actes du Huitième Congrès de l'Association Internationale de Littérature Comparée*. Budapest: Akadem Kiado, 1981: 911-15.
- 1981b. Narrativity. In Daniel Rancour-Laferrière and Karl Menges (eds.), *Axia. Davis Symposium on Literary Evaluation*. Stuttgart: Akademischer Verlag: 61-76.
- 1982. *Narratology: The Form and Functioning of Narrative*. New York: Mouton.
- 1988. The Disnarrated. *Style* 22: 1-8.
- 1989. L'Alternarré. *Strumenti Critici* 4: 223-31.
- 1993. On Formalist Narratology. *Languages of Design* 1: 303-19.
- 1999. Revisiting Narratology. In Walter Grünzweig and Andrew Solbach (eds.), *Narratologie, Linguistik und Rhetorik*. Tübingen: Narr: 43-51.
- 2003. Surveying Narratology. In Tom Kindt, and Hans-Harald Müller (eds.), *What is Narratology? Questions and Answers Regarding the Status of a Theory*. Narratologia 1. Berlin/New York: de Gruyter: 1–16.
- 2005. On a Postcolonial Narratology. In James Phelan & Peter

J. Rabinowitz (eds.), *A Companion to Narrative Theory*. Maldlen, MA, Oxford & Victoria: Blackwell Press: 372-382.
– 2006. Narratologie classique et narratologie post-classique. *Vox Poetica*. http://www.vox-poetica.org/t/prince06.html
– 2008. Narrativehood, Narrativeness, Narrativity, Narratability. In John Pier and José Angel García Landa (eds.), *Theorizing Narrativity*. Berlin: Walter de Gruyter: 19-27.
– 2011. Story Grammars. In Patrick Colm Hogan (ed.), *The Cambridge Encyclopedia of the Language Sciences*. Cambridge: Cambridge University Press: 806-808
Propp, Vladimir. 1970. *Morphology of the Folktale* [1927]. Austin: University of Texas Press.
Rabinowitz, Peter J. 1977. Truth in Fiction: A Reexamination of Audiences. *Critical Inquiry* 4: 121-41.
– 1981. Pleasure in Conflict: Mahler's Sixth, Tragedy, and Musical Form. *Comparative Literature Studies* 18.3: 306-313.
– 1992. Chord and Discourse: Listening Through the Written Word. In Steven Pearl Scher (ed.) *Music and Text: Critical Inquiries*.
– 1994. 'Betraying the Sender': The Rhetoric and Ethics of Fragile Texts. *Narrative*. 2.3: 201-13.
– 1998. *Before Reading*. Second Edition. Columbus: Ohio State University Press. First edition: Ithaca, N.Y.: Cornell University Press, 1987.
– 1999. 'Singing for Myself': Carmen and the Rhetoric of Musical Resistance. In Elaine Barkin and Lydia Hamessley (eds.), *Audible Traces: Gender, Identity, and Music*. Zurich: Carciofoli, 1999. 133-151.
– 2004. Music, Genre, and Narrative Theory. *Narrative Across Media: The Languages of Storytelling*. Lincoln: University of Nebraska Press: 305-328.
– 2007. The Rhetoric of Reference; or, Shostakovich's Ghost Quartet. *Narrative* 15.2: 239-56.
– forthcoming. Shakespeare's Dolphin, Dumbo's Feather, and Other Red Herrings: Some Thoughts on Intention and Meaning. *Style*.
Rabinowitz, Peter J. and Michael W. Smith. 1998. *Authorizing Readers: Resistance and Respect in the Teaching of Literature*. New York: Teachers College Press/NCTE.
Radway, Janice. 1984. *Reading the Romance: Women, Patriarchy, and Popular Literature*. Chapel Hill: University of North Caroline Press.

Rajewski, Irina O. 2007. Von Erzählern, die (nichts vermitteln): Überlegungen zu grundlegenden Annahmen der Dramentheorie im Kontext einer transmedialen Narratologie. *Zeitschrift für französische Sprache und Literatur* 117: 25-68.
Richardson, Alan. 2004. Studies in literature and cognition: A field map. In Alan Richardson and Ellen Spolsky (eds.), *The work of fiction: Cognition, culture, and complexity.* Aldershot: Ashgate: 1-29.
Richardson, Brian. 1997. Beyond Poststructuralism: Theory of Character, the Personae of Modern Drama, and the Antinomies of Critical Theory. *Modern Drama* 40: 86-99.
 – 2000. Narrative Poetics and Postmodern Transgression: Theorizing the Collapse of Time, Voice, and Frame. *Narrative* 8.1: 23-42.
 – 2002. Beyond Story and Discourse: Narrative Time in Postmodern and Nonmimetic Fiction. In Brian Richardson. (Ed.), *Narrative Dynamics: Essays on Time, Plot, Closure, and Frames.* Columbus: Ohio State University Press: 47-63.
 – 2006. *Unnatural Voices: Extreme Narration in Modern and Contemporary Fiction.* Columbus: Ohio State University Press.
 – 2007. "Narrative and Drama," Cambridge Companion to Narrative Theory, (ed.) David Herman, Cambridge UP: 142-56.
 – 2007. "Singular Text, Multiple Implied Readers," Style 41.3: 257-72.
Ricoeur, Paul. 1984-8. *Time and Narrative.* 3 vols. 1983-5. Trans. Kathleen McLaughlin and David Pellauer. Chicago: University of Chicago Press.
Rimmon-Kenan, Shlomith. 1977. *The Concept of Ambiguity, The Example of James.* Chicago: The University of Chicago Press.
 – 1983; (2002). *Narrative Fiction: Contemporary Poetics.* London and New York: Methuen, Routledge.
 – 1987. Ed., *Discourse in Psychoanalysis and Literature.* London and New York: Methuen.
 – 1996. *A Glance beyond Doubt: Narration, Representation, Subjectivity.* Columbus, Ohio: The Ohio State University Press.
 – 2002. The Story of 'I': Illness and Narrative Identity. *Narrative* 10.1: 9-27.
 – 2006a. In Two Voices, or Whose Life/ Death/ Story Is It, Anyway? In James Phelan and and Peter J. Rabinowitz (eds.), *A Companion to Narrative Theory.* Oxford: Blackwell Publishing: 399-412.
 – 2006b. What Can Narrative Theory Learn from Illness Nar-

ratives? *Literature and Medicine*, 25.2: 241-254.
– 2009: Place, Space, and Michal Govrin's Snapshots. *Narrative* 17.2: 220-234.
Robinson, Jenefer. 2005. *Deeper than reason: Emotion and its role in literature, music, and art.* Oxford: Clarendon Press.
Pascal, Roy. 1977. *The Dual Voice: Free Indirect speech and its functioning in the nineteenth century European novel.* Manchester: Manchester University Press.
Royle, Nicholas. 2003. The Telepathy Effect. In Nicholas Royle, *The Uncanny*, Manchester and New York: Manchester University Press/Routledge.
Ryan, Marie Laure. 1991. *Possible Worlds, Artificial Intelligence, and Narrative Theory.* Bloomington: Indiana University Press.
– (ed.) 2004. *Narrative across Media: The Language of Storytelling.* Lincoln: University of Nebraska Press.
– 2006. From Parallel Universes to Possible Worlds: Ontological Pluralism in Physics, Narratology, and Narrative. *Poetics Today* 27.4: 633-74.
– 2009. Temporal Paradoxes in Narrative. *Style* 43.2: 142-64.
Salway, Andrew, and David Herman (forthcoming). "Digitized Corpora as Theory-Building Resource: New Methods for Narrative Inquiry." In Ruth Page and Bronwen Thomas, (eds.), *New Narratives: Stories and Storytelling in the Digital Age.* Lincoln: University of Nebraska Press.
Schank, Roger C. 1995. *Tell Me a Story: Narrative and Intelligence.* Evanston: Northwestern University Press.
Scholes, Robert. 1982. *Semiotics and Interpretation.* New Haven: Yale University Press.
Schulz, Volker. 2005. *A Structuralist-generative Model of Literary Narrative*, Frankfurt /M.: Peter Lang.
Searle, John. 1975. The Logical Status of Fictional Discourse. *New Literary History* 6.2: 319-332. Reprinted in *Expression and Meaning: Studies in the Theory of Speech Acts.* Cambridge: Cambridge University Press: 58-75.
Seilman, U., and S.F. Larsen. 1989. Personal resonance to literature: A study of remindings while reading. *Poetics* 18: 165-177.
Sell, R.D. 2004. Blessings, benefactions, bear's Services: *Great Expectations* and communicational narratology. *European Journal of English Studies* 8.1:49-80.
Semino, Elena, and Michael Short. 2004. *Corpus Stylistics:*

Speech, Writing and Thought Presentation in a Corpus of English Narratives. London: Routledge.
Shields, Christopher. 1991. The First Functionalist. In J.C. Smith (ed.), *Historical Foundations of Cognitive Science*. Dordrecht: Kluwer.
Shklovsky, Victor. 1965. Art as Technique [1916]. In Lee T. Lemon and Marion J. Reis (eds.), *Russian Formalist Criticism*. Lincoln: University of Nebraska Press. 3-24.
– 1990. *Theory of Prose*. Trans. Benjamin Sher. Elmwood Park, IL: Dalkey Archive Press [1925].
Sibley, Frank. 1962. Aesthetic Qualities. In Joseph Margolis (ed.), *Phil-o-sophy Looks at the Arts*. New York: Scribner: 63-87 [1959].
Snow, C. P. 1959. *The Two Cultures and the Scientific Revolution*. Cambridge: Cambridge University Press, 1959.
Sperber, Dan and Deirdre Wilson. 1995. *Relevance: Communication and Cognition*. 2nd ed. Oxford: Blackwell, 1995.
Spolsky, Ellen. 1993. *Gaps in Nature: Literary Interpretation and the Modular Mind*. Albany: State University Press of New York
Stanzel, Franz Karl. 1955. *Die typischen Erzählsituationen im Roman*. Wien, Stuttgart: Braumüller.
– 1964. *Typische Formen des Romans*. Göttingen: Vandenhoeck und
– 1984. *A Theory of Narrative* [1979]. Transl. Charlotte Goedsche, with a Preface by Paul Hernadi. Cambridge: Cambridge University Press.
– 1990. A Low Structuralist at Bay? Further Thoughts on *A Theory of Narrative*. *Poetics Today*: 805-816
– 2002. *Unterwegs. Erzähltheorie für Leser*, Göttingen: Vandenhoeck & Ruprecht.
Sternberg, Meir. 1978. *Expositional Modes and Temporal Ordering in Fiction*. Baltimore: Johns Hopkins University Press.
– 1982. Proteus in Quotation-Land: Mimesis and the Forms of Reported Discourse. *Poetics Today* 3.2: 107-56.
– 1987. *The Poetics of Biblical Narrative. Ideological Literature and the Drama of Reading*. Bloomington: Indiana University Press.
– 2003. Universals of Narrative and Their Cognitivist Fortunes (I-II). *Poetics Today* 24: 297-395; 517-638.
– 2008. If-Plots: Narrativity and the Law-Code. *Theorizing Narrativity*. In John Pier and José Ángel Garciá Landa (eds.), *Nar-*

ratologia 12. Berlin: de Gruyter: 52-91.
Sternberg, Meir & Menachem Perry. 1967. The King through Ironic Eyes: The Narrtor's Devices in the Biblical Story of David and Bathsheba and Two Excursuses on the Theory of the Narrative Text. *Hasifrut* 1: 263-292.
Stockwell, Peter (2000) *The Poetics of Science Fiction,* London: Longman.
– 2002. *Cognitive Poetics*, London: Routledge.
– 2003. Schema poetics and speculative cosmology, *Language and Literature* 12.3: 252-71.
– 2007. Cognitive poetics and literary theory. *Journal of Literary Theory* 1.1: 135-52.
– 2008a. Cartographies of cognitive poetics. *Pragmatics and Cognition* 16.3: 587-98.
– 2008b. Situating cognitive approaches to narrative analysis. In Geert Brône and Jeroen Vandaele (eds.), *Cognitive Poetics: Goals, Gains and Gaps*, Berlin: Mouton de Gruyter, pp.119-23.
– 2009a. *Texture: A Cognitive Aesthetics of Reading*, Edinburgh: Edinburgh University Press.
– 2009b. The cognitive poetics of literary resonance. *Language and Cognition* 1.1: 25-44.
– 2010a. Ethics and imagination in literary reading. In Rodney Jones (ed.), *Discourse and Creativity*, London: Pearson.
– 2010b. Authenticity and creativity in reading lamentation. In Joan Swann, Rob Pope and Ronald Carter (eds.), *Creativity in Language*, Palgrave: Basingstoke
Tammi, Pekka. 2006. Against Narrative ('A Boring Story'). *Partial Answers* 4.2: 19-40.
– 2008. Against 'Against' Narrative. In Lars-Åke Skalin (ed.). *Narrativity, Fictionality, and Literariness: The Narrative Turn and the Study of Literary Fiction.* Örebro: Örebro University Press. 37-55.
Todorov, Tzvetan. 1966. Les catégories du récit littéraire. *Communications* 8: 125-151.
– 1969. *Grammaire du Décameron*. The Hague: Mouton.
Tomashevsky, Boris. 1965. Thematics. In Lee T. Lemon and Marion J. Reis (eds.), *Russian Formalist Criticism: Four Essays*. Lincoln, Nebraska: University of Nebraska Press: 61-95.
Toolan, Michael J. *Narrative: A Critical Linguistic Introduction*. 2nd ed. London: Routledge, 2001.
Tsur, Reuven. 1975. Two Critical Attitudes: Quest for Certitude and Negative Capability. *College English* 36:776-788. reprinted in

Tsur 2008: 511–529
– 1977. *A Perception-Oriented Theory of Metre.* Tel Aviv: The Porter Institute for Poetics and Semiotics.
– 1992. *What Makes Sound Patterns Expressive: The Poetic Mode of Speech-Perception* (the Roman Jakobson series). Durham N. C.: Duke University Press.
– 1998. *Poetic Rhythm: Structure and Performance—An Empirical Study in Cognitive Poetics.* Bern: Peter Lang.
– 2003. *On the shore of nothingness.* Exeter: Imprint Academic.
– 2006. *"Kubla Khan"—Poetic Structure, Hypnotic Quality and Cognitive Style: A Study in Mental, Vocal, and Critical Performance.* Amsterdam: John Benjamins.
– 2007. "The Structure and Delivery Style of Milton's Verse: An Electronic Exercise" in *Vocal Performance. ESC:English Studies in Canada* 33: 149–168. (appeared in 2009).
– 2008. *Toward a Theory of Cognitive Poetics.* Second, expanded and updated edition. Sussex Academic Press: Brighton and Portland.
Turner, Mark. 1996. *The Literary Mind: The Origins of Thought and Language.* New York: Oxford University Press.
– 2006. Ed., *The Artful Mind: Cognitive Science and the Riddle of Human Creativity.* Oxford: Oxford University Press.
van Peer, Willie. 1986. *Stylistics and psychology: Investigations of foregrounding.* London: Croom Helm.
Verstraten, Peter. 2009. *Film Narratology.* Trans. Stefan van der Lecq. Toronto: University of Toronto Press.
Vygotsky, Lev. 1986. *Thought and Language.* Translated by Alex Kozulin. Cambridge, MA.: MIT Press.
Walsh, Richard. 1995. *Novel Arguments: Reading Innovative American Fiction.* 179pp. New York: Cambridge University Press.
– 1997a. Why We Wept for Little Nell: Character and Emotional Involvement. *Narrative* 5.3: 306-21.
– 1997b. Who Is the Narrator? *Poetics Today.* 18.4: 495-513.
– 2000. The Novelist as Medium. *Neophilologus* 84.3: 329-45.
– 2001. Fabula and Fictionality in Narrative Theory. *Style* 35.4: 592-606.
– 2003. Fictionality and Mimesis: Between Narrativity and Fictional Worlds. *Narrative* 11.1: 110-21.
– 2005. The Pragmatics of Narrative Fictionality. In James Phelan and Peter Rabinowitz (eds.), *A Companion to Narrative Theory.* Oxford: Blackwell, 2005:150-64.
– 2006. The Narrative Imagination across Media. *Modern Fic-*

tion Studies 52.4: 855-868.
– 2007. *The Rhetoric of Fictionality: Narrative Theory and the Idea of Fiction.* Columbus: Ohio State University Press.
– 2010. Dreaming and Narrative Theory. In Frederick Luis Aldama (ed.), *Toward a Cognitive Theory of Narrative Acts.* Austin: University of Texas Press: 141-57.
– 2010. Person, Level, Voice: A Rhetorical Reconsideration. In Jan Alber and Monika Fludernik (eds.), *Postclassical Narratology: Approaches and Analyses.* Columbus: Ohio State University Press: 35-57
– 2011. Emergent Narrative in Interactive Media. *Narrative* 19.1: 72-85
Warhol, Robyn R. 1989. *Gendered Interventions.* New Brunswick: Rutgers Univ. Press, 1989.
– 1999. Guilty cravings: What feminist narratology can do for cultural studies. David Herman (ed.) *Narratologies: New Perspectives on Narrative Analysis.* Columbus: Ohio State University Press: 218-246.
– 2003. *Having a Good Cry: Effeminate Feelings and Pop-Culture Forms.* Columbus: Ohio State University Press.
Watt, Ian. 1957, *The Rise of the Novel.* Berkeley: University of California Press
Wellek, René and Austin Warren. 1956. *Theory of Literature.* New York: Harcourt, Brace & Co.
Werth, Paul. 1999. *Text Worlds: Representing Conceptual Space in Discourse.* Harlow: Longman.
White, Hayden. 1973. *Metahistory: The Historical Imagination in Nineteenth-Century Europe.* Baltimore, MD: Johns Hopkins University Press.
– 1987. *The Content of the Form: Narrative Discourse and Historical Representation.* Baltimore: Johns Hopkins University Press.
Wittgenstein, Ludwig. 1958. *Philosophical Investigations.* Oxford: Blackwell.
Wolf, Werner. 1993. *Ästhetische Illusion und Illusionsdurchbrechung in der Erzählkunst: Theorie und Geschichte mit Schwerpunkt auf englischem illusionsstörenden Erzählen.* Tübingen: Max Niemeyer Verlag.
– 1999. *The Musicalization of Fiction: A Study in the Theory and History of Intermediality.* Amsterdam: Rodopi.
– 2003. Narrative and Narrativity: A Narratological Reconceptualization and its Applicability to the Visual Arts. *Word & Image*

19.3: 180-97.
Wolfe, Cary, (ed.). 2003. *Zoontologies: The Question of the Animal.* Minneapolis: University of Minnesota P.
Zunshine, Lisa. 2006. *Why We Read Fiction: Theory of Mind and the Novel.* Columbus: Ohio State University Press, 2006.
Zwaan, Rolf A. 1994. Effect of genre expectations on text comprehension. *Journal of Experimental Psychology: Learning, Memory, and Cognition.* 20: 920-933.
Zwaan, Rolf A.,Joseph P. Magliano, and Arthur C. Graesser. 1995. Dimensions of situation model construction in narrative comprehension. *Journal of Experimental Psychology: Learning, Memory, and Cognition* 21: 386-397.

About the Editors

Peer F. Bundgaard, (*1967). Ph.D. in General Semiotics 1996. Since 2005 Associate Professor at the Center for Semiotics, Aarhus University, Denmark.
Major publications: Kunst-Semotiske beskrivelser af æstetisk oplevelse og betydning (2004), Kognitiv Semiotik (ed., 2003); articles and book chapters on cognitive semiotics, cognitive aesthetics, phenomenology and cognitive linguistics. Has co-edited (with Frederik Stjernfelt) Signs and Meaning: Five questions in the present series.

Henrik Skov Nielsen, (*1972), Professor at Department of Aesthetics and Communication, Aarhus University. Head of the research group Narrative Research Lab. and of Centre for Fictionality Studies.
Recent publications: "Natural Authors, Unnatural Narratives" in Monika Fludernik and Jan Alber (eds.): Post-Classical Narratology 2010.
A Poetics of Unnatural Narratology (Editor and contributor with Brian Richardson and Jan Alber.

Frederik Stjernfelt, (*1957). Professor, Ph.D., Center for Semiotics, Aarhus University.
Recent books: "Diagrammatology (Springer, 2007), "Semiotics. Critical Concepts" (I-IV, ed. with Peer Bundgaard, Routledge 2010), "The Democratic Contradictions of Multiculturalism" (Telos Press, in press).

www.ingramcontent.com/pod-product-compliance
Lightning Source LLC
Chambersburg PA
CBHW030807230426
43667CB00008B/1101